GREATEST
WOMEN
in HISTORY

COURAGE CALLS TO COURAGE EVERYWHERE

sona
BOOKS

**First published in the UK 2019 by Sona Books
an imprint of Danann Publishing Ltd.**

WARNING: For private domestic use only, any unauthorised Copying,
hiring, lending or public performance of this book is illegal.

Published under licence from Future Publishing Limited a Future PLC
group company. All rights reserved. No part of this publication may be
reproduced or stored in a retrieval system or transmitted in any form or
by any means without the prior written permission of the publisher.

Editor: Hannah Westlake, Designer: Laurie Newman
Copy editor for Danann Juliette O'Neill

© 2018 Future Publishing PLC

CAT NO: SON0442
ISBN: 978-1-912918-07-2
Made in EU.

CONTENTS

26

Politics & activism

42

Arts & culture

68

128

POLITICS & ACTIVISM

16

14

22

The USA's Founding Mothers

From negotiating peace treaties to shooting at the British, these women had a unique part to play in the War of Independence

They say history is written by the winners, and the heroic victories of the American rebels against the British colonists have certainly been well documented. It was a hard won battle, and rightly holds a revered place in the story of the United States.

But for every great man, there is an equally great woman, whose actions to help - or hinder - the American Revolution are frequently left out of the spotlight and pages of the history books. At the time of the revolution, women were largely confined to the home, socialising with genteel company and raising children - watching the war from the sidelines. Their husbands, brothers and fathers returned with epic tales of danger and destruction.

The Declaration of Independence is telling of contemporary attitudes towards women. "All men are created equal", it says, omitting the female gender entirely. Keeping women out of politics was of paramount importance to a number of the Founding Fathers, who believed that women lacked the intelligence and integrity to conduct the serious business of government. John Adams even stated "we know better than to repeal our masculine systems", intending to keep women firmly in their place.

But finding ever more ingenious and inventive ways to ensure that their voices were heard, many women played a significant part in the revolution anyway. They boycotted British goods and taxes, or followed the army into battle as cooks, nurses and water carriers.

Some even went to exceptional lengths, and defied gender norms to show their dedication to the cause. Radical women threw themselves into politics and war, whether the Founding Fathers liked it or not. Women from across the nation - regardless of ethnicity, social status, wealth, or region - threw off their shackles, aprons and fears. In their eyes, they had important work to do, and that was gaining liberty for both themselves and the fledgling United States of America.

This painting of Freeman was done by Susan Ridley Sedgwick, one of her pupils, in 1812

Elizabeth Freeman
c1742 - 1829

This maltreated slave used the climate of the revolution to emancipate herself from bondage

While the Founding Fathers were fighting to achieve freedom for their nation, Elizabeth Freeman (once known as Bet) was simply fighting for her own. Born into slavery in Massachusetts, the family she worked for were abusive. When they tried to attack her child with a heated shovel in 1780, Bet dived in front, receiving a deep scar to the arm. As proof of her cruel treatment, she left the wound uncovered, for all the world to see.

It's said that when she heard the words "all men are created free and equal" when the new US Constitution was being read in her master's home, Bet decided to escape slavery once and for all. With the help of Theodore Sedgwick, an abolitionist, she took her case to the Massachusetts Supreme Court in 1781.

The jury ruled in Bet's favour, and her case set an important precedent — slavery was abolished in the state of Massachusetts. She also became the first woman to be emancipated there. As a symbol of her hard-won status, Bet changed her name to Elizabeth Freeman. She worked in Sedgwick's home as a governess, before buying a house for herself and her daughter, then becoming a midwife. She died a well-respected and valued pillar of her community in 1829.

Abigail as a young woman, close to the time she married future president John Adams

Abigail Adams
1744 -1818

Adams was an early supporter of women's rights, and set her husband on the path to the presidency

Abigail Adams was no ordinary First Lady. A witty, wealthy and intelligent young woman, Abigail was not someone to be trifled with. When she decided to marry John Adams, a lawyer with poor prospects, that was that — regardless of what her father said.

When her husband rebelled against the British, Abigail took the reins of his career, managing his finances and schedule. Her letters to him reveal her sharp mind and fervent support for the revolution. In 1776, as the Continental Congress came together, she implored him to "remember the ladies" in drafting a new Constitution. John laughed at this suggestion and dubbed female agency as the "despotism of the petticoat", but Abigail was determined.

When John was elected to the USA's highest office in 1797, she found herself in a position of unprecedented influence. Never content to simply sit pretty and look after the house, as First Lady Abigail blazed a trail for women to participate in political discussion. She championed female education and the abolition of slavery.

However, she was mocked by John's colleagues — partly because Abigail was so astute, she could see through the political manoeuvring her husband didn't, and they felt threatened. She died in 1818, leaving a legacy of fascinating letters, providing a unique female voice in the turmoil of revolution.

While no contemporary images of Nanye'hi survive, she was commemorated in 1923 by the Daughters of the American Revolution

© Getty

Nanye'hi (Nancy Ward)
1738 - 1822

Cherokee woman Nanye'hi was beloved by both her people and white settlers

Even while American soldiers and settlers were pillaging their land, Native Americans played a key part in the American Revolution. The names of a few men have been remembered, but the contribution Native American women offered is often lost to history.

Nanye'hi — known as Nancy Ward to English speakers — was a wise woman from the Cherokee tribe. During a battle with the Creek, her husband was killed, and she took his place in the fighting. This won her a great deal of respect, and she was able to play a role in tribal councils and decisions. As tensions between white settlers and the Cherokees reached fever pitch, Nanye'hi is said to have warned the settlers of an oncoming attack in 1776. She helped to save a white woman from being burned at the stake by fellow tribesmen, so the American militias spared her village from destruction during their fight.

When the time came to make peace with the now United States in 1785, Nanye'hi made a passionate plea for mutual friendship, negotiating the Treaty of Hopewell — one of the earliest agreements between the US and the Cherokee. However, when the US purchased the lands she lived on in 1819, Nanye'hi — now an old woman — was forced to relocate.

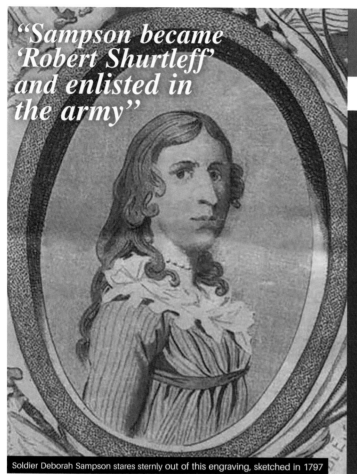

"Sampson became 'Robert Shurtleff' and enlisted in the army"

Soldier Deborah Sampson stares sternly out of this engraving, sketched in 1797

Deborah Sampson
1760 - 1827

From servant, to soldier, to speaker, Deborah Sampson had a colourful career

When the going gets tough, the tough get going. Deborah Sampson was a hard-as-nails young woman, with a taste for patriotism and a bravery that took her to the front lines of the Revolutionary War.

Sampson's family was large, and her parents were destitute. Seeing no other option, they sent some of their children to work for wealthier families as indentured servants. Ten-year-old Deborah found herself on a Massachusetts farm belonging to Benjamin Thomas, and worked hard on the fields. In her down time, she would educate herself. Soon, Sampson found her tranquil life disturbed by the campaign for independence. Throwing her lot in with the revolutionaries and binding her breasts to disguise her gender, Sampson became 'Robert Shurtleff' and enlisted in the army.

'Shurtleff' excelled, and even led a raid on the house of a British supporter, capturing 15 men. Though they applauded Shurtleff's bravery, their colleagues nicknamed Shurtleff 'Molly' because of her beardless face. For almost two years, Molly fought tirelessly, her true gender undetected.

When Deborah Sampson was exposed by a visit to the military hospital, she was honourably discharged. She was granted a full military pension, and she later toured the US, giving lectures about her experiences in the army and in the Revolutionary War.

Ann Bates
c.1748 - 1801

While the Founding Fathers fought for liberty, Ann Bates stood in their way

Not all women were fervent revolutionaries. Indeed, some of them actively worked against the rebels, and gave their service to the British. One such woman was the loyalist spy, Ann Bates.

A schoolteacher by trade, her husband fought in the British Army. When the British and their allies were forced to evacuate Philadelphia and head for New York, Ann went with them. Since women were widely assumed to know nothing of military technology and strategy, Bates had relatively easy access to crucial American information.

On her first mission, Bates dressed as a peddler and infiltrated George Washington's camp, relaying some of their military secrets — such as the position of cannons — back to the British Army. She deliberately kept a low profile to avoid exposure, and the tactic largely worked. In 1781, when it appeared her cause was lost, she migrated to England and lived the rest of her days in poverty.

Bates didn't stand out from the crowd - which turned out to be the perfect disguise

Ona Judge

c.1773 - 1848

The woman who defied George Washington to live truly free

George Washington was notorious for his ownership of a slave plantation at Mount Vernon, but he was not nearly as effective a master as he was a president. In 1796, Ona 'Oney' Judge, a mixed race domestic slave, escaped from his clutches permanently as a fugitive. She simply walked out of the house as the family were eating dinner, never to be seen again.

Judge stepped onto a ship and sailed north to New Hampshire. Having been exposed to free black men and women, she knew that a better life might be found away from the president's home. However, the loss of a favourite slave was a humiliation Washington wasn't going to let go of easily, so Judge became a wanted fugitive.

Washington even sent assistants to convince her to return, but Judge was smarter than Washington gave her credit for. She attempted to bargain with them, and the president viewed this as the deepest insolence. She never did go back, but when she died she was still legally a slave — as were her children.

May 23 No. 43, ſouth Water ſtreet. dtot

Advertiſement.

ABSCONDED from the houſhold of the Preſident of the United States, ONEY JUDGE, a light mulatto girl, much freckled, with very black eyes and buſhy black hair, ſhe is of middle ſtature, ſlender, and delicately formed, about 20 years of age.

She has many changes of good clothes, of all ſorts, but they are not ſufficiently recollected to be deſcribed—As there was no ſuſpicion of her going off, nor no provocation to do ſo, it is not eaſy to conjecture whither ſhe has gone, or fully, what her deſign is;—but as ſhe may attempt to eſcape by water, all maſters of veſſels are cautioned againſt admitting her into them, although it is probable ſhe will attempt to paſs for a free woman, and has, it is ſaid, wherewithal to pay her paſſage.

Ten dollars will be paid to any perſon who will bring her home, if taken in the city, or on board any veſſel in the harbour;—and a reaſonable additional ſum if apprehended at, and brought from a greater diſtance, and in proportion to the diſtance.

FREDERICK KITT, Steward.

May 23 d2t

To-morrow will be landed,

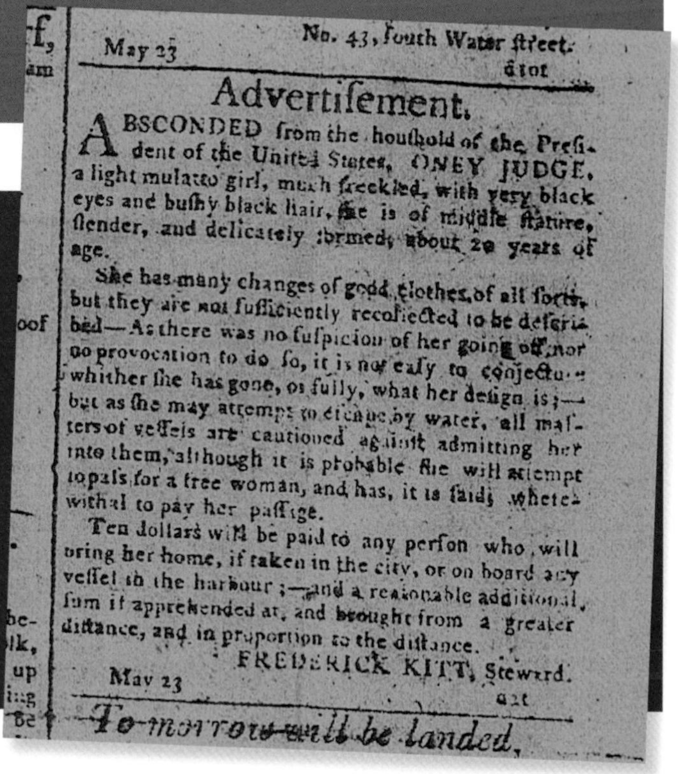

This newspaper advert offers a hefty prize of ten dollars for returning Ona to the president

Mercy Otis Warren

1728 - 1814

Warren's sharp wit and aptitude for politics made her a prominent chronicler of the era

Despite growing up in a well-to-do Massachusetts family, the young Mercy Otis Warren was denied the formal education given to her brothers. So, she convinced her uncle to let her sit in on their lessons. Her fascination with history and politics would soon serve her well.

After her brother was brutally beaten by British soldiers, Warren threw herself into the political sphere. Using an extensive network of contacts in the political elite, she organised protests at her home, and bore witness to some of the greatest events in American history — like the Stamp Act crisis and the Boston Tea Party.

To attract support, Warren used her keen political knowledge and skill for writing to publish satirical, pro-revolutionary columns and plays in prominent American newspapers. For instance, in 1772, her play The Adulator showcased grievances with the British government. Her witty style won her great popularity, and she counted Abigail Adams among her friends. They even exchanged letters on the nature of women's oppression, though Warren's opposition to John Adams' politics led to a fracture in their friendship.

After the revolution, Warren turned her hand to history writing, and her works have been of invaluable use ever since. Ever the firebrand, she continued her political correspondence until she died aged 86.

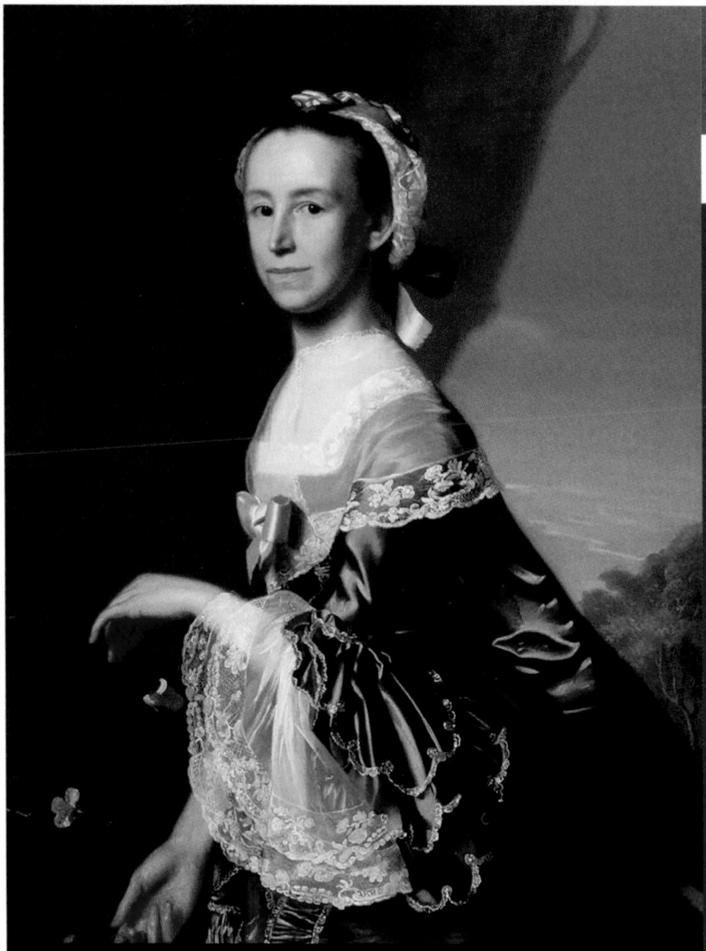

Warren helped set a precedent that female writers could, and should, be published

This portrait from her anthology describes her simply as a "negro servant to Mr John Wheatley"

Phillis Wheatley

c.1753 - 1784

The African woman whose poetry inspired Washington

To free oneself from slavery was an incredible act of bravery by itself, but to become the US's first African American poet puts Phillis Wheatley in a league of her own.

Born in West Africa, she was kidnapped and enslaved. Bought by the tailor John Wheatley in Boston in 1761, Phillis was treated kindly by her master's family. They taught her how to read and write in English, and before long, she had mastered Greek and Latin, too.

As a young woman, Wheatley was known for her translations of classic texts, and her poems about morality and liberty. In On Being Brought from Africa to America (1768), she told the story of her journey in beautiful rhyme. Wheatley was even sent to London to publish an anthology.

Her English friends implored the Wheatley family to free their brilliant slave, so as soon as Wheatley returned, she was emancipated. In 1775, she wrote To His Excellency General Washington, wishing the future President great military success. He was so pleased, he replied, inviting her to come and visit his headquarters.

Wheatley married a free black man in 1778, but he abandoned her. By the time of her death, she was once again reduced to servitude, and died a poor — but free — woman.

This statue of Phillis Wheatley at the Boston Women's Memorial shows her deep in thought

Having shot one of them, Nancy Hart threatens the British home invaders with one of their own rifles

Nancy Hart

c.1735 - 1830

How this cunning 'war woman' made a fool out of British soldiers

A fanatical Whig from North Carolina, Nancy Hart would stop at nothing to rid her homeland of the rapacious British. Allegedly, she was a fiery redhead who towered over everyone at around six feet, and could handle a gun like a pro. Even the local Cherokee tribe were afraid of her, and nicknamed her 'War Woman'.

One story goes that some Tory soldiers came into Hart's home one day, and demanded this woman cook them a meal. They evidently didn't know whose threshold they had crossed, so Hart took advantage of their stupidity. She cooked them a meal and plied them with alcohol, while her daughter went out to alert the local Whigs.

Hart, meanwhile, stole some of their rifles. When they found out, they tried to attack her, but she killed one of their number and wounded another. The rest were lynched by the Whigs.

Many other legends tell of Hart's belligerency, and she remained a thorn in the side of the British until they were eventually ousted.

Margaret Corbin

1751 - 1800

"Corbin wasn't afraid to get her hands dirty"

After watching her husband be killed, this pioneer kept calm and carried on

Frontierswoman Margaret Corbin wasn't your average country housewife. Life for pioneers was tough away from the major towns and cities, but women were still largely kept away from the action. Some women like Corbin, however, were not afraid to get their hands a little dirty.

Orphaned at the age of five by a Native American raid, Corbin learned to be steady in the face of danger. So, when her husband went to join the revolutionary cause, Corbin insisted on following him.

But in 1776, the new recruit was killed during a Hessian advance. Margaret Corbin, having observed how soldiers used heavy artillery, took her dead husband's place on the cannons and fired away at the enemy. Unfortunately, she was wounded and taken as a prisoner of war.

After her release, the now disabled Corbin struggled all the way from New York to Philadelphia. She continued to assist wounded troops until the war was over. Grateful for her brave service, the Continental Congress granted her a military pension — although it amounted to only half what male combatants received.

Margaret Corbin's grave at the West Point military cemetery

c.1822 – 1913

Harriet Tubman

Harriet Tubman escaped a life of slavery and saved dozens of other slaves from the same fate

Harriet Tubman was born into slavery and a life of unrelenting cruelty. Beaten and brutalised, her only comfort came from her faith and she prayed for freedom.Those prayers were answered when Harriet made a daring escape after 27 years as a slave. She travelled to freedom via the Underground Railroad, an abolition organisation that provided escaping slaves with resources and protection so that they could make their way to freedom.

After a fraught and dangerous trip Harriet arrived in Pennsylvania and here, for the first time, she could relax. Yet now she was free, Harriet wasn't content to rest. The thought of those who still suffered the brutalities that she had known haunted her and Harriet adopted the code name Moses in order to join the Underground Railroad herself and help others to reach freedom too.

Acting as a guide along dangerous roads, Harriet initially spirited away members of her own family but she didn't stop there. She worked tirelessly to assist around 300 escaping slaves over little more than a decade, risking her life time and again to lead them through the dangerous states where all were wanted men and women. She used the spiritual song, Go Down Moses, as she led the group, altering the tempo of the song to let her companions know whether the road ahead was safe or they should tread with more care to avoid detection. Faith wasn't Harriet's only weapon though, and she carried a gun, both for protection and to make sure that none of the escaping slaves in her group dropped out of the mission and left those who remained in jeopardy.

Harriet became one of the most wanted women in America but she evaded capture, as did all of those whom she helped to escape. She became a figurehead of the abolition movement and gave impassioned talks to her supporters but in 1860, Harriet gave up her calling. Her last experiences had been unhappy and despite her best efforts, she had been unable to rescue her sister, Rachel, who died in slavery. She was also unable to rescue Rachel's children and they remained as slaves.

When the American Civil War broke out, Harriet gave her support to the Union cause and toured camps, meeting escaped slaves and offering them her assistance. She spearheaded a raid on the Combahee River plantations, for which she enjoys the distinction of being the first woman to lead an armed attack during the American Civil War. Thanks to her decisive actions, more than 700 slaves were freed in that assault.

Sadly, Harriet never received any official recognition for her bravery and lived in penury. She petitioned Congress for a Civil War pension but received nothing until 1899, by which time she had become a vocal supporter for women's suffrage. Harriet died in 1913, having spent two years in a nursing home due to her ill health. In the century since her death she has become an icon of the abolitionist movement and a guiding light for generations.

A life's work

1849
Born into slavery, Tubman escapes after nearly three decades of labour. She flees Maryland for Philadelphia.

1851
Tubman returns to Dorchester County to rescue her husband, John, only to find that he has remarried.

1858
Tubman meets abolitionist John Brown, who is later executed for treason. She supports his call for direct action and joins him as a speaker.

1863
After working as a nurse and spy for the Union Army, Tubman leads the raid at Combahee Ferry, liberating over 700 slaves in the process.

1896
Tubman is the keynote speaker at the first meeting of National Federation of Afro-American Women. She gains new recognition as a suffragist.

Running the rail

Harriet Tubman was one of the most successful "conductors" on the Underground Railroad, escorting slaves to safety. During the decade following her own escape she made 19 perilous return trips to the South and conducted more than 300 slaves to freedom, including her own parents.

Known by the codename Moses, Tubman was inspired by the religious visions she experienced during narcoleptic attacks to continue her work despite the dangers she faced. After her retirement, Tubman proudly stated that she was rare indeed among conductors of any railroad, as she never lost a passenger from her train.

Harriet Tubman is pictured with a handful of the slaves she rescued during her illustrious career

Known as the Moses of her People, Harriet Tubman was a fearless conductor of the Underground Railroad.

Five things to know about... Harriet Tubman

1 A narcoleptic heroine
Tubman suffered from narcolepsy after being struck with a metal weight by an overseer in her youth. She was inspired by the vivid religious dreams she had during narcoleptic spells.

2 She said no to anaesthetic
Tubman's sleep issues became so serious that she opted to have brain surgery. She refused anaesthesia and instead elected to chew on a bullet during the operation.

3 A cure for dysentery
Tubman's extensive knowledge of Maryland's flora enabled her to cure Union soldiers who were suffering from dysentery. She could also relieve the symptoms of other conditions, including cholera.

4 A wanted woman
A bounty of $100 was put on Tubman's head when she escaped. Later, her supporters claimed that $40,000 was offered for the capture of the saviour known as "Moses".

5 An unblemished record
Harriet Tubman enjoyed a 100% success rate. None of the slaves rescued by Tubman were recaptured, nor was she ever apprehended on her missions.

IN MEMORY OF
HARRIET TUBMAN
BORN A SLAVE IN MARYLAND ABOUT 1821
DIED IN AUBURN, N.Y. MARCH 10TH, 1913
CALLED THE "MOSES" OF HER PEOPLE
DURING THE CIVIL WAR, WITH RARE
COURAGE, SHE LED OVER THREE HUNDRED
NEGROES UP FROM SLAVERY TO FREEDOM,
AND RENDERED INVALUABLE SERVICE
AS NURSE AND SPY.
WITH IMPLICIT TRUST IN GOD
SHE BRAVED EVERY DANGER AND
OVERCAME EVERY OBSTACLE, WITHAL
SHE POSSESSED EXTRAORDINARY
FORESIGHT AND JUDGMENT SO THAT
SHE TRUTHFULLY SAID-
"ON MY UNDERGROUND RAILROAD
I NEBBER RUN MY TRAIN OFF DE TRACK
AND I NEBBER LOS' A PASSENGER."
THIS TABLET IS ERECTED
BY THE CITIZENS OF AUBURN
·1914·

1899
Tubman is finally awarded a Civil War pension in recognition of her nursing work, after years of struggle to see her wartime exploits recognised.

1913
Harriet Tubman dies in the Harriet Tubman Home for the Aged. She is buried with military honours at Fort Hill Cemetery, Auburn, New York.

1914
Booker Washington unveils a plaque in Tubman's honour on the courthouse of Auburn, New York, where she settled.

1944
The SS Harriet Tubman is launched by the United States Maritime Commission. Tubman's name is given to schools and other buildings.

2013
President Obama signs a proclamation creating Maryland's Harriet Tubman Underground Railroad National Monument.

1847 – 1929

Millicent Fawcett

Suffragist and educator Millicent Fawcett might have been a moderate, but she was still a force to be reckoned with

Millicent Fawcett came from a pioneering family. Her sister, Elizabeth Garrett Anderson, was Britain's first female doctor and she certainly wouldn't be the only daughter of the family to make her mark; Millicent was inspired by her sibling's fighting spirit. Fawcett developed an interest in women's suffrage in her teens and at just 19, she was already secretary of the London Society for Women's Suffrage. She became known as a passionate and erudite speaker and as the years passed, established a respected reputation as a supporter of suffrage. Thanks to her work as a speaker she became a member of Lectures for Ladies, an education group that originated in Cambridge and as such, in 1871 she became a co-founder of Newnham College, Cambridge, only the second college to grant entrance to women.

Though Fawcett was a dedicated campaigner on behalf of women's suffrage and was eventually appointed leader of the National Union of Women's Suffrage Societies, she advocated only peaceful protest and activism. Fawcett looked darkly on the Women's Social and Political Union's use of direct action. She actively distanced herself from the actions of more militant suffragettes and spoke out against those who advocated what she considered extreme means to achieve their common aim.

Fawcett, however, didn't limit her campaigning to England. In 1901 she was appointed to head a commission of women who were sent to South Africa to report on the conditions in concentration camps where the families of Boer soldiers were being held. It was the first time a woman had been given such a responsibility and Fawcett took up the cudgels on behalf of those who were suffering in the camps, campaigning to improve conditions for the women and children who were interred there. She also regularly campaigned on behalf of her husband, Liberal MP Henry Fawcett, and became a familiar figure on the hustings in his Brighton constituency where the couple both spoke out in favour of women's suffrage.

For decades, Millicent Fawcett remained dedicated to the causes to which she had devoted her public life. She toured schools to talk to girls about suffrage and the opportunities they might enjoy and campaigned for women to have the right to be awarded degrees at Cambridge. Though her campaigns didn't always enjoy success, she became a figurehead for female education and as head of the NUWSS, played a pivotal role in securing the vote for the women of Britain. Though this side of her work culminated with the Representation of the People Act, Fawcett occupied any free time she now had by writing the biography of Josephine Butler, a forerunner in the suffrage movement.

Millicent Fawcett died in 1929 but her name lives on today in The Fawcett Society, which continues to educate young people on the story of suffrage, as well as leading campaigns for gender equality. Today her statue stands in Parliament Square, forever immortalised as the pioneering woman she was.

A life's work

1865
Millicent Fawcett founds the Kensington Society, a group dedicated to the pursuit of women's suffrage.

1866
At just 19 years old, Fawcett is appointed secretary of the London Society for Women's Suffrage.

1890
After the death of Lydia Becker, Fawcett becomes the leader of the National Union of Women's Suffrage Societies. She holds the post until 1919.

1901
Fawcett travels to South Africa to investigate Emily Hobhouse's reports of conditions in concentration camps, the first woman to do so.

1918
The Representation of the People Act 1918 is passed, awarding the vote to 8.4 million women over the age of 30 in the UK.

Fawcett welcome suffragists from across the world to the 1909 Suffrage Alliance Congress in London

Five things to know about...
Millicent Fawcett

1 Don't call her a suffragette
Though Millicent Fawcett campaigned for suffrage from her teenage years, she was a suffragist as opposed to a suffragette, and rejected the latter's more militant methods of persuasion.

2 She believed in domesticity
Fawcett didn't encourage women to reject a domestic life but instead argued that their experiences in the home were valuable to the nation and should be considered by policymakers.

3 She co-founded a college
Fawcett was one of the co-founders of Newnham College, Cambridge. Newnham allowed women to study flexibly, so they didn't have to abandon other commitments to do so.

4 She was a pioneering campaigner
Fawcett campaigned on numerous issues including her fight to repeal the Contagious Diseases Act, which allowed sex workers to be prosecuted for infecting their clients with STIs but not vice versa.

5 She lived to see victory
When women over 21 were given the vote in 1929, Fawcett was in Parliament to witness the historic moment. She died the following year, after six decades of tireless campaigning.

The Suffrage Fight

From the age of 19, Millicent Fawcett fought to see women given the right to vote. It was a battle that she stayed with to the very end of her life, campaigning passionately but peacefully for women's right to vote.

Though she was too young to sign it herself, Fawcett organised the very first petition in support of suffrage and during her leadership of the National Union of Women's Suffrage Societies, it grew to 50,000 members.

Fawcett's work was a key factor in the awarding of votes to women in 1918 and she is honoured today as a pioneering voice in British politics.

Dame Millicent Fawcett devoted her life to the fight for women's suffrage and emerged victorious

1925
Fawcett is appointed a Dame of the Grand Cross of the Order of British Empire in the 1925 New Year Honours list.

1929
Millicent Fawcett Hall is constructed in Westminster. Owned by Westminster School, the hall is a place for women to meet and debate issues.

1933
The London Society for Women's Suffrage is renamed as The Fawcett Society. It continues to campaign under this name today.

2016
Caroline Criado Perez, who campaigned to see Jane Austen on a banknote, campaigns to have a statue of Fawcett erected in London.

2018
A statue commemorating Millicent Fawcett is unveiled in Parliament Square, the first statue of a woman to be erected in this location.

"Despite their freedom, life for a young black family in the Deep South was extremely harsh"

1913 – 2005

Rosa Parks

A small act of defiance, caused by a community pushed too far, would be the catalyst for the nationwide Civil Rights Movement

When the Civil Rights Movement is mentioned, few people would fail to think of the woman who almost single-handedly kick-started the national movement: Rosa Parks. Many aspects of 1950s American society were strictly segregated and while Parks was not the first person who refused to obey the laws, she was the spark that lit the fire of civil rights throughout the land.

In what was just another day for Parks, riding home on the Montgomery city bus after work, she was asked to give up her designated seat to a white person. She refused, was arrested, and her court case gained the support of the local chapter of the National Association for the Advancement of Colored People (NAACP), who organised a citywide bus boycott that ran for 381 days. This nonviolent protest gained national coverage, acting as a catalyst to spread the Civil Rights Movement across the entire country, headed by the newly appointed head of the NAACP, Dr Martin Luther King Jr. To attribute this to the actions of one person seems unfair but Parks' act of defiance is often seen as the straw that broke the camel's back. It was one injustice too far that inspired a large chunk of the population to rise up and fight for equality.

Parks herself came from humble beginnings, having been born in Tuskegee, a small town near the Alabama state capital Montgomery, on 4 February 1913. Her parents, Leona and James McCauley, a teacher and carpenter, valued education and were strong advocates of racial equality. Despite their freedom and strong views, life for a young black family in the Deep South was extremely harsh. The black community of Alabama relied almost entirely on the white population for work, but the jobs were often menial and offered very little in the way of a living wage and perks.

Rosa grew up attending segregated schools, but was forced to drop out of high school at 16 to care for her sick grandmother and later her mother. She would return to school years later, encouraged by her husband, to gain her high school diploma. It is a testament to her will, and others sharing her plight, that despite her oppressive

ROSA PARKS HAS BEEN CALLED "THE FIRST LADY OF CIVIL RIGHTS"

beginnings, she grew up with a great sense of self-worth. Those that knew her explained that she was softly spoken but carried with her a quiet strength and determination that saw her fight hard whenever she was challenged.

Parks found a job as a seamstress at a textile factory in Montgomery and in 1932, aged 19, married Raymond Parks. Raymond, lacking a formal education of his own, was actively involved in the NAACP and Rosa would soon become involved as well. Her actions on 1 December 1955 reflect her passion for the cause, as she was not just a person who decided not to give up her seat, but a committed activist working to better the lives of black people in Alabama and throughout the United States.

The incident in December was, to many, a routine occurrence. Buses in Montgomery were segregated by colour, with the front reserved for white people and the back for black people. This meant that a black person would need to pay for their ticket at the front of the bus, get off and walk to the back door to find a seat. The bus drivers held ultimate authority in their vehicles, being able to move the segregation line back and force any black person to give up their seat in busy periods. Failure to do so would mean getting thrown off the bus and having the police called. Parks had already had a run-in with the driver, James Blake, a few years beforehand when Blake had driven off while Parks exited the bus to walk to the back doors.

Parks, who had just finished a long shift, was seated on the crowded bus but in a row with three other black people. When Blake noticed a white man standing he ordered Parks and the others to give up their seats. While only one seat was needed, the law stated that whites and blacks couldn't be seated in the same row. The four at first refused, to which Blake replied, "You'd better make it light on yourselves and let me have those seats". While the others complied, Parks would not budge, stating that as she was not in the white section she didn't think she should have to give up her seat. When remembering the incident in later life, Parks said: "When that white driver stepped back toward us, when he waved his hand and ordered us up and out of our seats, I felt a determination to cover my body like a quilt on a winter night". With steely resolve, Parks refused to move an inch, forcing Blake to call his supervisor, asking for advice. The response was simple: "Well then, Jim, you do it, you got to exercise your powers and put her off, hear?" Parks was then arrested as she had technically broken the law by not giving up her seat. While she was being arrested, she asked the police officer a question: "Why do you push us around?" The question and response of "I don't know, but the law is the law," along with Parks' actions, are widely credited as one of the catalysts for the Civil Rights Movement in America.

She was held in the police station for violating chapter 6, section 11 of the Montgomery city code that dealt with segregation. She was bailed out that evening by the president of the local NAACP chapter, Edgar Nixon. Nixon saw an opportunity to use Parks' arrest to further their cause and immediately began planning a boycott of the city's buses that night. The next day, the city was saturated with newspaper ads and over 35,000 handbills, produced the night before, were distributed around black neighbourhoods. The boycott called for all black people to avoid using the buses until they were treated with the same level of respect as the white passengers while on board, the segregated seating was removed and black drivers were hired. The Montgomery Improvement Association (MIA) was formed to spearhead the initiative and at its head was Dr Martin Luther King Jr, quite a recent newcomer to

PARKS, AND OTHER MEMBERS OF THE BOYCOTT, WOULD RECEIVE DEATH THREATS FOR THEIR ACTIONS

Edgar Nixon played an instrumental role in the bus boycott and bailed Rosa Parks out of jail

Women of the Civil Rights Movement

Fannie Lou Hamer
Having faced brutal beatings in jail campaigning for equal rights, Hamer spoke candidly of her experiences live on air in 1964, prompting President Lyndon B Johnson to organise an impromptu press conference to draw media coverage away from this embarrassing insight into racist America. Hamer spoke of her terrible experiences at the 1964 Democratic conference.

Dorothy Height
President of the National Council for Negro Women for 40 years, Dorothy worked tirelessly to help low-income schools and provide for poor families. Her efforts led President Obama to describe her as the "godmother of the Civil Rights Movement" in 2010. Height is seen by many as one of the key figures of the Civil Rights Movement.

Daisy Bates
An iconic member of the civil rights campaign, Bates' most famous achievement was leading the Little Rock Nine to enrol in the Little Rock Central High School in 1957. After Little Rock, Bates worked tirelessly to improve living conditions in her poor community.

Septima Clark
With her work including securing equal pay for black teachers, Septima Clark was dubbed the "mother of the movement" by Martin Luther King Jr and had been fighting for equality since 1919. Clark would continue her work with the SCLC until her retirement in 1970.

Bernice Robinson
Robinson was a civil rights activist who recognised the importance of education in the fight for equality. She helped set up Citizenship Schools in South Carolina and worked with the SCLC across the South to teach adult reading skills to help black Americans pass literacy tests in order to vote.

Diane Nash
As the founder of the Student Nonviolent Coordinating Committee (SNCC), Diane Nash was one of the most influential figures of the entire Civil Rights Movement. She helped organise sit-ins and the now legendary Freedom Riders. Nash worked tirelessly around Nashville and beyond to win equal rights and end segregation.

Parks became a figurehead for the Civil Rights Movement and continued to fight for equality throughout her life

Formation of the SCLC

The Southern Christian Leadership Conference (SCLC) was an organisation born out of the success of the Montgomery Bus Boycott. Headed by Martin Luther King Jr, the group sought to capitalise on the victory in Alabama and advance the cause of civil rights in a nonviolent manner. Black communities in the South at this time were formed around the church, so having a minister as the figurehead was an obvious choice. King himself stated, "The SCLC is church orientated because of the very structure of the Negro community in the South."

Combining various smaller civil rights groups under one spiritual umbrella, the SCLC formed three main goals which would be the bedrock of the organisation. The first was to encourage white Southerners to join their cause. Although a staggering amount of hate and vitriol was levelled against blacks in the South, the SCLC believed that not all people harboured racist views. All black people were also encouraged and asked to "seek justice and reject all injustice". The final and perhaps most important point for the group was a strict belief and adherence to nonviolent protest. The unofficial motto of the group became "not one hair of one head of one white person shall be harmed".

Montgomery and the man who saw a chance to use Parks' case to take the struggle nationwide.

The first day of the boycott coincided with Parks' trial, where she was fined $14. Continuing for another 380 days, the boycott saw many black people shun the bus in favour of using black taxi companies, carpooling or simply walking to work – with some people walking up to 32 kilometres (20 miles) a day. It soon began to have the desired effect as the bus company's profits slumped, leading to much of the fleet sitting idle for over a year. The successes were tempered by the backlash, however, as black churches were burned and both King and Nixon's houses were attacked. The authorities also tried to break the boycott through other means, with the taxi companies that took black people to work having their insurance revoked and arrests made under antiquated anti-boycott laws.

These heavy-handed reactions did little to sway the MIA who went on the legal offensive. Only a year before, the Brown v Board of Education Supreme Court ruling had found that segregated schools were unconstitutional. Armed with this, their legal team sought to challenge the segregation laws for public transport. In June 1956 they were ruled unconstitutional and despite resistance the decision was upheld by the Supreme Court in November 1956. With the law on their side and both the bus company and city businesses suffering financial losses, the city had little choice but to end segregation on public transport. The boycott was formally ended on 20 December 1956.

Rosa Parks' resistance ignited one of the largest and most successful protests against racial segregation in the South. Its nonviolent means saw it gain national coverage and helped to send the struggle for civil rights nationwide.

BLACK TAXI COMPANIES REDUCED THEIR FARES TO THE PRICE OF A BUS TICKET IN SUPPORT OF THE BOYCOTT

The SCLC is still active today with Charles Steele Jr the current president, a position previously held by Dr King's daughter Bernice

1936 – 2018

Winnie Mandela

As controversial as she was celebrated, Winnie Madikizela-Mandela remains a divisive figure in South Africa

Winnie Madikizela-Mandela might be best known for her nearly four-decade-long marriage to Nelson Mandela, but she was far more than just a wife. The couple married in 1958 and five years later, Nelson Mandela began his 27-year jail sentence. Winnie Madikizela-Mandela, however, didn't sit at home and mourn her husband's absence. Instead, she devoted herself to anti-apartheid movement and to securing Nelson Mandela's freedom.

Madikizela-Mandela became a campaigning force to be reckoned with and in doing so, attracted the persecution of the South African government. Detained, tortured and held in solitary confinement, Madikizela-Mandela emerged from prison stronger than ever and began her work again. Even when she was exiled to the isolated town of Brandfort, Madikizela-Mandela refused to go quietly. Instead, she worked to establish clinical and childcare facilities in the area, endeavours that won the attention of the international media. Shrewd and well aware of the power of PR, Madikizela-Mandela capitalised on the publicity to raise awareness of the African National Congress and their battle against apartheid.

Winnie Madikizela-Mandela, however, was not without controversy. When she returned to Soweto from Brandfort she was accompanied by a protection force known as the Mandela United Football Club. The group shared her home and swiftly became implicated in violent attacks in the area, including the murder of a 14-year-old boy, Stompie Seipei. Though her imprisoned husband urged her to denounce the club and local people protested at her support of

them, Madikizela-Mandela refused to do so. As a result, she became the subject of a later investigation by the the Truth and Reconciliation Commission that found her guilty of kidnapping Seipei, as well as raised concerns about her involvement in numerous other murders and disappearances.

Despite these controversies, Madikizela-Mandela served as a Member of Parliament for more than 20 years and was celebrated for her work on behalf of the ANC as well as her efforts to secure her husband's freedom. The marriage, however, didn't survive long after Nelson Mandela's release in 1990 and just two years later the couple were divorced. Winnie Madikizela-Mandela continued to be an important figure in the post-apartheid government but her political career remained mired in controversy. Dismissed from her position as head of social welfare development for the the ANC due to corruption, subsequent appointments were met with protests. When the Truth and Reconciliation Commission found her responsible for human rights violations in 1998, it seemed as though her once illustrious career was over.

Madikizela-Mandela emerged from retirement in 2009 to once again serve as an MP. Although she was increasingly sidelined by the ANC in an effort to distance itself from the criticisms her name attracted, Winnie Madikizela-Mandela remains forever associated with the party and the battle to overcome apartheid.

Following her death in April 2018, her reputation and legacy is as hotly debated as ever and it remains to be seen how history will judge Winnie Madikizela-Mandela.

A life's work

1958
Winnie Madikizela and Nelson Mandela marry. They are a formidable force against apartheid in South Africa.

1964
Nelson Mandela is sentenced to life in prison. Madikizela-Mandela begins her campaign to secure his release.

1969
After several shorter jail sentences, Madikizela-Mandela is imprisoned. She spends most of her sentence placed in solitary confinement.

1977
In an effort to silence her, Madikizela-Mandela is exiled to Brandfort. Distance does nothing to stop her campaigning for civil rights.

1990
Nelson Mandela is released from prison. Winnie Madikizela-Mandela is at the gates to greet her husband and walks at his side as he emerges.

The freedom fight

When her husband was sentenced to life imprisonment in 1964, Winnie Madikizela-Mandela was determined to keep fighting for the things they had stood for. Though she suffered imprisonment and endured torture and separation from her family, she never lost sight of her goal and strove to end apartheid.

Despite the danger to herself Madikizela-Mandela visited her husband throughout the period of his imprisonment on Robbin Island. Even death threats and repeated incarceration couldn't silence her and she became a lifelong campaigner for equality in South Africa and across the world, fighting apartheid for long, tumultuous decades.

Madikizela-Mandela became a spokesperson for the anti-apartheid movement

Just as she had fought for Nelson Mandela, when Madikizela-Mandela went on trial, her husband supported her

Five things to know about...
Winnie Mandela

1 A social care trailblazer
With her appointment by Baragwanath Hosptal in Soweto, Madikizela-Mandela became the first qualified black social worker in South Africa.

2 Defying a fashion ban
When Madikizela-Mandela wore traditional tribal dress while supporting Nelson Mandela in court, the outfit was banned. She responded by wearing ANC colours instead.

3 Solitary confinement
Madikizela-Mandela was jailed in 1969 and held in solitary confinement for much of her imprisonment, while being subjected to brutal beatings.

4 The walk to freedom
When Nelson Mandela was released from prison in 1990, Winnie Madikizela-Mandela was at his side. The couple later separated and divorced in 1996.

5 Controversy
Winnie Madikizela-Mandela is a polarising figure around the world. Regarded as a criminal by some, her supporters accuse her opponents of treason.

1991 Madikizela-Mandela is accused of the kidnapping and assault of 14-year-old Stompie Seipei. She protests her innocence but is found guilty.

1993 Madikizela-Mandela is elected president of the African National Congress Women's League, a feat she repeats in 1997. She holds office until 2003.

1994 Nelson Mandela appoints his now estranged wife as Deputy Minister of Arts, Culture, Science and Technology.

2007 Following her conviction for fraud, Madikizela-Mandela is re-elected to Parliament, but her influence within the ANC has declined.

2018 Winnie Madikizela-Mandela dies after suffering ill health. Amid an outpouring of public grief, she is laid to rest in Johannesburg.

"*Pankhurst believed that the women's right to influence policy-making was the only way society would be reformed*"

EMMELINE PANKHURST WAS SENT TO FINISHING SCHOOL IN PARIS

1858 – 1928

Emmeline Pankhurst

Discover the makings of a militant as we look back on the incredible story of the suffragette leader

We are here, not because we are law-breakers; we are here in our efforts to be law-makers." Those immortal words by Emmeline Pankhurst encapsulated the Suffragette Movement. As their iron-willed leader, she fought for women's right to vote in the United Kingdom – by any means. The motto was "Deeds, not words", and a campaign of vandalism, violent protests and arson reigned. Pankhurst saw it as her duty to break the law in order to draw attention to the reasons behind her actions; a belief that would see her arrested on countless occasions and even cause a rift within her own family. She argued that unless women were given political power, the laws of the country wouldn't have an equal standard of morals. Articulate and strong, Pankhurst would enter the history books for influencing how women were perceived within society – a role she seemed almost destined to fulfil from an early age.

Much of Pankhurst's political education took place at her home in Manchester, England. Her parents Robert Goulden and Sophia Crane were involved in many social movements such as the abolition of slavery, and her grandfather had even been in the crowd at the Peterloo Massacre in 1819. Unsurprisingly, she was barely into her teens when a young Emmeline Pankhurst followed in their footsteps. "I was 14 years old when I went to my first suffrage meeting," she wrote in her autobiography, *My Own Story*. "Returning from school one day, I met my mother just setting out for the meeting, and I begged her to let me go along."

Her childhood was a happy one, surrounded by a loving family in a comfortable home, but she couldn't help but sense the inequality between genders. It started when Pankhurst and her brothers were sent to school. While her father spent a great deal of time discussing the boys' education, hers and her sister's were scarcely mentioned at all. While feigning sleep one night, she overheard her father mutter, "What a pity she wasn't born a lad." His words stuck with her for days before she concluded that men saw themselves as superior to women, and that she didn't regret her sex one bit. "I suppose I had always

BORN ON 15 JULY 1858, PANKHURST CLAIMED HER BIRTHDAY WAS 14 JULY, BASTILLE DAY

been an unconscious suffragist," she reflected. "With my temperament and my surroundings, I could scarcely have been otherwise."

Before Pankhurst joined the fight, suffrage – the right to vote in political elections – had been stirring for years. In 1866, a group of women presented a petition to MPs and an amendment to the Reform Act was proposed. It was defeated in Parliament by 196 votes to 73 and women's suffrage groups started to form all over the country. In 1897, 17 of these groups banded together to create the National Union of Women's Suffrage Societies. Led by Millicent Fawcett, they were characterised by their peaceful campaign tactics, holding public meetings and distributing posters and leaflets, but without progress. Pankhurst, however, would wash her hands of this approach when she founded the Women's Social and Political Union in 1903.

It was the horrors she witnessed while working as a Poor Law guardian that drove her to believe that "Deeds, not words" was the way forward. Regular visits to the Manchester workhouses exposed her to many elderly women who had been domestic-servant class, unmarried and who had lost their job only to wind up with no other option than to slave away in the workhouse. Pregnant women would be separated from their babies after two weeks if they wanted to remain in the workhouse, or leave without a home or hope. It was these women who stoked the fire in Pankhurst, giving her the fervent belief that the women's right to influence policy-making was the only way society would be reformed. "Women have more practical ideas about relief... than men display," she said.

During this time, Pankhurst was supported by her husband, who did a great deal to bolster her beliefs. As a radical liberal barrister 24 years her senior, Dr Richard Pankhurst was a socialist and stoic supporter of women's suffrage. They married in 1879 and became a formidable team. They founded the Women's Franchise League – an organisation to secure the vote for women in local elections. But tragedy soon struck as Richard's untimely death left her alone with five children to support. In spite of such odds, she threw herself into the suffrage movement

The Poor Law

The 1800s saw the introduction of the Poor Law – a lifeline to the impoverished. According to the law, each parish had to set money aside for those who were unable to work. However, changes to the law in 1834 saw the cost of looking after the poor dramatically reduced. The Poor Law Amendment Act meant that money was only given to the poor in exceptional circumstances and, if they wanted help, they had to go to a workhouse and earn it. Food and shelter was given in exchange for manual labour, but the conditions were so dreadful that only the truly desperate would turn to this solution.

Emmeline Pankhurst would witness the horrors first-hand, after joining the Independent Labour Party and being elected as Poor Law guardian in Chorlton-on-Medlock in Manchester, England. "The first time I went into the place I was horrified to see little girls seven and eight-years-old on their knees scrubbing the cold stones of the long corridors," she said. "I found that there were pregnant women in that workhouse, scrubbing floors, doing the hardest kind of work, almost until their babies came into the world." At once, she began to use her position on the board of guardians to try and change these conditions for the better. This activism lit a fire that would spur her on to becoming the leader of the suffragettes.

Members of the Women's Social and Political Union campaigning for women's suffrage in Kingsway

and later, so would her daughters. A crucial step was transforming the Women's Franchise League into a women-only activist group – the Women's Social And Political Union.

It was Emmeline Pankhurst's eldest daughter Christabel who persuaded her mother that the WFL she had set up some 14 years before had fallen hopelessly out of touch. She had inherited her parents' indomitable values and became a leading member of the WSPU, and in 1905 was one of the first suffragettes to be thrown in prison. Her crime was interrupting a Liberal Party meeting, shouting demands for women's votes and reportedly assaulting a police officer, but the acts of the WSPU would grow to be much more violent, eventually using arson as a tactic. It proved a step too far for two of Pankhurst's daughters, Adela and Sylvia, and they left the activist group. Those who remained cut phone lines, sent letter bombs and attacked the home of Chancellor David Lloyd George. "I have never advised the destruction of life, but of property,

ONE OF HER HOMES IN MANCHESTER WAS OPENED AS A MUSEUM

Defining moment
Birth of first child
22 September 1880

Richard and Emmeline Pankhurst's first child, Christabel, is born less than a year after their marriage. Christabel grows up to be very close to her mother, co-founding the Women's Social and Political Union and spending 15 years working alongside her. Other siblings notice the bond, as younger daughter Sylvia notes in 1931: "She was our mother's favourite; we all knew it, and I, for one, never resented the fact." In 1959, Christabel writes *Unshackled: The Story Of How We Won The Vote*, and lauds her mother's dedication.

Timeline

1858

Born
Emmeline Pankhurst is born in Moss Side in Manchester, England, to politically active parents. She has 11 siblings, but three tragically die before the age of two.
15 July 1858

Married
After returning from finishing school in Paris, she meets the lawyer Richard Pankhurst, who shares her views on women's suffrage. They marry in Salford.
18 December 1879

Women's Franchise League begins
Emmeline Pankhurst and her husband found the Women's Franchise League, aiming to give women the vote in local elections.
1 January 1889

Richard dies
Richard Pankhurst dies suddenly of stomach ulcers, leaving Emmeline and five children. In his lifetime, he did much for women's suffrage, including writing the Married Women's Property Act of 1870.
5 July 1898

WSPU is launched
Pankhurst forms the National Women's Social and Political Union in Manchester, with the help of her eldest daughter. Their motto is "Deeds, not words" and their aim is to win the vote for women. The women-only activist group is independent of government and political parties.
October 1903

yes," admitted Pankhurst.

In 1912, she was sent to Holloway Prison for smashing windows, a place she described as "at once the stuffiest and the draughtiest building" she had ever set foot in. While in prison, however, suffragettes were not recognised as political prisoners because the government didn't see their actions as such. To protest against what she saw as unjust and lengthy sentences (three months just for breaking a window, for instance), Pankhurst went on hunger strike, resulting in having to undergo violent force-feeding. She wasn't alone in her actions and the government retaliated with the 'Cat and Mouse' Act, where striking prisoners were released from prison until they grew strong enough to be re-arrested and put back into the prison system. These acts split public opinion, particularly when suffragette Emily Davison walked on to the course at the Epsom Derby and was trampled by King George V's horse, dying of her injuries four days later. Pankhurst later wrote that Emily "clung to her conviction that one great tragedy, the deliberate throwing into the breach of a human life, would put an end to the intolerable torture of women."

What would put an end to the militant activism, however, was war – the kind of which had never been seen before. On 4 August 1914 – just days after the First World War broke out – Pankhurst and her daughter ordered a truce between the WSPU and the government. Considering it their patriotic duty, they channelled their energies into helping the war effort and subsequently all suffragettes were released from prison. As Pankhurst pointed out, there was no use fighting for a vote when there might not be a country left in which they could cast one. So as men went to fight overseas, the suffragette leaders volunteered to take their place. It was an unexpected opportunity to prove that women were every bit as capable as their male counterparts, taking on important industrial roles, from working in munitions factories to labouring on farms.

Society's attitudes towards the sexes finally started to change and on 10 January 1918, the Representation of the People Act was passed. This granted the vote to all 'respectable' ladies over 30-years-old who were householders or married to householders. To this day, historians still debate whether it was the Great War that brought about the victory for the suffragettes, or whether the pre-war political movement should take the credit. Some also argue whether the militant campaign did more harm than good. Either way, Emmeline Pankhurst did a great deal to draw attention to her passionate belief that women deserved to be equal.

Sadly, she died in the month before the right to vote was extended to all women over 21 years of age on 2 July 1928 – finally on a par with men in the United Kingdom. Just two years after her death, Pankhurst's efforts were commemorated with a statue in London's Victoria Tower Gardens. At the unveiling, a crowd of former suffragettes gathered to pay their respects to such a dedicated foot soldier of the feminist movement.

PANKHURST WAS ENCOURAGED TO RUN FOR THE HOUSE OF COMMONS, BUT DECLINED

"The acts of the WSPU would grow to be much more violent, eventually using arson as a tactic"

Defining moment
Demanding votes
21 June 1908

500,000 activists storm Hyde Park in London demanding votes for women. Prime Minister Asquith is unmoved, angering members of the WSPU. After the rally, 12 women gather in Parliament Square to speak on women's rights but are stopped. Two WSPU members, Edith New and Mary Leigh, hurl rocks at the windows of 10 Downing Street. Pankhurst is pleased, despite denying WSPU involvement.

Emmeline Pankhurst in 1911, jeered by a disapproving crowd in New York

1930

Hunger strikes
The WSPU protest against what they perceived as unfair prison sentences by going on hunger strike. Police officers resort to violently force-feeding the women using tubes.
1909

The Conciliation Bill
When the Conciliation Bill that would have given women the vote is dropped, Pankhurst starts a protest in anger. Over 100 women are arrested and charged for disturbing the peace.
18 November 1910

Truce
Two days after the outbreak of the First World War, Emmeline and Christabel call an immediate halt to suffrage activism and support their country in the war effort.
4 August 1914

Votes for men and women
The Representation of the People Act grants votes to all men over the age of 21 and to women over the age of 30.
6 February 1918

Emmeline dies
Emmeline Pankhurst dies just weeks before the vote is extended to all women over 21 years of age, on 2 July 1928.
14 June 1928

Commemorated
Two years after her death, Emmeline Pankhurst is commemorated with a statue in London's Victoria Tower Gardens. A crowd of radicals and former suffragettes gather to celebrate her.
6 March 1930

1884 – 1962

Eleanor Roosevelt

Controversial and principled, Eleanor Roosevelt entered the White House at a crucial moment and changed American politics

No other woman has held the position of first lady of the United States for longer than Anna Eleanor Roosevelt, who served from 1933 to 1945. The wife of Franklin Delano Roosevelt, himself the only president to win four presidential elections, she was first lady for 12 years, one month, one week and one day during a period of unprecedented turmoil, both at home and abroad. No other first lady, before or since, has used her position to pursue policy goals with such ambition and success – or with such controversy.

A first lady lives in a paradoxical position. She enters the USA's most famous house unelected, her title is unofficial, with no salary. She does not feature in the Constitution's division of powers between the presidency, the Supreme Court and Congress. Yet as a president's wife, she is in a position of unparalleled status and responsibility. She has the president's ear, and the eyes of the world are upon her.

The essentials of a first lady's work were established in the earliest days of the American republic, when Martha Washington planned and hosted receptions for George. But how to address her among equals, in a society that had dispensed with aristocratic titles? Martha Washington, the first 'first lady', preferred to be called 'Lady Washington'. Some of her successors preferred 'Mrs President'. In the 1840s, President John Tyler's wife Julia called herself 'Mrs Presidentress' when she was in the White House, and 'Mrs ex-President Tyler' after she left it.

The title 'first lady' seems to have appeared in the mid-19th century, but it did not settle on the president's wife until the early-20th century. The timing is significant. In the age of the New Woman and the suffragette, women asserted their right to take part in public life, and to be more than social secretaries to their husbands. Eleanor Roosevelt was a product of that age. Earlier first ladies had wielded influence, but Eleanor was the first to enter the White House as a public figure in her own right.

For more than two decades, since Franklin Delano Roosevelt's entry into politics in 1910 as a senator for New York State, Eleanor had studied the workings of government and developed tactics for advancing those causes that were close to her heart. During World War I, when FDR was assistant navy secretary in Woodrow Wilson's administration, Eleanor immersed herself in wartime relief

and successfully lobbied for the improvement of conditions at Saint Elizabeth's – the military psychiatric hospital in Washington, DC.

After the war, FDR's sickness accelerated Eleanor's growth as a public figure. When the Democrats lost the 1920 election, FDR, the Democratic nominee for vice-president, returned to private practice as a lawyer. The following year, he contracted polio. Eleanor believed that FDR's happiness depended on returning to politics. While he convalesced, she supervised his care, and managed the upbringing of their five children. But his absence from the public stage allowed her to forge her own role.

Protocol had prevented Eleanor from speaking when she joined FDR on the 1920 campaign trail. But now, she could speak publicly on causes such as race and gender equality in the workplace, and the plight of the poor and unemployed. Through the Depression years, Eleanor accumulated experience and prestige on the boards of the Women's City Club of New York, the League of Women Voters, the World Peace Movement and the Women's Trade Union League. She set up a furniture factory in upstate New York to create local jobs, and took over and taught in a school in New York City. She also began a lifelong career as a pundit on the radio and in print.

When FDR returned to politics as governor of New York State in 1928, Eleanor suspended her political affiliations, but not her political activity. Sometimes, as in her support for striking garment workers, she was ahead of her husband; at other times, especially when he was ill, she described herself as his "eyes, ears, and legs" at meetings and visits across the USA.

FDR's rise to the presidency in March 1933 forced a further curtailment of Eleanor's freelance activities, but it permitted an often-controversial expansion of her semi-official work for her husband. Previous first ladies had come to the White House intending to publicise apolitical issues. Grace Coolidge worked for the deaf, and Lou Hoover for the Girl Scouts; Michelle Obama's advocacy for healthy eating and exercise fits this pattern of using the position for non-partisan improvements to American life.

Eleanor came to the White House as an active campaigner on partisan issues, and at a time when the Great Depression was bringing misery to millions. Two days into FDR's presidency, she broke the

Roosevelt (second left) and 'Hick' (far right) in 1933

Behind closed doors
The enigmatic private life of the first lady, the other man and the other woman

Even before FDR was crippled by polio, Eleanor had refused to sleep with him because of his infidelity. Biographers continue to argue over the nature of two subsequent relationships. The first, with her bodyguard, an ex-circus acrobat named Earl Miller, began in 1928. Friends of the Roosevelts noticed their intimacy. Miller never discussed his years with Eleanor, but he did admit to having dated other women in order to reduce gossip.

It is highly likely Eleanor had an affair with journalist Lorena Hickok. They met when 'Hick' was covering FDR's first election campaign. Soon, they were writing to each other daily. "Oh! I want to put my arms around you. I ache to hold you close," a note from Eleanor read. It seems the feeling was mutual. "Most clearly I remember your eyes, with a kind of teasing smile in them," Hickok wrote, "and the feeling of that soft spot just north-east of the corner of your mouth against my lips."

Roosevelt holds a copy of the Universal Declaration of Human Rights, 1949

"She broke the mould by holding her first press conference – inviting only female members of the media"

mould by holding her first press conference – inviting only female members of the media. White House press conferences had traditionally been a male preserve, but all-female ones became a regular feature of Eleanor's tenure. They allowed her to advertise the competence of women in an almost entirely male-dominated profession – and by extension suggest that women could succeed in many other previously closed vocations.

Similar symbolic acts told Americans where the first lady stood on racial discrimination. At a time when many whites were candidly racist, Eleanor was the first white resident of Washington, DC to join the National Association for the Advancement of Colored People (NAACP).

While attending a conference in Alabama in 1938, where the seating was divided into separate areas for whites and blacks, she moved her chair into the aisle.

In Congress, Eleanor's critics did not see a balancing act in her advocacy, so much as blatant partisanship, and the politicising of a privileged position. She, however, believed that if she was acting in the national interest, there could be no conflict of interest. The late 1930s offered a unique opportunity for an activist first lady. To dig the American economy out of the Great Depression, FDR had committed to the New Deal, a collection of massive government programmes to create jobs.

The first ladies before the first lady

★★★

ADAMS
1797-1801

ABIGAIL ADAMS
1744-1818
The wife of the first president to live in the White House, Abigail Adams advised her husband on policy and corresponded with him as he negotiated the shape of the American government at the Continental Congresses in Philadelphia.

★POLK★
1845-1849

SARAH POLK
1803-91
Sarah Childress Polk was her husband's trusted adviser during his political career, editing his speeches and advising him on policy. Concerned for his health while he was president, she reduced the scale of White House entertainments, which earned her the nickname "Sahara Sarah".

TAFT
1909-1913

HELEN 'NERVOUS NELLIE' TAFT
1861-1943
Known as 'Nervous Nellie' because of her perfectionism, Taft attended her husband's cabinet meetings, and sat in the front row at his rival's nomination in case he insulted her husband.

Eleanor used her connections and prestige to prioritise key issues in New Deal programmes. She held conferences at the White House to examine the needs of unemployed women, on the 'Participation of Negro Women and Children in Federal Welfare Programs', and, in 1944, on the role of women in post-war policy making. She ensured that key New Deal organisations, such as the Civil Works Administration as well as the Federal Emergency Relief Administration, contained divisions devoted to alleviating female unemployment, and picked the heads of their offices.

Working with NAACP president Walter White, she harnessed the New Deal to her long-standing campaign for the equal rights of African Americans. She addressed NAACP conferences, successfully lobbied for increased federal funding for African-American institutions, and ensured that key acts of legislation acknowledged racial inequities. Most dramatically, in 1939, she resigned from the Daughters of the American Revolution, a group whose members claim descent from the generation of 1776, when the Daughters refused to rent their auditorium for a concert by the African-American opera singer Marian Anderson.

FDR's presidency oversaw the Depression, the New Deal and World War II – experiences that reshaped American society. Eleanor's activism for the rights of women and African Americans was vital in creating two long-term alliances from which the Democratic Party continues to benefit. Through her radio and newspaper work, she was vital in securing a majority of female voters for the Democratic Party. In 'If You Ask Me', her monthly column in *Ladies' Home Journal*, she became the USA's most elevated agony aunt. Her daily column, 'My Day', was a very human running commentary, mixing politics with her daily experience as the president's emissary to the people. Also, Eleanor's highly visible campaigning for the rights of African Americans was vital in drawing African-American voters away from a historic alliance with the Republicans, the party of Lincoln, and towards the Democrats.

World War II brought the economy back to health, and women and African Americans into the workplace. The first lady spoke to the nation on the night of the attack on Pearl Harbor; FDR did not address the public until the next day. She devoted herself to the war effort, speaking bluntly against the Axis in her broadcasts and digging up the White House lawn to plant a Victory Garden.

When FDR died in April 1945, the first lady announced her retirement from public life. But by the end of the year, she was the only woman among President Truman's five-person delegation to the newly created United Nations. She rose to the chair of the Human Rights' Commission, and in December 1948, presented the Universal Declaration of Human Rights for the UN member states' approval. She died in 1962, having campaigned to the end on labour rights and racial equality.

Interpreters of the American Constitution include 'originalists', who try to establish the founders' original intentions, and 'activists', who see

President Roosevelt?

Eleanor was the niece of one president, Theodore Roosevelt, and the wife of another, Franklin Delano Roosevelt. After his death in 1945, she was rumoured to be planning a run for office. In July 1946, however, she published a disclaimer in Look magazine listing several reasons for not running. She hoped that her work at the new United Nations might prevent future wars. She was elderly, and felt that young people deserved an opportunity. She enjoyed her newly recovered privacy, and "the freedom in being responsible only to yourself." As an "onlooker" and a "help" in FDR's career, she had seen "the worst and best of politics and statesmanship," and had "absolutely no desire" to participate further. But "the plain truth," she admitted, was simpler.

"I am influenced by the thought that no woman, has, as yet, been able to build up and hold sufficient backing to carry through a program," she said. "Men and women both are not yet accustomed to following a woman and looking to her for leadership. If I were young enough, it might be an interesting challenge." Hillary Clinton, the woman who, at the time of writing, has come closest to winning a presidential election, was born just over a year after Eleanor Roosevelt wrote this letter.

Roosevelt at a United Nations conference, Lake Success, New York

EDITH WILSON
1872-1961

When Woodrow Wilson suffered a stroke in October 1919, his second wife Edith Galt Wilson – who had married the president while he was in office in 1915 – effectively ran the executive branch of the government for the last two years of his second term.

WILSON 1915-1921

FLORENCE HARDING
1860-1924

Known as 'The Duchess', Edith Wilson's successor was five years older than President Warren Harding and, observers noted, much more intelligent. Among other accolades, Harding was the first first lady to vote and the first first lady to invite movie stars to the White House.

HARDING 1921-1923

Fundraising for a Red Cross War Relief drive, 1940

Keeping up appearances with FDR in the 1930s

WIT AND WISDOM
FROM THE
WHITE HOUSE

Eleanor Roosevelt's
philosophies for life

No one can make you feel inferior without your consent

" GREAT MINDS DISCUSS IDEAS;
AVERAGE MINDS DISCUSS EVENTS;
SMALL MINDS DISCUSS PEOPLE "

The future belongs to those who believe in the beauty of their dreams "

"A WOMAN IS LIKE A TEA BAG – YOU CAN'T
TELL HOW STRONG SHE IS UNTIL YOU PUT
HER IN HOT WATER "

" ## Do one thing every day that scares you "

" IN THE LONG RUN,
WE SHAPE OUR LIVES, AND WE SHAPE
OURSELVES. THE PROCESS NEVER ENDS
UNTIL WE DIE. AND THE CHOICES WE MAKE
ARE ULTIMATELY OUR OWN RESPONSIBILITY "

the Constitution as a document whose meaning changes as time and society progresses. Eleanor was an activist, responding to the shifting meaning of relations between men and women, blacks and whites, in an era of dramatic change. There is no doubt she used her position for partisan ends. During the FDR presidency, she insisted that her broadcasts and journalism were separate from her husband's policies. Later, she admitted that FDR's office had used her to break difficult news or advocate for unpopular policies.

In retrospect, many of those policies were right. Today, Eleanor pressuring her husband to pass a law against lynching looks less dubious than his decision to overrule her because he did not want to alienate white voters in the south. Eleanor's blunt statements were vital

"Roosevelt used her privileged position to alleviate poverty and racism"

assets in FDR's careful campaign to convince the Isolationist majorities in Congress and the American public of the danger represented by German and Japanese territorial ambitions.

At a time of national crisis, desperate need and on-going discrimination, Eleanor Roosevelt used her privileged position to alleviate poverty and racism, and pull together the American nation in a global war for freedom. She had become the 'First Lady of the World'.

Her legacy, however, was another paradox. She had expanded the possibilities of being a first lady, but also demonstrated its limits. Today, the first lady is under greater scrutiny. But the candidacy of Hillary Clinton itself is part of Eleanor Roosevelt's legacy too.

Eleanor at the Philadelphia headquarters of a civil rights organisation, the Citizens Campaign Committee, 1956

The founding father
Claes emigrated from Holland around 1638. A few years later, he bought a farm in what is now midtown Manhattan. The farm included the site of the modern Empire State Building.

Claes Martenszan van Rosenvelt unknown- 1659

Nicholas 1658-1742

The Democratic Roosevelts of Hyde Park
Eleanor's controlling mother-in-law was the second wife of James 'Squire James' Roosevelt, the horse-breeding scion of the Democrat-voting Hyde Park side of the Roosevelt family.

The Republican Roosevelts of Oyster Bay
Claes's grandson Johannes, a New York businessman and manufacturer of linseed, founded the Oyster Bay branch of the family. They voted Republican: in 1901, Johannes's great-great-great-grandson Theodore became a Republican president.

Johannes 1689-1750

Jacobus 1724-77

James 1759-1840

Cornelius Van Schaack 1794-1871

Theodore Sr 1831-78
m

Martha Bulloch 1835-84

Jacobus 1692-1776

Isaac 1726-94

James 1760-1847

Isaac 1790-1863

James 1828-1900
m

Rebecca Howland 1831-78

Sara Delano 1854-1941

THE ROOSEVELT FAMILY TREE

Eleanor and Franklin were kissing cousins – fifth cousins, once removed, to be precise

The 26th president of the United States
'TR' was the great-grandson of Johannes, the founder of the Oyster Bay branch. A Republican, he held office from 1901 to 1909.

Theodore 1858-1919
m

Alice H Lee 1861-84

Anna 1855-1931

Corinne 1861-1933

Elliott 1860-94   m   **Anna Hall 1863-92**

James 1854-1927

Edith K Carow 1861-1948

Anna Eleanor 1884-1962   m   **Franklin D 1882-1945**

Eleanor's tragic father
Elliott, TR's unstable brother and Eleanor's father, was a hopeless alcoholic who had several nervous breakdowns. In 1894, when Eleanor was nine years old, he died after jumping from a window.

The 32nd president of the United States
The 32nd president, and the only incumbent to have been elected four times, FDR was Claes's great-great-great-great-great-grandson.

Alice 1884-1980

Theodore 1887-1944

Kermit 1889-1943

Ethel 1891-1977

Archibald 1894-1979

Quentin 1897-1918

1910 – 1997

Mother Teresa

Controversial, celebrated and ultimately revered as a saint, Mother Teresa devoted her life to philanthropy

When she was growing up in what is now the Republic of Macedonia, little Anjezë Gonxhe Bojaxhiu dreamed of becoming a missionary. Better known today as Mother Teresa, Anjezë left home at 18 to travel to Ireland. It was there that she took holy orders and adopted the name by which she is now sainted.

Mother Teresa as we know her, dressed in a plain white sari with simple blue edging, came into being in 1948 when she started her missionary work in India. She became an Indian citizen and spent her days working in the grinding poverty of the Kolkata slums, where she championed education and healthcare, as well as helping people face the day to day privations of life.

Mother Teresa's work inspired those who saw her and by 1949 she was at the head of a burgeoning community of novices, all of whom wanted to follow her example and minister to the poorest people in Kolkata. This became the Missionaries of Charity, the organisation with which Mother Teresa is most associated, and as word spread of her work among the poor and dying, support for her cause began to flood in.

Within 20 years the Missionaries of Charity counted hospitals, orphanages, retreats for lepers and international offshoots among its achievements. As foundations in the name of the Missionaries of Charity began following Mother Teresa's examples and values all over the world, donations and would-be missionaries poured through the doors, all dedicated towards alleviating the suffering of the poor.

Eventually Mother Teresa's message had spread to over 500 missions across the globe, but she wasn't immune to controversy. She has been accused of overstating the work of her mission in Kolkata and of ignoring basic safety requirements when administering medical care.

At the same time, her comments on the immorality of abortion jarred with commentators who questioned her claims to be without any political bias. She also accepted donations from controversial figures and laid flowers on the grave of the late prime minister of Albania, Enver Hoxha, whose regime had employed methods of torture and violent repression.

Despite the criticisms levelled at her, more than two decades after her death Mother Teresa continues to be feted for her charitable work. Though letters published posthumously revealed that she had suffered a crisis of faith that lasted years, the campaign to beatify Mother Teresa began almost immediately after she died. In order to satisfy the requirement that the candidate for sainthood must have performed a miracle, her supporters submitted the fact that a locket containing Mother Teresa's picture had cured a tumour that had threatened the life of Monica Besra. Despite Besra's doctor and family claiming that her survival owed more to her medical treatment than the late nun, Besra swore that a beam of light had shone from the picture and healed her. This was all the proof that was needed.

Mother Teresa was eventually canonised on 4 September 2016. From that day forward, Anjezë Gonxhe Bojaxhiu became Saint Teresa of Calcutta.

A life's work

1928
Anjezë Gonxhe Bojaxhiu goes to Ireland to begin her instruction as a novice. She changes her name to Sister Teresa.

1937
Sister Teresa takes her final vows. She is called Mother Teresa for the first time, a name that later becomes famous.

1948
After teaching in Loreto for years, Mother Teresa is given permission to leave her order and follow her calling to work in the Kolkata slums.

1950
The Missionaries of Charity is officially founded as a religious congregation. Over the ensuing decades it will a vast worldwide organisation.

1952
The Missionaries of Charity open a home for the dying in Kolkata. The following year Mother Teresa opens the Missionaries of Charity's first orphanage.

A lifetime's work

Despite the controversies attached to her name, Mother Teresa's achievements are many. Perhaps her greatest was the sheer amount of attention and awareness her work brought to the poorest people of Kolkata, those who were trapped in the most dire poverty imaginable with no hope of escape.

She struggled against her own self-doubt as well as the privations of the lifestyle she had elected to live and emerged as a champion of the poor and sick, including raising awareness of the plight of leprosy sufferers and orphans.

Mother Teresa's work took her around the world, and won her meetings with world leaders

"Teresa's picture had cured a tumour"

Mother Teresa's work amongst the world's poorest people saw her rewarded with the Nobel Peace Prize

Five things to know about... Mother Teresa

1 A life-long calling

Mother Teresa was fascinated by stories of missionaries from infancy and decided to enter a religious order and devote her life to her faith.

2 A career in education

Mother Teresa was a teacher at the Loreto convent school in India and became its headmistress in 1944, a role she left to work in the slums.

3 A home for the dying

The first establishment Mother Teresa opened was the Kalighat Home for the Dying. It opened its doors in 1952 as a place for the ailing poor to die in peace.

4 It wasn't just women

The Missionaries of Charity Brothers was formed in 1963 to allow men to follow Mother Teresa's teachings and carry out missionary work just as the sisters did.

5 A global mother

Though she abided by her vow of poverty, Mother Teresa toured the world undertaking missionary work. She visited Chernobyl and Ethiopia, and met with the most powerful world leaders.

1962
Mother Teresa wins the first of many humanitarian prizes for her work. She ploughs any prize money that she receives back into her mission.

1979
Mother Teresa is awarded the Nobel Peace Prize in recognition of her humanitarian work not just in Kolkata, but across the globe.

1990
After years of ill health, Mother Teresa considers retirement but is convinced to remain active by her supportive followers.

1997
Mother Teresa dies in Kolkata. She is given a state funeral and across the world, people mourn her passing and fete her name.

2016
Following her 2003 beatification, on 4 September 2016 Mother Teresa is canonised by Pope Francis before a crowd in St Peter's Square.

Heroines of politics & activism

From underground resistance to the pinnacle of government, these are the political trailblazers

Indira Gandhi
Indian 1917 – 1984

Indira Gandhi is, to date, the only woman to serve in office as prime minister of India, a position that she held from 1966 to 1977 and again from 1980 until her death. She led her country to a victory in the war with Pakistan, which resulted in the liberation of Bangladesh, but also presided over a disastrous state of emergency, leading to her removal from office. When Gandhi returned to power in 1980, it was on the back of a massive wave of popular support. Her time in power was short and she was assassinated in 1984, just months after her pioneering nation sent its first astronaut into outer space.

Ruth Bader Ginsburg
American 1933 – now

When Ruth Bader Ginsburg embarked on her legal studies at Harvard Law School, she was asked how she had the nerve to take a place that might better have been awarded to a man. It was the first of many challenges that she'd face in her rise to become associate justice of the Supreme Court of the United States. Bader Ginsburg, however, met her doubters head on and became not only one of the world's most respected legal scholars, but also one of America's most celebrated attorneys. She battled for gender equality and now sits in the country's highest court, helping to define the law of the land.

Malala Yousafzai
Pakistani 1997 – now

Growing up in Pakistan, Malala Yousafzai became a well-known speaker on the importance of education for girls. It was an issue she had already experienced firsthand in her homeland of Swat Valley, where the Taliban had banned girls from schools. In 2012 she was travelling home by bus in Pakistan after sitting an exam when a Taliban gunman shot her in the head. She was rushed to hospital and later transferred to Birmingham, UK for specialist treatment. Since then, Yousafzai has become an international speaker for the rights of women, a recipient of the Nobel Peace Prize and a spokesperson in the fight against oppression.

Irena Sendler
Polish 1910 – 2008

Irena Sendler used her position in the Social Welfare Department to gain access to the Warsaw ghetto. She smuggled in medication and other essentials and smuggled out babies, children and adults, spiriting them to safety under the noses of the Nazis. In 1943, Sendler was interrogated by the Gestapo. She refused to speak and escaped execution only because an associate bribed her guards. Though highly honoured in Israel and Poland, she remained virtually unknown in the West. Today she is recognised for her humanitarian efforts and was twice nominated for the Nobel Peace Prize.

Josephine Baker
French 1906 – 1975

Famed as an entertainer and civil rights activist, Josephine Baker lived a secret life during WWII as an informer for the Free French movement, charming those she met at parties into giving away information. Under the cover of touring her show, she was able to move information across the continent, carrying secrets written on her sheet music in invisible ink. After the war, Baker became a spokesperson for the Civil Rights Movement, refusing to perform in segregated venues and speaking on platforms alongside Martin Luther King. She was buried in France with full military honours.

Benazir Bhutto
Pakistani 1953 – 2007

As Pakistan's prime minister from 1988 to 1990 and 1993 to 1996, Benazir Bhutto was the first woman to be elected head of state in a Muslim nation. Her rise to power was remarkable given her youth and the fact that she had once faced exile from Pakistan following the overthrow and execution of her father. Bhutto championed education and healthcare and was devoted to establishing democracy in Pakistan. Though she was a devout Muslim, her work earned her the ire of religious fundamentalists. Though her murder by suicide bomber devastated her supporters, they continue her work to this day.

Golda Meir
Israeli 1898 – 1978

Golda Meir was prime minister of Israel from 1969 to 1974 and is to date the only woman to hold that office. Although her time at the helm ended in disappointment, Meir's political career had been nothing short of glittering. A committed Zionist, she had held numerous positions within government including labour minister and foreign minister, and was a key player in the founding of the Jewish state. A committed politician dedicated to her nation and beliefs, Meir was respected by all who met her, even if they didn't share her ambitions.

Madeleine Albright
American 1937 – now

When Madeleine Albright was appointed as US secretary of state in 1997, she was the first woman ever to hold the office. Before that she had served as US ambassador to the United Nations. Albright's appointment as secretary of state made her the highest-ranking woman in American history, a remarkable achievement considering that she didn't have a government position until she was nearly 40 years old. She remains active as a member of several peace initiatives and chair of the Albright Stonebridge Group, an international strategy consultancy.

Margaret Thatcher
British 1925 – 2013

Margaret Thatcher was the first female leader of the Conservative Party, the first female prime minister of the United Kingdom and the longest-serving prime minister of the 20th century, with a term of office that began in 1979 and ended in 1990. Thatcher came to power with promises to end the 'Winter of Discontent' and won huge public support following her handling of the Falklands War. Yet rising unemployment, increased poverty and a series of deeply unpopular policies combined to see her forced into resignation by her own party in 1990.

ARTS & CULTURE

46

40

50

58

60

52

1907 – 1954

Frida Kahlo

Enduring a life of physical and emotional pain, this iconic Mexican artist reinvented herself through her surreal portraits

Her cheek pressed against the cool glass of the window, little Frida Kahlo gazed wistfully at the outside world. Confined to her bed to recover from a severe bout of polio, Frida had been deemed too fragile to step outdoors – and in her solitude, she found herself longing for a friend. She pulled her head back and exhaled on the windowpane. If she couldn't see her own friends, she'd just have to make up her own. Raising a frail finger, she drew a door in the misted glass and slipped through it. Walking across a field, she reached a small dairy shop – Pinzón – and clambered through its letter 'O' into the innards of the Earth. Here, she stood face-to-face with a girl, beaming.

In young Frida's make-believe world, her imaginary friend waited for her daily. Endlessly joyful and lively, this imaginary friend was the polar opposite of the sickly six-year-old that created her. Where Frida was morose, her friend was happy; where Frida limped and struggled with her ailing right leg, her friend danced. It was in this fictitious land where Frida felt most happy.

Born in 1907 to Guillermo Kahlo and his second wife, Matilde, Frida was the third of four daughters born to the couple. A photographer by trade, Frida's German father had emigrated to Mexico in 1891 after a severe epileptic fit and disagreements with his stepmother put a swift halt to his education in his homeland. Having been consigned to her bed for months after contracting polio at the age of six, Frida grew close to her father, whose shared experience of severe illness bonded the two. While Frida recovered, Guillermo shared his passion for creativity and philosophy with her, and once she was strong enough, he encouraged her to take up sports to strengthen her right leg, which was stunted and skinny as a result of polio.

Despite starting her education later than her peers, by 1922 Frida was one of 35 girls that had been accepted into the National Preparatory School, an elite academy of 2,000 students. The school's headteacher claimed the young girl was the leader of a "band of juvenile delinquents who raised such uproars in the school that [he] had considered quitting

IN HER SICKBED, FRIDA CONSIDERED A CAREER AS A MEDICAL ILLUSTRATOR

his job". While she may have been mischievous, Frida also thrived academically and harboured dreams of becoming a doctor.

But while Frida's formative years began to mould her, Mexico was in chaos. Its president, 80-year-old Porfirio Díaz, had vowed to stand down from the 1910 elections, only to backtrack and then rig the vote to ensure that he won an eighth term. In being so brash, he insulted those who dreamed of democracy in Mexico. Díaz triggered what became known as the Mexican Revolution from 1910-20, and by 1911 he had been ousted, his oppressive regime in ruins. But Díaz's successors were no more successful - power was

Self Portrait with Thorn Necklace and Hummingbird, 1940

Frida's wheelchair and specially designed easel in the Blue House, now a museum to her art

Frida and Diego in their New York home after he was fired in May 1933

juggled between tyrants, puppets and incapable politicians. By 1917, the Mexican Constitution was drafted, and the revolution largely slowed in the years that followed. In the ensuing years, citizens demanded the reforms promised to them by the Constitution, and the newly elected President Alvaro Obregón was seemingly the man to deliver them. Obregón instigated the rebirth of Mexican culture, encouraging a sense of nationalism that filtered through all walks of Mexican society. His reforms provided stability and security to Mexico's peasants, while his left-leaning cultural endeavours meant that like-minded artists, such as the famous muralist Diego Rivera, thrived. Even after Obregón's assassination, his successors continued his semi-socialist vision for Mexico, and Mexico rapidly became a mecca for liberal thinkers, including philosophers, artists and writers alike. For Frida, this burgeoning renaissance was the epitome of Mexican identity. She identified herself as a child of the revolution, even moving her birth year forward by three years to coincide with the Mexican Revolution.

On 17 September 1925, Frida's life changed forever. On her way back home from school, her bus catastrophically crashed with a streetcar,

> *"Frida was sickened by America's wealth and the nation's obsession with capitalism"*

leaving several people dead and almost killing Frida. The force of the impact had shattered her already feeble right leg, crushed her feet and fractured several ribs and her collarbone, as well as dislodging three vertebrae. The streetcar's handrail had also impaled Frida, entering through her abdomen and coming out through her groin. She spent months recovering, first at hospital and later at home, confined to the same bedroom of her youth. Forced to abandon higher education, any dreams of becoming a doctor lay shattered among the debris and bodies that fateful day.

As she lay bed-ridden, however, Frida sought a means to keep her mind and body occupied. Having shown promise in painting before the accident, a custom-made easel was set up on Frida's bed, with a mirror pointing towards Frida hanging from above. While she recovered, she painted anything she could – self-portraits, her sisters, friends – even decorating her stifling body cast and orthopaedic corsets.

By 1927, however, Frida had recovered well. Her injuries would haunt her for the rest of her life, but soon her mind would be occupied with happier thoughts. That year, Frida joined the Mexican Communist Party, where she became acquainted with a new and elite circle of intellectuals and creatives. One of these was Diego Rivera, whose patriotic art had seen him shoot to fame and glory in the wake of the Mexican Revolution. Diego was 20 years Frida's senior, twice married and a reputed womaniser, but Frida was smitten. It wasn't Frida's first brush with the famed muralist – in 1922 he had painted at her school, where the young student had allegedly remarked that she would marry him

This was a gift to her doctor

Frida painting in 1931

Her 1946 *Tree of Hope* shows her both as a victim and survivor

Making Her Self Up

For the first time, many of Frida Kahlo's personal belongings are being exhibited outside of her homeland. V&A Museum curator Circe Henestrosa reveals what these long-forgotten treasures can tell us about the artist

Where were the 50 artefacts in the 'Frida Kahlo: Making Her Self Up' exhibition before this, and why haven't they left Mexico before?

These objects came all the way from the Museo Frida Kahlo in Mexico City, where they have been since their discovery in 2004. Some of them have been included in an exhibit at the Museo Frida Kahlo curated by myself called 'Appearances Can Be Deceiving', which was in 2012.

The V&A exhibition [on until November] will include a number of self-portraits, numerous photographs, film and sound, and provide context about the political and artistic circles that Frida and Diego Rivera were at the centre of in post-Revolutionary Mexico.

What can we learn about Frida's life from these exhibits?

The exhibition will show some of her personal belongings such as her dresses, jewellery, make-up, orthopaedic devices and medicines, to reveal more about Frida's life. Frida Kahlo has become a countercultural and feminist symbol, well known for her self-portraits and stylised look. This exhibition, entitled 'Frida Kahlo: Making Her Self Up' definitely looks to explore some of the deeper issues relating to her life. This will be the first exhibition outside of Mexico to display her clothes and intimate possessions, reuniting them with key self-portraits and photographs to offer a fresh perspective on her compelling life story. We will present an unparalleled insight into Frida Kahlo's life, even revealing some objects that have never been on show to the public before.

How did Frida use make-up and fashion to craft her own identity?

I think Kahlo's powerful style is as integral to her myth as her paintings. It is her construction of identity through her ethnicity, disability, political beliefs and art that makes her such a compelling and relevant icon today. Her self-portraits make us remember her through her self-image. In the collection of personal belongings found at the Blue House back in 2004, we found a Revlon eye pencil called 'Ebony' that she used to darken her eyebrows. We also have other surviving objects, such as different lipsticks, her blush, a cigarette case and more. Her famous husband, Mexican muralist Diego Rivera, recalled his first meeting with Kahlo: "dark and thick eyebrows met above her nose. They seemed like the wings of a black bird, their black arches framing two extraordinary brown eyes." They became her defining feature, alongside her moustache.

Did Frida conform to the expectations of a Mexican woman at the time?

Frida Kahlo is the very model of the bohemian artist: unique, rebellious and contradictory, a cult figure that continues to be appropriated by feminists, artists, fashion designers and popular culture. I think she was unconventional, and very much ahead of her time, and that's what makes her so relevant today. We want to show that side of Frida Kahlo, that different side of her. Kahlo never let her disabilities and personal circumstances define her. She defined who she was in her own terms. So in this show, my co-curator Claire Wilcox and I want to emphasise Kahlo's unconventional spirit. We want to show her non-conforming ways of being that she expressed through art, dress and in her life.

After her death, Frida was revered as a kind of champion of feminism – is that a fair portrayal?

I think she has been appropriated by feminists due to what she represents today – again, that intersectionality. A Mexican, female artist who was disabled, looking for a place as a female artist in a highly male-dominated environment in Mexico City. Aren't we fighting as women for the same today? How much more relevant and refreshing for our times can she be?

Frida painted her corsets and individualised her prosthetic leg – why did she do that?

Frida's clothes became part of her armour, to deflect, conceal and distract from her injuries. She included them in her art and in the construction of her style as an essential wardrobe item. Her relationship to the corset was one of support and need – her body was dependent on medical attention – but also one of rebellion. Far from allowing the corset to define her as an invalid, Kahlo decorated and adorned her corsets, making them appear as an explicit choice. She included them in the construction of her looks as an essential piece and as her second skin.

Did Frida play a role in shaping Mexico at the time?

Frida very much incorporated a strong sense of cultural pride following the Mexican Revolution (1910-20). She even changed her birth date to align with the start of the Mexican Revolution. She was part of the circle of intellectuals of the post-revolutionary period al the way until she passed away in 1954. Her Tehuana dresses symbolised her 'mexicanidad', her political beliefs and her will to portray herself as a Mexican artist.

After her right leg was amputated in 1953, Frida added a striking red leather boot with a bell on the laces to her wooden leg

Frida poses with an Olmec figurine, a product of a highly advanced ancient Mexican culture

Frida wore clothing from a variety of indigenous styles

This jewellery was inspired by indigenous designs

The Many Faces of Frida Kahlo

Frida was more than just an artist - she was a force of nature

The Communist

Frida wasn't afraid to use her political voice to express her standpoint. A firm believer in the socialist reforms following the Mexican Revolution, Frida joined the Communist Party early in her life, and became a devout member in her final years. In 1953, she described herself as "an unconditional ally of the Communist revolutionary movement. For the first time in my life my painting is trying to help in the line set by the Party."

The Disabled

After recovering from polio at the age of six, Frida's right leg remained shorter and skinnier than her left, and she was ridiculed by her peers, who called her 'Frida the peg-leg'. But this cruel nickname hardened the young girl, and even after the horrific accident in 1925, Frida had learnt to hide her pain. Instead of merely accepting her injuries, she embraced them as a vital part of her identity.

The Feminist

In recent decades, Frida has been championed as a symbol of women's expression thanks to her frank and emotional depictions of her own trauma, but also for defying gender norms of the time. Frida's intimate paintings reveal a woman determined to break the mould, so it's no wonder that she's lauded as a feminist icon today.

The Surrealist

Revered today as one of the great surrealist painters of the mid-20th century, Frida herself was keen to keep a certain amount of distance between her personal, intimate self-portraits and the kooky artistic movement, explaining, "I never painted dreams. I painted my own reality."

The Two Fridas, painted by Kahlo in 1939

one day. The two quickly fell in love, and by 1929 the couple had wed. Diego's work saw them travel to the United States, first to San Francisco, where Frida's work was exhibited for the first time at the Sixth Annual Exhibition of the San Francisco Society of Women Artists, and later to Detroit and New York.

Frida never truly took to life in America. She was sickened by the wealth and appalled by the nation's obsession with capitalism. In a letter written during her time in the US, she was "convinced it's only through communism that we can become human". She longed for home. In December 1933, her wish was granted. After Diego was fired from a commission in the Rockefeller Center for refusing to remove the face of Lenin from a mural, the pair returned to Mexico, with Diego's reputation in the United States in tatters.

Frida and Diego's marriage was the very antithesis of conventional. Back in Mexico, they lived in two separate houses joined by a bridge, and both were notorious adulterers. Despite her own infidelities, Frida was devastated to discover her husband's affair with her own sister, Cristina. For weeks she contemplated divorce, before eventually reconciling with them both.

All might have been forgiven, but it certainly wasn't forgotten. When the exiled Leon Trotsky and his wife, Natalia, arrived in Mexico in 1937, it was only a matter of time before Frida sought retaliation for her husband's indiscretions. Housed in La Casa Azul - meaning 'The Blue House', Frida's childhood home - Trotsky was quickly seduced by the vivacious and intelligent Frida. Their affair was brief but passionate.

Frida and Trotsky secretly exchanged love letters hidden beneath the covers of books, and the pair spoke only in English to their spouses' bafflement - but by the end of the year, it was all over. Natalia and Diego had uncovered the truth, and after months of bitter disagreements between the men, Trotsky and his wife moved out of the Blue House in April 1939. Just over a year later, Trotsky was assassinated in Mexico.

In 1939, Frida and Diego's marital problems proved to be too much, and the pair divorced in November. Frida moved back into The Blue House, where she fondly reflected on her happy memories - in particular, recollections of her childhood imaginary friend inspired her to create The Two Fridas. But while Frida retreated from the world, her heartbreak proved the perfect fodder for her creativity, and from 1939-40 she painted some of her most acclaimed masterpieces, including Self Portrait With Cropped Hair and The Wounded Table, depicting the emotional

"While Frida retreated from the world, her heartbreak proved the perfect fodder for her creativity"

Frida greets Trotsky and his wife Natalia as they arrive in Mexico

devastation that she'd experienced at the hands of her husband. Their separation was only temporary, however, and in 1940 Diego and Frida remarried.

By this time, Frida had made a name for herself as an artist in her own right. No longer just the wife of Diego Rivera, Frida's work was in demand. But with her steep rise in popularity came a sharp decline in her health. In almost constant agony and unable to stand or sit for long periods of time because of her back, Frida turned to alcohol and drugs to self-medicate. In 1945 Frida flew to New York to receive state-of-the-art surgery on her spine, but the operation was a disaster and left Frida in even more pain. This was yet more inspiration for her creativity, and arguably her most famous work – *The Broken Column* – expresses the emotional and physical pain that Frida suffered in the aftermath of the surgery. Further surgery in 1950 failed, with multiple follow-up operations required to combat the onset of infection.

Despite the crippling pain of her back, Frida rekindled her passion for politics. She rejoined the Mexican Communist Party (having revoked her membership in solidarity with her husband following his expulsion from the Party back in 1929), and once again became active in voicing her socialist dreams for Mexico through her art. In 1954, Frida painted *Self Portrait With Stalin*, an ode to the communist leader who had ordered the assassination of Leon Trotsky over a decade before.

In 1950, Frida took another turn for the worse, and she was diagnosed with gangrene in her right foot. In spite of her failing health, Frida was determined to continue working. The following months were tumultuous, with Frida in and out of hospital, or confined for months on end to bed rest. When her 1953 solo exhibition launched at the Contemporary Art Gallery of Mexico in April, her doctors had expressly forbidden her to attend, insisting that she remain in bed. Famously, she obeyed their orders by having her four-poster bed transported into the gallery.

Frida never recovered from the past decade of illness, and in August 1953 her right leg was amputated at the knee. In the face of such trauma, Frida seemed defiant, determined to exude power and strength to the very end – but behind the curtain another scene was unravelling. With her health deteriorating, Frida spiralled into a depression. In February 1954, Frida wrote, "They amputated my leg six months ago. It seemed to me centuries of torture and at times I nearly went crazy. I still feel like committing suicide. Diego prevents me from doing it in the vain belief that maybe he will need me. He has told me so and I believe him. But I have never suffered so much in my life. I'll wait a while."

Less than six months later, Frida was dead. Though officially recorded as a pulmonary embolism, it's thought that she committed suicide by overdose. Her last diary entry reveals the face that Frida hid behind a mask of bravado: "Thanks to the doctors... Thanks to the nurses, to the stretcher-bearers, to the cleaning women and attendants... I hope the exit is joyful – and I hope never to return."

In life, Frida Kahlo's reality was cruel and unkind; beneath the powerful and defiant facade, Frida was fragile and self-conscious of her ailing, shattered body. But in death, Kahlo has indeed returned – as an iconic figure, a champion of women, and as Mexico's greatest artist.

Frida kept unconventional pets, such as this monkey

Frida shows herself as a wounded, but still strong, deer in this 1946 painting

1928 – 2014

Maya Angelou

A prolific and heartfelt activist, Maya Angelou's writings have become a cornerstone of American culture

Maya Angelou lived many lives. Actor, dancer, journalist and more, she has became revered as a legend, with a body of work that is recognised as one of the most important in modern literature. Angelou endured a brutal and unsettled childhood. Subjected to horrifying sexual abuse at the hands of her mother's partner, Angelou confided in her brother, and as a result her abuser was convicted – but he was jailed for just one day. When he was later murdered, the young Angelou, believing that her confession of the abuse had resulted in his killing, became an elective mute.

For five years, Maya Angelou was silent. It was a teacher, Bertha Flowers, who helped her to find her voice again and introduced her to the wonders of literature, sharing the works of Dickens, Shakespeare and more with her young pupil. Angelou never forgot the lessons she learned with Bertha Flowers and when she left home, she had an abiding love of literature.

A mother at just 17 years old and a wife at the age of 23, Maya Angelou initially entered showbiz as a singer, dancer and actor, but in the early 1960s, she met Malcolm X and agreed to work with him on the Organization of Afro-American Unity. His subsequent murder shattered her and when her burgeoning friendship with Martin Luther King was ended by his assassination, she sank deeper and deeper into misery.

Angelou wrote her most famous work, *I Know Why the Caged Bird Sings*, in 1969. It was the first of seven volumes of autobiography and was hailed as a seminal work. Billed as autobiographical fiction, the book followed Angelou's life from infancy to the age of 17 and focused on her experience as a young black woman growing up in America, unflinchingly discussing questions of identity and race, as well as the traumatic abuse that she had endured in her youth.

When the book was published, it was immediately hailed as a revolutionary approach to autobiography. Angelou purposefully moved away from the traditional trappings of the genre and captured not only her own experience as a young black woman in an often racist society, but a wider sense of oppression and hopelessness that spoke to readers across the world.

Angelou went on to tell the rest of her story in a series of bestselling autobiographies, as well as penning poems, essays and other works. She worked as an educator and became a celebrated spokesperson for women and black people, as well as a seminal cultural figure in America.

When she recited her poetry at the inauguration of President Bill Clinton, she became only the second poet in history to do so. Richly honoured, she received innumerable awards including the Presidential Medal of Freedom, awarded by President Barack Obama.

News of Maya Angelou's death in 2014 was met with an outpouring of grief and love from across the globe. Today her writings are as popular as ever and her legacy lives on in her remarkable body of work and the autobiographies that changed the face of American literature.

A life's work

1942
After years of selective mutism following childhood sexual abuse, Maya Angelou learns to speak again.

1952
Following the breakdown of her marriage she adopts the name Maya Angelou and begins her career as an entertainer.

1959
Angelou accepts an invitation from Martin Luther King Jr to become the northern coordinator for the Southern Christian Leadership Conference.

1964
After four years in Africa, Angelou returns to the US to work alongside Malcolm X as he establishes the Organization of African Americans.

1969
I Know Why the Caged Bird Sings is published. It becomes a best-seller immediately, and from that day forward, never goes out of print.

The Caged Bird

Although she was a civil rights activist, an entertainer, a filmmaker, an educator and more, it is for her seven volumes of autobiography that Maya Angelou is most celebrated. Without a doubt it is the first of these, *I Know Why the Caged Bird Sings*, that remains her masterpiece.

The book is a hard-hitting examination of race and gender, unflinching in its depiction of Angelou's suffering in childhood and her struggle to find her way in the world. To this day it attracts controversy and is among the ten books most frequently banned in American high schools.

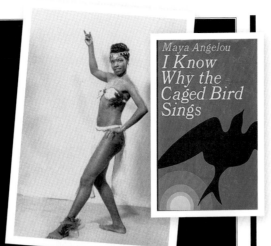

I Know Why the Caged Bird Sings unflinchingly tells the story of Angelou's early tormented life

At the inauguration of President Clinton in 1993, Angelou performed her poem, *On the Pulse of the Morning*

Five things to know about... Maya Angelou

1 What's in a name?
Maya Angelou was baptised Marguerite Johnson. Her brother nicknamed her Maya, which means 'my sister'. She adopted it as her professional name, adding Angelou, her marital surname.

2 A decorated woman
Though Maya Angelou never attended college, she was the recipient of over 50 honorary degrees, many of them from some of the world's foremost educational institutions.

3 A civil rights icon
Following the assassination of Martin Luther King Jr on her birthday, Angelou chose not to celebrate her birthday for many years. Instead, she sent flowers to King's widow.

4 A productive routine
When working on a book, Angelou followed a set routine. She checked into a local hotel, removed the pictures from the walls and wrote by hand on yellow legal pads.

5 Travelling the world
Angelou lived in Egypt and edited *The Arab Observer*. She followed this with a move to the University of Ghana, where she taught in the School of Music and Drama.

1977
Angelou appears in Roots, adding to a CV that includes not only literature but also stints in academia, as well as credits as a composer and actress.

1993
Angelou recites her own poem On the Pulse of the Morning at President Clinton's inauguration. Her recording of the poem wins a Grammy Award.

2013
Mom & Me & Mom, the 7th volume of Angelou's autobiography, is published. It is the last full-length autobiographical work that Angelou publishes.

2014
Angelou dies while writing the next volume of her autobiography. At her memorial, speakers include Michelle Obama and Bill Clinton.

2015
Maya Angelou is memorialised on a stamp by the US Postal Service, adding to numerous other honours.

1759 – 1797

Mary Wollstonecraft

Thanks to her husband's memoirs, it took more than a century for Mary Wollstonecraft to receive the recognition she deserved

When it came to life, Mary Wollstonecraft was anything but traditional. Her unorthodox lifestyle and her husband's efforts to memorialise her after her death saw this remarkable woman remembered not for her groundbreaking work, but for her love affairs. A century after her death she was finally recognised as one of the first feminist philosophers and took her place beside her daughter, Mary Shelley, in the pantheon of female literary greats.

Mary Wollstonecraft began her literary career writing about education but it was for her *Vindications* that she became famed. The first, *A Vindication on the Rights of Men*, was published in 1790 and was her response to the French Revolution. In it she refutes the concept of monarchy and calls instead for a republican nation. The book was a response to Edmund Burke's monarchist work, *Reflections on the Revolution in France*, and Wollstonecraft was frustrated at his depiction of women as passive vessels in a male-dominated world.

The work brought Wollstonecraft to fame and she followed it with *A Vindication on the Rights of Woman*, the book that has since become recognised as one of the most important works of the Enlightenment. Published in 1790, *A Vindication of the Rights of Woman* is one of the first feminist works and calls for women to be given a full education and not to be sidelined as ornamental wives to educated husbands. She made a plea for women to recognise their own abilities and push against society's determination to pigeonhole them, beseeching them to recognise that they might achieve recognition for more than just their beauty.

A Vindication on the Rights of Woman was a success on its release, but Wollstonecraft's popularity wouldn't last. When she died in 1797 her husband, William Godwin, published *Memoirs of the Author of A Vindication of the Rights of Woman*, detailing her tempestuous love life and attempts at suicide. His intention had been to preserve the memory and reputation of the woman he loved but instead the reception to the book and to Mary Wollstonecraft was vicious. She was held up as a creature without morals whose influence could only be damaging to decent women and for decades, scholars sought to distance themselves from her work for fear of becoming as reviled as Wollstonecraft was.

Mary Wollstonecraft's reputation was in tatters for over a century but by the dawn of the 20th century, the tide had begun to turn. She was championed by such seminal figures as Virginia Woolf and as feminist theory rose to prominence in the 1960s, Wollstonecraft's writing was recognised as the pioneering work it truly was. She was hailed as an early warrior for the rights of women and today, is lauded as one of the foremost thinkers of her age. Her writings continue to influence scholars to this day and across the world, the name of Mary Wollstonecraft has become forever associated with the plight of women as they battle for equality in all areas of life.

A life's work

1784
Wollstonecraft opens a school with her friend, Fanny Blood. The following year Blood dies and the school closes.

1789
Wollstonecraft publishes The Female Reader, an anthology for the improvement of young women. She uses a male pseudonym, Mr Cressick.

1790
Wollstonecraft writes A Vindication of the Rights of Man, a counter-argument to Burke's work. It brings her into the public eye.

1792
A Vindication of the Rights of Woman is published. Its reception is warm, though some male readers find the content shocking.

1797
Mary Wollstonecraft dies just days after the traumatic birth of her daughter, Mary. The little girl later achieves fame as Mary Shelley.

Mary Wollstonecraft's Vindications

Though she wrote novels, letters, and even a book for children, it is as the author of A Vindication of the Rights of Woman that Mary Wollstonecraft is quite rightly lauded in the 21st century. She was inspired to write the book as an answer to Charles Maurice de Tallyrand-Périgord's assertion that women needed no education beyond the domestic. She dedicated the book to him, arguing that women should be educated so that they might contribute fully to society. Wollstonecraft's work became a rallying cry for feminists in the early 20th century.

The groundbreaking *A Vindication of the Rights of Woman* made Mary Wollstonecraft's name

Wollstonecraft's only children's book contained engravings by William Blake

This portrait was painted by John Opie

Five things to know about... Mary Wollstonecraft

1 The reluctant governess

Though she didn't enjoy the work, Wollstonecraft had a short career as a governess. She shared her experiences in her only children's book, *Original Stories from Real Life*.

2 A different take on revolution

Wollstonecraft viewed the French Revolution with pride, believing it marked the start of a new chapter of democratic history in which monarchy would be pushed aside.

3 A notorious woman

Though it is popularly thought that *A Vindication of the Rights of Woman* was a controversial flop on its first release, it was actually well-received by its readers.

4 Other literary works

Wollstonecraft was a novelist and prolific letter writer who collected together *Letters Written in Sweden, Norway and Denmark*, a series of correspondence that offers a unique insight into her travels and character.

5 The well-meaning widower

When William Godwin set out to write a posthumous biography of his late wife, he hoped to honour her. Instead, her unorthodox lifestyle saw her rejected as a pariah.

1798
Wollstonecraft's widower, William Godwin, publishes Memoirs of the Author of a Vindication of the Rights of Woman, inadvertently destroying her reputation.

1884
The first full biography of Wollstonecraft is written by Elizabeth Robins Pennell. It marks the start of her rehabilitation and sparks new interest in her.

2004
A blue plaque in Mary Wollstonecraft's honour is unveiled at 45 Dolben Street, Southwark, her home from 1788 to 1791.

2010
The Mary on the Green campaign opens amid wide support, dedicated to raising money to erect a statue in Wollstonecraft's honour.

2018
As the Mary on the Green campaign nears its financial goal, sculptor Maggi Hambling is chosen to design the statue.

1874 – 1946

Gertrude Stein

In her work as an avant-garde writer and as a dedicated patron to modern artists, Gertrude rebelled against the patriarchy and proved that women deserved to be heard

Born into a wealthy Jewish family in Pennsylvania, Gertrude's early years were as unconventional as the rest of her life. Spending her formative years travelling Europe with her family, they eventually settled in California. Here, school bored Gertrude, and she passed her time reading Shakespeare and Wordsworth among others.

Her mother's and father's deaths in 1888 and 1891 respectively meant that Gertrude was sent to live with her aunt and uncle in Baltimore. Here, Gertrude met Claribel and Etta Cone, whose own salons would inspire those held by Gertrude herself in her later years.

Gertrude had a natural intellect and an appetite to learn, and she excelled at her degree in psychology at Radcliffe College. Encouraged by one of her professors, celebrated psychologist William James, Gertrude reluctantly took up a place at Johns Hopkins School of Medicine, but her disinterest meant her grades plummeted, and she eventually dropped out.

Instead, Gertrude sought the cultural decadence she'd glimpsed as a child. She travelled around Europe, eventually settling in Paris with her brother, Leo. Here, Gertrude could craft an identity for herself, far from the oppressive and stifling rigidity of American society.

Paris gave Gertrude the freedom she craved to explore her own creativity and she began to write, drawing on her experiences both at college and medical school. Meanwhile, Leo and Gertrude had acquired a windfall from their trust funds and the pair began collecting

art in earnest, particularly works by contemporary avant-garde artists. Alongside their art collections, they cultivated relationships with Parisian bohemians at their Saturday-night salon, inspired by that of the Cone sisters. In time, invites to the Stein salon became the most sought after in all of Paris.

By 1914, two events occurred that came to define Gertrude's life. Her brother moved to Italy, and the pair bitterly split their art collection – in his stead, Gertrude's partner, Alice B Toklas, moved in. Secondly, war broke out on an international scale. After World War I ended, the Stein salon became a popular haunt for young American expats, who Gertrude came to call the "Lost Generation" – so called because these young men lived an aimless existence in the wake of the brutality of the war.

> *"Invites to the Stein salon became the most sought after in all Paris"*

By now, having published several of her experimental writings, Gertrude's unique approach was intriguing the literary world – not only celebrated authors, but academics, too. Despite this interest, Gertrude remained a little-known figure outside of the literary world. Her 1933 memoir, curiously named *The Autobiography of Alice B*

A life's work

1892
Gertrude goes to Radcliffe College in Boston, where she studies psychology under William James.

1897
Having completed her studies, Gertrude enrols in Johns Hopkins Medical School. The studies don't interest her, and she drops out.

1903
After travelling Europe for two years, Gertrude settles in Paris with her brother. They live at 27 Rue de Fleurus, where her salon later took place.

1904-1914
Gertrude and Leo begin collecting art. When Leo moves to Italy in 1914, the pair split the collection.

1909
Gertrude publishes her first book, Three Lives. It doesn't sell particularly well but it's talked about in literary circles for its unique style.

Cubism in words

At her salon, Gertrude welcomed some of the greatest avant-garde artists of the era – but this entirely modern approach to art was something she tried to replicate in her writing. Eschewing conventional means, Gertrude embraced a completely new style of writing, falling back on her studies on unconscious automatic writing during her psychology degree to influence her new and very conscious style.

It wasn't necessarily a success for Gertrude. Her experimentations, including Tender Buttons, lacked meaningful plots or dialogue and they were commercially unsuccessful, being widely panned by many critics at the time. However, the theory behind her new approach fascinated and inspired her contemporaries, including Ernest Hemingway and F Scott Fitzgerald among others.

Gertrude's writing style was considered to be the literary equivalent of cubism, like Picasso's *Girl With A Mandolin*

Toklas, changed that. Suddenly Gertrude became a name and face recognised across the globe. Unlike her experimental pieces, her memoirs were largely narrative and conventional – and she questioned whether commercial success had compromised her true identity.

By the outbreak of World War II, Gertrude's fame ensured her a certain amount of security as a Jewish lesbian living in Nazi-occupied France. Rather than leave her adopted nation, she remained with Alice, only agreeing to move as far south as Bilignin, near Lyon, where they were offered a certain amount of protection from friends with political ties to the Vichy government. In 1946, Gertrude died of stomach cancer, leaving most of her precious art collection to her loyal partner, Alice.

Felix Edouard Vallotton's 1907 portrait of Gertrude

Five things to know about... Gertrude Stein

1 Unrequited love

While studying at Johns Hopkins, Gertrude became infatuated with Mary Bookstaver, who was already in a relationship with Mabel Haynes. This love triangle became fodder for Gertrude's 1903 novel, *Q.E.D.*

2 The writer of the opera

Working with Virgin Thomson, Gertrude provided librettos to several operas, including *Four Saints in Three Acts*. Despite a mixed reception from critics, it was a resounding success.

3 A family divide

When Leo moved to Italy, he and Gertrude split the collection they had amassed. While Leo left with the Renoirs and Gertrude kept the Picassos, the Cezannes were a sticking point. Aside from a chance encounter after World War I, they never spoke again.

4 The fate of the art

After Gertrude died, she bequeathed her collection to her life partner, Alice B Toklas. Sadly, as their relationship was not legally recognised, Gertrude's relations took legal action to claim them. Alice died in poverty 20 years later.

5 The godmother

When Ernest Hemingway's first son, Jack, was born in 1923, he asked Gertrude to be his godmother, despite their tumultuous relationship. She accepted.

1914
Tender Buttons is published. It is entirely unconventional in its style but it absolutely fascinates Gertrude's literary contemporaries.

1914-1918
WWI breaks out. Gertrude and her partner, Alice B Toklas, volunteer with the American Fund for French troops, driving supplies to French hospitals.

1920s
Gertrude's salon welcomes what she calls "the Lost Generation" – young American writers in the wake of WWI like Ernest Hemingway.

1926
Invited to lecture at the Oxbridge universities, Gertrude travels to England to discuss her writing and the theories behind her work.

1933
Gertrude's only bestselling book, The Autobiography of Alice B Toklas, is published. She is catapulted to fame.

GERTRUDE STEIN
1874 – 1946
ÉCRIVAIN AMÉRICAIN
Vécut ici avec son frère LÉO STEIN
puis avec son ALICE B. TOKLAS
elle y reçut de nombreux
artistes et écrivains
de 1903 à 1938

1775 – 1817

Jane Austen and Regency trailblazers

How Regency women sparked a revolution in arts, culture and politics

AUSTEN'S NOVELS WERE PUBLISHED ANONYMOUSLY, BY "A LADY"

Two hundred years after her death, one woman remains the centrepiece of British Regency literature. Jane Austen is a literary legend and a figure to whom millions still turn to for entertainment, a little romance and the occasional pithy put-down. Her polite comedies of manners, featuring militamen eloping with rich young heiresses and social-climbing gorgons prowling the lawns of eligible young bachelors, spear social conventions and can be as savage as they are romantic.

Rather than being demure drawing room dramas, Austen held up a mirror to the social reality of her class and time that did not shy away from difficult truths. This included her understanding that women's lives in the early 19th century were limited in opportunity, even among the gentry and upper middle classes, and that marriage was often a means to financial security and social respect.

Austen was a remarkable woman in an era when the world was dominated by men. Her path to success was far from easy and she fought to make her voice heard. The Prince Regent purchased a copy of *Sense and Sensibility* two days before it was advertised But her most famous work, *Pride and Prejudice*, was completed in 1797 but didn't see the light of day until 1813, so Jane was no overnight sensation. The Age of Enlightenment only went so far, after all!

Yet she didn't struggle alone, and all around the world, women just as remarkable as her were battling convention, society and expectation to be heard. They came from mansions and hovels, from Britain, Europe, China and further afield, lone voices crying out in a worldwide chorus that couldn't be ignored. From suffragists to abolitionists, pirates, authors and even proud advocates of free love, here are eleven women who would give any feisty fictional heroine a run for her money.

Mary Shelley

30 August 1797 — 1 February 1851

Author, traveller and all-round scandalous sort, Mary Shelley gave us much more than a monster!

Mary Shelley had form from the moment of her birth. She was the daughter of pioneering feminist Mary Wollstonecraft and anarchist thinker William Godwin. At 16 she ran away with Romantic poet and married man Percy Bysshe Shelley and together began one of the world's most celebrated and tumultuous romances.

Mary fell pregnant by her lover, but their child was born prematurely in February 1815 and didn't survive. She rode out a storm of criticism and social isolation to remain with Percy and when his wife, Harriet, committed suicide in 1816, the couple married.

In 1816, they travelled to Geneva to summer with Lord Byron and his friend Dr John Polidori in the Villa Diodati. When Byron suggested that the guests each write a ghost story, Mary experienced a waking dream that inspired her to write Frankenstein: Or, The Modern Prometheus.

The book took two years to complete while Mary was also busy writing an account of her travels in Europe. Yet it was Frankenstein, a masterpiece of Gothic literature and trailblazer for science fiction, that caused a sensation. Sadly Mary, afflicted with depression, could never fully enjoy her success. She died more than 30 years after her husband yet lives on today as a literary legend, the creator of one of fiction's most famous monsters.

After Percy's death, Mary worked hard writing more books to support herself and her only surviving son, Percy Florence

Charlotte and Sarah lived together in Plas Newydd near Llangollen for over 50 years and their letters were jointly signed

Plas Newydd in 1840. Today it's a museum dedicated to the women

The Ladies of Llangollen: Eleanor Charlotte Butler & Sarah Ponsonby

11 May 1739 — 2 June 1829 (Eleanor)
1755 — 9 December 1831 (Sarah)

Faced with forced marriages, two ladies eloped to live life on their own terms

Eleanor and Sarah were two young ladies from Ireland with a dream: they wanted to live together, free from meddling husbands. Their dream became a reality in 1780 when they fled Kilkenny for Llangollen in Wales and set up home in a Gothic house called Plas Newydd.

Here they indulged their love of botany and architecture, plunging headfirst into a total restructure of their home. They cultivated the gardens and rebuilt the house to their own specifications, creating a Gothic architectural fantasy. Rejected by their families, they needed only each other, and together they created the idyll that they had always dreamed of sharing.

With little interest in society or traditional feminine pursuits, these unusual ladies became unlikely celebrities thanks to their unconventional relationship. They were given a royal pension and visitors flocked to see them in their own little piece of rural heaven.

Although the nature of Eleanor and Sarah's relationship was never confirmed, the ladies of Llangollen lived together for half a century as though they were a married couple. They died within two years of one another and the people of their adopted homeland honour them to this day.

Sojourner Truth

C. 1797 — 26 November 1883

This former slave went to court to free her child

Sojourner Truth made history when she escaped slavery and discovered that her five-year-old son remained in chains. She had been sold at the age of nine for the price of $100 and a flock of sheep, and her life had been hard as she was passed around owners throughout New York.

Following her daring escape from captivity, her life changed forever. In a groundbreaking legal case, Sojourner took the man who owned her child to court and won, becoming the first black woman to legally challenge a white man and emerge victorious.

Sojourner was celebrated among abolitionists for her remarkable achievement and became a public speaker who was in high demand. Wherever she was due to lecture, she was a hot ticket. Her speeches were on slavery and suffrage and she became famed for her passionate speech Ain't I A Woman, which was widely published across America.

Sojourner wasn't content with simply giving speeches, though, and campaigned for years to secure territory from the government for those who had once been held captive as slaves. Her fight was unsuccessful, but she never gave up her crusade and is celebrated across the world to this day.

Sojourner, shown here in c.1870, collected food and clothing for black troops in Michigan during the American Civil War

Elizabeth Fry

21 May 1780 — 12 October 1845

The 'Angel of the Prisons' pioneered penal reform

When Elizabeth Fry attended a speech on the matter of the plight of the poor given by William Savery, her life changed forever. Barely 18 years old, she devoted the rest of her life to helping those who lived in poverty. However, it was a visit to Newgate Prison, London, in 1813 that set her on the crusade that shaped her legacy.

Elizabeth was horrified by the conditions she saw in Newgate — particularly the fate of children who had been incarcerated in dreadful conditions alongside their mothers. She established the British Ladies' Society for Promoting the Reformation of Female Prisoners, aimed at teaching the women how to sew. This, she hoped, would greatly enhance their employability when they were released.

Not content with this, though, Elizabeth was instrumental in the campaign against penal transportation. She faced loud criticism for her efforts to reform the prison system and was accused of neglecting her husband and children in favour of her work. When her husband was bankrupted, her enemies even falsely claimed that Elizabeth had siphoned money from her charities to bail him out. But through her endeavours, Elizabeth won the backing of no less a woman than Queen Victoria herself, who made contributions of her own to Elizabeth's charities.

Elizabeth donated food and clothes to the women and children at Newgate Prison. She eventually funded a prison school there

Queen Victoria contributed money to Elizabeth's cause after ascending the throne

Anna Wheeler

1780-1848
Married to a brute at 16, Anna turned to socialism to better the rights of women

When teenaged Anna Doyle was married off to a drunken husband, she wasn't about to take it lying down. Instead, she bucked convention and left him to his booze, fleeing their Irish home for England. But this wasn't far enough for the adventurous Anna, so she upped sticks with her daughters and took a trip through France.

Anna started a new life and was independent of her penniless husband. Instead, she financed herself by translating French philosophy texts into English. Desperate to see other women enjoy the freedom she had fought for, she mixed with reformers including Fanny Wright and Jeremy Bentham and argued tirelessly for women's rights. She was both respected and feared in England and France for her outspoken views and she was a formidable public speaker and opponent.

She never stopped fighting for girls to have a right to education and women to have the vote and was even invited to join the 1848 revolution in France, though ill health prevented her from doing so. Her descendants — writers and scholars — continued the fight on her behalf, even including the famous suffragette, Lady Constance Bulwer-Lytton, who was repeatedly imprisoned for her part in the struggle for the vote.

Anna was invited to take part in the French Revolution of 1848 but was unable to take part due to her ill health

Tall, Darcy & Handsome

Building the perfect Jane Austen hero from their raw materials

Good sense
If a man seems flighty, he's better avoided. A Regency chap like Pride And Prejudice's Fitzwilliam Darcy might seem to be far too serious, but those frowns mask a passionate heart of gold.

Good looking, but not too good looking
A strong jaw, casually fashionable haircut and soulful eyes will take a hero far. Avoid dashing heroes such as Sense And Sensibility's John Willoughby, though – they're usually up to no good.

A snappy dresser
Ask any 21st century Jane Austen fan what their must-have is and they'll probably tell you it's a wet shirt and not George Wickham's red coat, as seen in Pride And Prejudice.

Taste
A true hero doesn't prop up the bookies and flit about houses of ill repute. Like Emma's George Knightley he has taste in all things, from interior decor to music to art.

Money
A gentleman should be well off, ideally in possession of a good fortune gained by honest means. Avoid chancers, charmers and show-offs at all costs. After all, when Henry Crawford arrives at Mansfield Park, he brings nothing but trouble.

Bravery
In Persuasion, Captain Frederick Wentworth turns around a rocky start by his brave showing against the massed forces of Napoleon's navy. From zero to hero on the ocean waves!

Frances Wright

6 September 1795 — 13 December 1852
This Scot fought for abolition and free love in America

Dundee-born Fanny Wright was the daughter of wealthy political radicals, and what she learned in infancy she put into practice in adulthood. When she was in her early 20s, the orphaned Fanny took her inheritance and financed a passage for herself and her sister to America, where they travelled widely across the country. Here she developed an unshakeable belief in the principles of suffrage, education, emancipation and the rights of women to govern their own bodies.

Fanny published an eye-opening political critique of American society and was sure that she could come up with a better way of life. Her dream took the form of the Nashoba Commune, which was intended to educate slaves in preparation for their emancipation. She sank her inheritance into the commune and dreamed of a community free of class or the shackles of society's expectations. The commune proved to be an expensive white elephant, however, and its belief in free love regardless of race or creed caused a scandal. Although Fanny was forced to close it down and re-house its inhabitants at her own expense, she continued to argue passionately for the rights of all until her dying day.

Many approved of Frances's ideas because she had found a way for slaves to prepare to be self-supporting citizens

Sacagawea

May 1788 — 20 December 1812
Lewis and Clark didn't undertake their groundbreaking expedition across America alone

Sacagawea was born into a Lemhi Shoshone tribe and sold as a bride to a trapper called Toussaint Charbonneau when she was just 13. When Charbonneau was hired to join the Lewis and Clark expedition in 1804, his young wife went along to serve as a translator.

Lauded for her intelligence and bravery, Sacagawea played a vital role in smoothing relations between the explorers and the Shoshone people whose land they wished to cross. She was even reunited with her brother, who she had lost when they were abducted as children. The young woman was a valued and respected member of the party and knew the land better than any of them. She had a natural affability that often headed off conflict.

Sacagawea's fate remains unknown. While most sources record her death as 1812, some indigenous tales claim that she lived into the 1880s. Efforts to confirm this have so far proven elusive and, though her grave at Fort Washakie is marked by a statue of the remarkable young woman who helped Lewis and Clark seal their place in American history, whether she really rests there remains a tantalising mystery.

Sacagawea was pregnant when she undertook the Lewis and Clark expedition

Anne Lister

3 April 1791 — 22 September 1840
Out and proud, Anne was an industrialist to be reckoned with

Anne Lister, the châtelaine of Yorkshire's Shiben Hall, had no time for convention. When she took control of her family estate in 1826, she proved herself to be a business brain to be reckoned with and turned the Lister agricultural empire into a multi-industry portfolio including property, mining and transport interests. With a keen scientific and mathematical brain, she left male business rivals in her wake and earned herself the mocking nickname 'Gentleman Jack'.

Anne's diary totalled more than 4 million words and detailed her love affairs

Yet it wasn't only business for which Anne had a passion. She lived at Shibden with her lover, Ann Walker, a wealthy woman who Anne Lister considered her wife. The two women made no secret of their relationship and though Ann was the most serious in a long string of affairs going back to adolescence, emotional affairs between women were dismissed as a simple rite of passage in the 19th century.

When they were discovered years after her death, Anne's diaries revealed her passionate personality and devotion to her partner. Written partially in code, they proved that the two women were far more than best friends, and today Anne Lister is lauded as a woman who lived by her own rules, regardless of convention.

Sarah Moore Grimké

26 November 1792 — 23 December 1873

From her early teens, Sarah fearlessly fought slavery with education

When a young South Carolinian girl called Sarah watched her brother receiving a full classical education, she wondered why she couldn't enjoy the same privilege. She shared his ambition of becoming a lawyer, but instead she was tutored in the ways of a lady, with an emphasis on more dainty pursuits.

But Sarah longed to do more and as a teenager she secretly tutored the family slaves, teaching them to read despite it being against the law to do so. Left at home when her brother went to Yale University, she immersed herself in books, training herself to be a lawyer despite what society may think.

When Sarah's brother died, she learned that he had fathered three children by a slave and raised them as her own. She became a loud and proud abolitionist, yet found herself shunned by members of her Quaker community who didn't think much of this noisy, opinionated woman. But Sarah wouldn't be silenced, writing and speaking extensively in favour of abolition.

Soon she was speaking out for women, too, challenging the Quakers to practise what they preached and allow women to join the clergy. To Sarah, life wasn't about master and slave, nor man and woman, but equality for all.

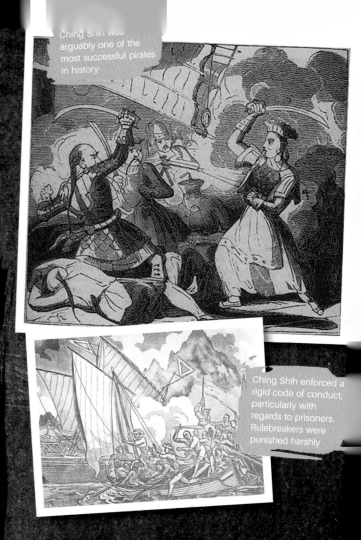

Ching Shih was arguably one of the most successful pirates in history

Ching Shih enforced a rigid code of conduct, particularly with regards to prisoners. Rulebreakers were punished harshly

When she was 12 years old, Sarah began to spend her Sunday afternoons teaching Bible classes to her parents' slaves

Ching Shih

1775-1844

Married into a pirate dynasty in 19th century China, Ching Shih ruled the waves

When Ching Shih inherited her late husband's business, she took to it like a duck — or pirate — to water. She was working as a prostitute when she was captured by pirate captain Cheng I. They hit it off and were soon married, with Ching Shih becoming an enthusiastic member of the crew.

When her husband died in 1807, Ching Shih inherited command of his pirate force. The Red Flag Fleet consisted of 300 ships crewed by more than 30,000 men. It was one of the most formidable fleets ever to sail.

Ching Shih ruled with a rod of iron and everyone was expected to follow the strict rules that she put in place. She seemed unstoppable and out-sailed every force, both Chinese and international, that attempted to take her down.

For Ching Shih, crime definitely paid. In 1810, she took advantage of an amnesty to leave her nautical life behind and settle down as a rich woman. She was allowed to keep her booty and lived in luxury for three more decades as mistress of an upscale gambling establishment, a far cry from her poverty-stricken early years.

1929 – 1945

Anne Frank

Over 70 years after her tragic death, the diary of one German teenager has become a global phenomenon

Anne Frank's diary begins unremarkably enough. On her 13th birthday, Anne received a small book that was covered with red and white cloth, its contents protected by a simple lock and key. She decided there and then that she would begin keeping a journal and in one of the first entries, catalogued the restrictions she was facing as a Jewish girl in Amsterdam, where her family had settled after the Nazis rose to power in Germany.

In her younger years Anne had lived a relatively normal life, but as the years passed and her family moved from place to place in the face of growing nationalism, Anne's horizons became more and more limited. Eventually, when Germany occupied the Netherlands and Margot, Anne's sister, was informed that she was to be sent to a work camp, the family decide to go into hiding.

Along with a small number of other friends, the Franks made their home in the Achterhuis, a hidden apartment secreted in the building where Otto Frank, Anne's father, kept his business offices. The entrance to their three-storey home was hidden behind a bookcase and for just over two years, Anne chronicled life in their secluded hiding place. Thrown together with her family and their fellow residents, her recollections are an evocative mix of coming-of-age trials and the sense of a life lived not so much in fear, but trepidation. Like many teenage girls she bickered with her mother, looked up to her elder sister even as she grumbled about the unfavourable

comparisons people made between them, and even shared her first kiss with Peter van Pels, the 16-year-old son of the family who was sheltering with the Franks.

Even though every day brought the danger of discovery, Anne continued her education and devoted herself to her diary, in which she reflected on her life and relationships. She even described her ambitions to become a journalist and writer when she was an adult.

Tragically, Anne would not live to see her career ambitions realised and on 4 August 1944 – three days after she wrote and edited the last entry in her diary – German police raided the Achterhuis and took its terrified residents into custody. Bep Voskuijl and Miep Gies, two of Otto Frank's employees who had helped the family during their concealment, rescued Anne's diary and notebooks as well as family photographs, all of which they intended to return to Anne when the war ended.

That day never came. Anne died at Bergen-Belsen just weeks before the camp was liberated by British soldiers. Her mother and sister died too, and Otto Frank alone survived to carry his daughter's legacy, overseeing the editing and publication of her diary. Anne is remembered today not just as a symbol of resistance and freedom, but as a bright young woman whose talent shines out of her journal, one of the most remarkable autobiographical works that the world has ever seen.

A life's work

1933
Months after Hitler becomes Chancellor of Germany, the Franks leave Germany for a new life in Amsterdam.

1942
On her 13th birthday, Anne receives an autograph book. She uses it as diary, a habit she maintains for two years.

1942
When Margot Frank is called up for internment in a Nazi labour camp, the Franks decide to go into hiding above Otto's business offices.

1942
The Franks are joined by the Van Pels family and Fritz Pfeffer. Anne gives them the pseudonyms Van Daan and Albert Dussel respectively in her diary.

1944
An anonymous informant reveals the whereabouts of the Franks and their hiding place is raided. They are arrested and sent to Auschwitz-Birkenau.

The secret diary

Anne Frank's remarkable, heartbreaking diary is one of the most significant literary publications of the last century, if not all time. In it Anne charts the path of her own maturity from a girl to a young woman, as well as the plight of the Jewish people and her own family in particular. Originally published as The Diary of a Young Girl in 1947, the journal has endured against censorship and accusations of forgery to remain a seminal text. It has been translated into more than 70 languages and to date, over 30 million copies have been sold worldwide.

Anne Frank took comfort in writing her diary, and longed to become a professional writer

Five things to know about... Anne Frank

The home of Anne Frank

Visitors to the house can experience her story through quotes, photos, videos, and original items

1 The Franks fled for Amsterdam

Anne was born in Frankfurt, Germany, but her family fled when the Nazis came to power. Anne was just four when she settled in the Netherlands.

2 The diary that wasn't

Though Anne used it as a diary, the red-and-white-checkered book she received for her 13th birthday was actually an autograph book.

3 Residents of the hidden annex

The Franks were joined in their hiding place by Hermann and Auguste van Pels and their son, Peter, as well as a dentist, Fritz Pfeffer. All perished during the war.

4 An escape through writing

Anne dreamed of becoming a professional writer. She wrote that all her cares and worries disappeared whenever she sat down to write.

5 A mother's sacrifice

When imprisoned in Auschwitz, Edith Frank gave her meagre rations to her children, Anne and Margot. Edith died of starvation just weeks before the death of her daughters.

1944
Separated from their father, Anne and Margot are sent on to Bergen-Belsen in Germany. The girls' mother, Edith, is left behind at Auschwitz-Birkenau.

1945
Anne, Margot and Edith die. Otto is freed by Soviet troops during the liberation of Auschwitz and begins the search for his family.

1947
Otto oversees the publication of Anne's edited diary as Het Achterhuis. It is a mix of the original and her 1944 rewrite.

1952
Anne's diary is saved from Doubleday's reject pile by editor Judith Jones. It is published for the first time in an English translation.

1995
Time magazine include Anne in their list of the most important people of the 20th century.

1921 – 2006

Betty Friedan

For decades, Betty Friedan stood at the vanguard of American feminism and her influence can still be felt today

On 26 August 1970, around 50,000 people gathered in New York City to support the Women's Strike for Equality. At the head of the march was Betty Friedan, a vocal activist who had fought her whole life for gender equality.

Betty Friedan began her career as a writer and it was here that she would feel the sting of inequality. For six years she worked for the *UE News*, the newspaper of the United Electrical, Radio and Machine Workers of America trade union, but her employment was terminated when she fell pregnant. Forced into a freelance role, Friedan published a series of articles detailing the experience of women in modern America and she was met with a tidal wave of response as housewives, frustrated by the sacrifices that they had been forced to make, came out in vocal support of her efforts.

Friedan's research turned up a world in which women had abandoned their own ambitions and careers to support those of their husbands, only to find themselves unappreciated and frequently abandoned. By the time they were able to return to a professional role they found themselves regarded as unemployable and left with nothing to show for their sacrifices.

In 1963 Friedan turned her research into *The Feminine Mystique*, the book that made her name. In it she skewered what she called "the problem that has no name", the plight of the dissatisfied suburban housewife in America. The book became a rallying point for women who wanted to take back control of their lives, and Friedan quickly became a spokesperson for those who felt that they had no voice.

Friedan parlayed her success into action and co-founded the National Organization for Women, serving as its first president. The NOW was committed to achieving and seeing legal recognition of gender equality. The organisation lobbied for equal pay and employment rights, the legalisation of abortion and the passage of the Equal Rights Amendment, which was voted into law by an overwhelming majority.

Yet Friedan wasn't without her critics. Her support of abortion was divisive and members of the NOW raised concerns that she had invoked the Civil Right Act on behalf of women while ignoring the fact that in practice if not in law, African Americans of both genders still enjoyed fewer rights than the privileged Caucasian women whom Friedan seemed to be focused on championing.

After she stepped down as president of the National Organization of Women in 1969, Friedan remained an influential and active figure in the feminist movement. She organised the Women's Strike for Equality in 1970 to coincide with the 50th anniversary of the Women's Suffrage Amendment and called on women across the USA to make their own protests, whether marching, striking or simply talking over the issues that had an impact on them.

The Feminine Mystique was credited with starting the second wave of American feminism and it certainly began a whole new conversation about equality. Following her death in 2006, Betty Friedan remains a divisive figure even within the movement that she championed.

A life's work

1952
A pregnant Friedan is dismissed from her position after working for six years as a journalist on the United Electrical Workers' journal, UE News.

1963
The Feminine Mystique is published in the US. It is a best-seller and attracts both plaudits and criticisms from women around the world.

1966
After scribbling the name on a napkin, Friedan co-founds the National Organization for Women. She is its first president for three years.

1970
Friedan leads the National Women's Strike for Equality, holding it on the 50th anniversary of the Women's Suffrage Amendment to the Constitution.

1970
Friedan founds the National Association for the Repeal of Abortion Laws and leads the campaign for a woman's right to choose.

The Feminine Mystique

When she was asked to conduct a survey of her former classmates at Smith College in 1957, Betty Friedan could little have expected the impact it would have on her life and legacy. She discovered that the women who were seemingly living comfortable lives were far from satisfied but were instead frustrated and unfulfilled as housewives and mothers.

Friedan intended to publish her findings as a magazine article but when publications rejected her, she turned her research into a book instead. The Feminine Mystique took America by storm and became the launching platform for feminists for years to come.

Supporters joined Friedan to march down 5th Avenue for the Women's Strike for Equality in 1970

In 1980, Betty Friedan led supporters of the Equal Rights Amendment to the US Constitution

Five things to know about...
Betty Friedan

1 It started as a class reunion
The Feminine Mystique was inspired by a survey Friedan took of her former college classmates at a reunion, which suggested that many were dissatisfied with their lives.

2 A middle-class manifesto
Friedan's critics felt that The Feminine Mystique spoke only to people like her, namely middle-class white women. Her research, they argued, seemed not to recognise any other group.

3 The second wave
Friedan's work has been credited with kickstarting the second wave of feminism and providing the mission statement for the groundswell of activism that followed it.

4 The homosexuality question
Though her stance later softened, Friedan admitted that she felt unease about homosexuality. She was reluctant to accept that sexuality was a factor in the women's movement.

5 A pro-choice spokesperson
Friedan helped found NARAL (National Association for the Repeal of Abortion Laws) Pro-Choice America, and was a lifelong supporter of a woman's right to choose abortion.

1971
Betty Friedan is one of the six founders of the National Women's Political Caucus, dedicated to supporting women in seeking office at all levels of government.

1975
The American Humanist Association names Betty Friedan its Humanist of the Year, recognising her "significant contribution to the human condition".

1981
The Second Stage is published, in which Friedan argues that feminism must evolve and adapt to a new generation of women.

1993
Friedan is inducted into the National Women's Hall of Fame in honour of her role in reshaping American attitudes to women and feminism.

2000
Six years before her death, Friedan publishes her autobiography, Life So Far. She continues to be active in politics, but it is her final book.

Heroines of arts & culture

Meet the women who exploded into the male-dominated world of art and redefined it

Sylvia Plath
American 1932-1963

From childhood, it was clear that Sylvia Plath was unlike her peers. By the age of eight, she had already published her first poem. After winning a scholarship to college in America, she later won another to study at Cambridge University where she met her future husband, fellow poet Ted Hughes. Among her acclaimed poetry, her most famous publication was her semi-autobiographical coming-of-age novel, The Bell Jar, released just a month before she took her own life. Over 50 years later, Sylvia Plath is considered one of the most original poets of the 20th century, as well as a champion for the acceptance of mental health treatment.

Peggy Guggenheim
American 1898-1979

After inheriting $2.5million dollars, Peggy Guggenheim jumped feet-first into the art world, befriending the bohemian community of Paris. She opened a gallery of modern art and started her own private collection in earnest in 1938. After World War II broke out she "[bought] one picture a day", including works from Picasso, Dali, Ernst, and more. In 1949 she settled in Venice, where she lived and exhibited her vast collection. The Peggy Guggenheim Collection on the Grand Canal is one of the most visited attractions in Venice, and has made Cubism, Surrealism and Abstract Expressionism accessible to so many people.

Angelica Kauffman
Swiss 1741-1807

In a world dominated by men, Angelica Kauffman proved that it didn't take a man to reveal the true face behind a façade. She showed promise beyond her years, learning several languages, as well as working as an assistant to her father, a modestly successful Austrian muralist. Having travelled to Italy following her mother's death, Kauffman set out on her career as an artist. In 1768, Kauffman became one of the founding members of the prodigious Royal Academy of Arts – one of two women of the 34 founders. Her work was championed alongside those of Sir Joshua Reynolds and Thomas Gainsborough.

Virginia Woolf
English 1882-1941

After a life plagued with mental illness, Virginia Woolf committed suicide on 28 March 1941. But in death, she left behind a legacy as one of the world's most innovative and influential writers, having embraced an entirely new approach to writing. She was inspired by her childhood haunts as well as her own personal traumas of death and sexual abuse. Alongside her famous novels, including To The Lighthouse and Mrs Dalloway, Virginia also wrote essays. One of these, A Room of One's Own, championed women's role in literature, and has since become part of the canon of feminist literature.

Lee Miller
American 1907-1977

Beautiful, reserved and chic, Lee Miller became the lover of surrealist photographer Man Ray in 1929 after a brief modelling stint. But Miller wanted to learn photography and became Man Ray's student. Upon the outbreak of World War II, she was determined to serve as a war correspondent and by 1942, she was capturing the conflict through a lens for Vogue, recording the use of napalm in France and the horrors of concentration camps. When the war ended, she returned with PTSD, and struggled with alcohol and drug addictions. Her now iconic photography only resurfaced after her death.

Zaha Hadid
Iraqi 1950-2016

Zaha Hadid was destined for greatness. Sent off to European boarding schools, she later studied at the Architectural Association School of Architecture in London and quickly became its most outstanding student. In 1980 she opened her own firm in London and was quickly singled out as the go-to modern architect, winning herself prized commissions. Her most notable works included the London Aquatics Centre and the Guangzhou Opera House. A heart attack in 2016 drew her exceptional life to a close, with her own firm remembering her as "the greatest female architect in the world today".

Charlotte Brontë
English 1816-1855

The eldest of three sisters, Charlotte Brontë's Jane Eyre courted controversy. Deemed "anti-Christian", the shocking tale outraged Victorian Britain. Since then, it has become an essential read, often ranking in the top ten books of all time. In the wake of such celebrated female authors as Jane Austen, the Brontë sisters' morbid tales were the antithesis of female sensibility – and all published under male pseudonyms, Charlotte's being Currer Bell. But by 1848, the trio revealed their true identities, and became celebrated figures in society.

Aphra Behn
English 1640-1689

Born into obscurity, Aphra Behn was a child of the English Civil War. It's thought that she may have served as a spy in her lost years, though little evidence confirms this. However, by 1665 she was indeed spying in the Dutch Netherlands, having come to the attention of King Charles II. Yet debt and death forced her back to England, where she wrote to make ends meet. This means to an end, however, proved to be the making of Aphra, and she became one of the leading figures of Restoration theatre, her most celebrated work being The Rover in 1677.

Simone de Beauvoir
French 1908-1986

Born into the French upper class, Simone de Beauvoir was a pampered child – until her family struggled to maintain its wealth after World War I. Relishing the opportunity for independence, Simone set to studying. In 1928 she became the ninth woman to earn a degree from Paris' Sorbonne, having studied philosophy. Simone's writings on feminism and existentialism catapulted her to fame, particularly She Came to Stay and The Second Sex. She was in a life-long relationship with John-Paul Sartre, though she had many affairs with both men and women.

SCIENCE & INGENUITY

76

84

72

1815 – 1852

Ada Lovelace

This unusual countess was one of the most influential figures in the history of technology, and one you may not have heard of

That the world's first computer programmer was a Victorian woman is remarkable in itself, but that she was the daughter of one of literature's most well-known poets adds such colour to the story it is difficult to understand how it isn't more widely known. Born in 1815, Ada Lovelace is not a name that draws the same reverence or even recognition as the likes of Alan Turing, Charles Babbage or Tim Berners-Lee – all undeniable innovators in technology. Yet she was the first to imagine the potential that modern computers held, and her predictions so accurately mirrored what later became the technological revolution that she is seen by many as a visionary, and even, by some, a prophet.

Understanding Ada's ancestry and childhood is key to discovering how this unlikely historical figure played her part in the creation and proliferation of the computer. Her mother, Anne Isabella 'Annabella' Byron, didn't want her daughter to grow up to be like her father, the eminent poet Lord Byron. He was tempestuous and prone to mood swings – the true picture of a popular poet. Annabella was terrified Ada would inherit her father's instabilities – a fear that would prove to be not entirely unfounded. As such, it was upon Annabella's insistence that her daughter be brought up completely in control of herself, able to apply logic and certainly not preoccupied with sensation and emotions in the same way that her father was.

If flights of fancy were Annabella's concern, there were signs early in Ada's life that her determination had not suppressed all of these tendencies. At the age of 12, Ada was already developing a curious scientific mind, and became obsessed with the idea of learning to fly. In the hope of achieving this lofty ambition, Ada undertook extensive and methodical research into materials that could be used to make effective wings and examined birds and insects for further inspiration. She gathered her findings in a volume and named it '*Flyology*'. At first, Annabella encouraged her daughter's enthusiasm for research and science, but as the obsession took hold, Ada was forced by her mother to abandon her project.

ADA'S MOTHER FORBADE HER FROM SEEING A PORTRAIT OF HER FATHER

Annabella's insistence on bringing up her daughter firmly rooted in logic was most likely inspired by her own interest in mathematics, and manifested itself in many, occasionally odd, ways. Part of Ada's 'education' was to observe the task of lying still for hours on end, an activity designed to teach her 'self control'. In addition, Annabella was not a particularly maternal force, referring to young Ada in letters as "it", and leaving Ada in the care of her grandmother, Lady Judith Millbanke. However, Judith died when Ada was six years old, and from then on her guardianship was covered by various nannies, and later, tutors, who had been chosen and approved by Annabella.

Lord Byron, Ada's father, had left two months after her birth for a life in Italy. His marriage to Annabella had ended abruptly, in a slew of scandalous rumours of affairs between Byron and a chorus girl, myriad financial troubles and rumoured violence and abuse. After travelling to Italy, where he stayed with Percy Bysshe and Mary Shelley, Byron's final years were spent in Greece, where he had joined the forces fighting for independence from the Ottoman Empire. It was here that he died in 1824, when Ada was just eight years old – the two never met.

While the mathematical passions of her mother meant Ada had endured some unorthodox methods in her upbringing, it also meant that she received an extraordinary gift, rare for women in the 19th century – a comprehensive mathematical education. Ada's tutors were a diverse group of academics, reading as a 'who's who' of early to mid-19th century intellectuals. Among the most notable were William Frend, a renowned social reformer; William King, the family's doctor, and perhaps most notably, Mary Somerville, a fellow female mathematician and astronomer.

Five years after her obsessive research into flight, Ada met a man who would prove integral to her life, and in particular, her intellectual pursuits. Charles Babbage was a technological innovator and had created the Analytical Engine – the device generally considered to be the first computer. Babbage was 42, and yet despite the gap of more than 20 years between them, a friendship would grow that would not

Enemies

Augusta Leigh

In 1841, Ada's mother informed her that her half-cousin Medora Leigh was in fact her half-sister, following an incestuous affair between Lord Byron and his half-sister Augusta Leigh. Ada wrote: "I am not in the least astonished," and blamed the affair on Augusta, writing: "I feel 'she' is more inherently wicked than 'he' ever was."

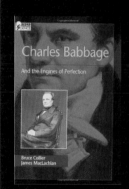

Bruce Collier

Ada's work has been the source of much contention, with many dismissing her part in the project. Historian Bruce Collier wrote: "It is no exaggeration to say that she [had] the most amazing delusions about her own talents, and a shallow understanding of both Babbage and the Analytical Engine."

Ada is believed to have written an algorithm for the Analytical Engine, designed by Babbage

only provide them with comfort and intellectual stimulation, but provide the world with its most revolutionary invention yet – the computer.

Babbage had been working under commission from the British government on a machine called the Difference Engine, but the Analytical Engine was something far more complex. Where the Difference Engine was essentially a calculator, designed to eliminate inaccuracies by fallible humans, the Analytical Engine could perform more complex calculations, stretching far beyond numbers. This was the first time any such machine had been conceived, let alone designed.

Babbage couldn't secure funding for his research into the new machine while the last project remained unfinished, but his determination to progress the Analytical Engine spurred him on, until he eventually found a sympathetic reception in Italy. In 1842, an Italian mathematician named Luigi Menabrea published an essay on the function of the machine. The text was in French, and Ada's talent for languages coupled with her mathematical understanding made her the perfect candidate to translate the document for Babbage. Over the course of nine months, she did this, but while the memoir was valuable, it paled in comparison to Ada's additions, which Babbage had suggested she should add in as she saw fit.

The notes that Ada made alongside the document were ground breaking. They exceeded the document she had translated, not just in length, but in depth and insight. One of the most quoted phrases, "the Analytical Engine weaves algebraic patterns just as the Jacquard loom weaves flowers and leaves," is a particularly feminine turn of phrase, strategically plucked from a much more lengthy, as well as technical, comparison of the machine to the Jacquard loom. In fact, most of the text is purely scientific, of a tone that wouldn't be out of place in a

"At the age of 12, Ada became obsessed with the idea of learning to fly'"

modern-day programming textbook. For example, she wrote: "When the value on any variable is called into use, one of two consequences may be made to result."

Ada also used the example of the complex numerical sequence known as Bernoulli numbers to prove the ability of the machine to calculate complex sequences from an original program. Detractors have used this against Lovelace, taking it as proof that the observations expressed in her notes weren't truly hers, but simply a relaying of information given to her by Babbage. Indeed, Ada did not have a full understanding of calculus, but even if Bernoulli numbers were the suggestion of Babbage, the principle of her assumptions remained the same. It was the insight for potential in her translation of this document that earned Countess Lovelace the moniker the

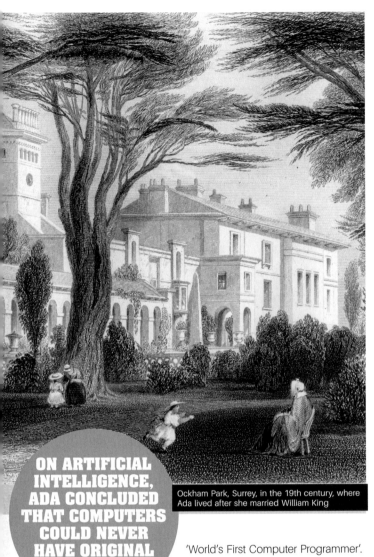

Ockham Park, Surrey, in the 19th century, where Ada lived after she married William King

ON ARTIFICIAL INTELLIGENCE, ADA CONCLUDED THAT COMPUTERS COULD NEVER HAVE ORIGINAL THOUGHTS

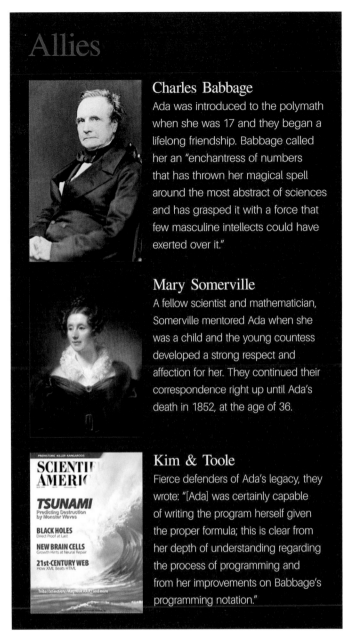

Allies

Charles Babbage
Ada was introduced to the polymath when she was 17 and they began a lifelong friendship. Babbage called her an "enchantress of numbers that has thrown her magical spell around the most abstract of sciences and has grasped it with a force that few masculine intellects could have exerted over it."

Mary Somerville
A fellow scientist and mathematician, Somerville mentored Ada when she was a child and the young countess developed a strong respect and affection for her. They continued their correspondence right up until Ada's death in 1852, at the age of 36.

Kim & Toole
Fierce defenders of Ada's legacy, they wrote: "[Ada] was certainly capable of writing the program herself given the proper formula; this is clear from her depth of understanding regarding the process of programming and from her improvements on Babbage's programming notation."

'World's First Computer Programmer'. Ada saw herself foremost as an "analyst and metaphysician," but while her scientific prowess earned her a place in history, she lived a generally unremarkable domestic life. In 1835, two years after her first meeting with Babbage, Ada married William King, 8th Baron of King, later to become the Earl of Lovelace. Ada and William would go on to have three children, the first, named Byron, born in May 1836. Two siblings shortly followed: Anne in September 1837 and Ralph in July 1839.

Ada suffered with health problems, both mentally and in the form of physical sicknesses, including cholera, from which she recovered. Annabella held Ada, William and the family in her financial thrall and as such, they lived on her terms. This, combined with William's sometimes controlling, even abusive, character, was at odds with Ada's friendly and fiercely independent nature. Affairs were rumoured, one in particular with the tutor to Ada's children, William Benjamin Carpenter, but there is no evidence that she ever embarked on an extra-marital relationship.

Ada died of uterine cancer aged just 36, the same age as her father, and was out-lived by her mother. In the years following her death, incredible advances have been made in the fields of technology, and her prophecies have been realised. The authenticity of her authorship has been questioned, but her findings proved invaluable to Alan Turing's work in the mid-20th century and were re-published at that time. Her legacy continues in the form of Ada Lovelace day, observed annually on 15 October. The day has the aim of raising awareness and interest for women in science. Ada was an unusual person in so many ways, and a remarkable one, and she continues to inspire those who feel that they must defy expectation to follow their passions.

"Lord Byron, Ada's father, had left two months after her birth for a life in Italy. His marriage to Annabella had ended abruptly"

1920 – 1958

Rosalind Franklin

How the work of the 'Dark Lady of Science' helped to solve the mystery of DNA

Rosalind Franklin was not the most popular figure in science. Nicknamed the 'Dark Lady' by her male colleagues for being hostile and troublesome, it's hard to say if this really described her nature or if it was a result of patriarchal prejudice. What is certain, however, is that she lived in the darkness of these men's shadows.

Born in London in 1920, Rosalind attended St Paul's Girls' School – one of the few institutions in the country at the time that taught chemistry and physics to girls. She excelled in these subjects and by the age of 15, she knew she wanted to become a scientist. Her father tried to discourage her, as he knew that the industry did not make things easy for women. But Rosalind was stubborn. In 1938, she was accepted into Cambridge University where she would study chemistry.

On graduating, Rosalind took up a job at the British Coal Utilisation Research Association. By this point the Second World War was in full swing, and Rosalind was determined to do something to help the war effort. Her research into the physical structure of coal was pivotal in developing gas masks that were issued to British soldiers, and it won her a PhD in physical chemistry as well.

In 1946, Rosalind moved to Paris to work as a researcher for Jacques Mering – a crystallographer who used X-ray diffraction to work out the arrangement of atoms in substances. Here she learnt many of the techniques that would aid her later discoveries.

Five years on, she was offered the role of research associate in King's College London's biophysics unit. Rosalind arrived while Maurice Wilkins, another senior scientist, was away. On his return, he made the assumption that this woman had been hired as his assistant. It was a bad start to what would become a very rocky relationship.

Despite the tense environment in the lab, Rosalind rose above and beyond the task, working alongside PhD student Raymond Gosling to produce high-resolution photographs of crystalline DNA fibres. The structure of DNA was a puzzle that Maurice and two friends – Francis Crick and James Watson – had been trying to piece together for years. But with a single photograph, simply labelled 'Photo 51', Rosalind and Raymond cracked it.

Without her permission, Maurice took this photograph and showed it to Watson and Crick. It was the final piece in their puzzle – DNA was indeed a double helix. The trio published their findings, and in 1962 they were awarded the Nobel Prize in Medicine.

In a tragic twist of fate, Rosalind died of ovarian cancer four years previous to that, at the age of 37. The doctors at the hospital she was treated at believed that prolonged exposure to X-rays was a possible cause of the disease. She had made the ultimate sacrifice for the sake of science, with no living reward.

"Rosalind rose above and beyond the task to produce high-resolution photographs of crystalline DNA fibres"

A life's work

1920
Rosalind is born in London to an affluent Jewish family.

1938
She begins her studies in chemistry at Newnham College, Cambridge.

1945
Awarded a PhD in physical chemistry for her research into the structure of coal.

1946
Moves to Paris to work as a researcher for crystallographer Jacques Mering.

1951
Joins King's College London as a research associate alongside Maurice Wilkins.

The big idea

Rosalind used X-ray diffraction to analyse the physical structure of substances. This involves firing X-rays at them. When the X-ray hits the substance, the beam scatters, or 'diffracts'. Rosalind recorded the pattern created by this diffraction in order to discover how the material's atoms were arranged.

The molecular structure of DNA had been puzzling scientists for years. Rosalind found that by wetting DNA fibres, the resulting images were a lot clearer. One photograph, called Photo 51, showed two clear strands. This indicated a double-helical structure, explaining how cells pass on genetic information.

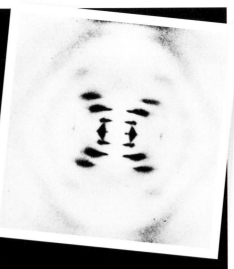

Crystalline DNA fibres, photographed

Five things to know about... Rosalind Franklin

1 Faking a death

Even during her experiments, Rosalind was unconvinced that DNA was helix-shaped, and even once sent her colleagues a notice commemorating the 'death' of helical DNA.

2 Beyond DNA

In addition to her work with DNA molecules, Rosalind also carried out pioneering research into the tobacco mosaic and polio viruses.

3 Girl power gone sour

Sexism was rife at King's College, where even Rosalind was accused of discriminating against female faculty. In a letter written to her parents, she allegedly referred to one of her lecturers as "very good, though female."

4 Not giving up

Rosalind tirelessly continued to work throughout her cancer treatment and was even given a promotion during the process.

5 No Nobel

Many people argue that the Nobel Prize should also have been awarded to Rosalind. But when the list of nominees was released 50 years later, it was revealed that, remarkably enough, she hadn't even been nominated for the award.

Rosalind's photographs of DNA fibres helped to establish its double helix structure

National Geographic sent a photographer to capture not just her work, but the woman behind it too

1952
Rosalind and her assistant Raymond Gosling take 'Photo 51', which proves the helical structure of DNA.

1953
Maurice shows Photo 51 to his friends James Watson and Francis Crick, who publish the findings.

1955
Rosalind reveals that tobacco mosaic virus particles are all the same length.

1957
Begins research into the polio virus, despite undergoing treatment for ovarian cancer.

1958
Rosalind dies of cancer, aged only 37, with no recognition for her groundbreaking discovery.

1867 – 1934

Marie Curie

A pioneer in nuclear physics and chemistry, Marie Curie made tremendous contributions to medical science and other fields

She coined the term 'radioactivity'; she was the first woman to win the Nobel Prize; and then, just for good measure, she won it a second time.

Marie Curie explored the properties of radioactivity, and discovered two elements: radium and polonium. She applied her acquired knowledge to the field of medical science through the use of diagnostic x-rays and early assessments of its capacity to fight cancer. Her achievements were remarkable; however, they were even more noteworthy because she was a woman whose intellectual and scientific prowess were undeniable in a professional arena dominated by men.

Born in the city of Warsaw, then a part of Imperial Russia, Maria Salomea Sklodowska was the fifth and youngest child of Wladyslaw and Bronislawa Boguska Sklodowski, both well-known educators who prized the pursuit of academic excellence. Her mother died of tuberculosis when Maria was only ten years old. Polish nationalism was a hallmark of the family's world view, and the loss of property experienced during support of such movements and periodic uprisings had left them struggling financially. Maria was educated in the local school system initially, while her father, a teacher of mathematics and physics, provided additional learning opportunities, particularly after the Russian authorities restricted laboratory instruction in the schools. Wladyslaw brought his equipment home and taught his children there.

A gifted student, Maria excelled in secondary school. However, she was prohibited from attending college because she was female. Along with her sister, Bronislawa, she enrolled in the 'Floating' or 'Flying' University, a clandestine college that conducted classes out of sight of the authorities, and also supported Polish nationalistic ideals. Prospects for higher education were more favourable to women in Western Europe, and the sisters came to an agreement: Maria would support Bronislawa while the latter obtained a degree, then the older sister would reciprocate. During the next five years, Maria worked as a tutor and a governess, falling in love with a man but being heartbroken when the family, distantly related through Maria's father, rejected the notion of marriage.

By 1891, Maria, who would become known as Marie in France, joined

CURIE RECEIVED TWO NOBEL PRIZES IN HER LIFE, ONE IN PHYSICS AND ONE IN CHEMISTRY

her sister and brother-in-law in Paris and enrolled at the Sorbonne. She was introduced to a community of physicists and chemists who were already establishing their own preeminence in these fields. Inspired, Marie worked tirelessly to obtain licensing in physical sciences and mathematics, and assisting in the laboratory of physicist and inventor Gabriel Lippmann, a future Nobel laureate. The long hours took their toll on Marie's health, as she subsisted primarily on tea, bread and butter. Within three years, though, she had achieved her immediate goals.

By 1894, Marie had secured a commission from the Society for the Encouragement of National Industry for research on the magnetic properties exhibited by numerous types of steel. Supposedly she needed a laboratory to work in, and was introduced to Pierre Curie by fellow physicist Józef Wierusz-Kowalski. Pierre made room in his personal living space, and a romance developed, but Marie returned to Poland that summer to visit her family, and hoped to gain a respectable teaching position at Kraków University. Gender discrimination again stood in her way, and Pierre persuaded her to return to Paris. The couple married on 26 July 1895, and a pivotal scientific partnership was poised for great achievement.

During this golden age of rapid scientific discovery, Marie searched for a worthy topic for further research, and the production of a thesis. German engineer and physicist Wilhelm Röntgen discovered the presence of x-rays in 1895, and the following year French physicist Henri Becquerel detected emissions of similar rays while researching uranium. News of the discoveries intrigued Marie. The rays did not depend on an external energy source. Apparently, they were produced within the uranium itself.

Using a spectrometer that Pierre and his brother had developed 15 years earlier, Marie determined that the level of activity present was solely dependent on the quantity of uranium being studied, and the activity remained constant regardless of the form of the element. She concluded that the energy was a product of the atomic structure of uranium rather than interaction between molecules, giving rise to the field of atomic physics.

Perhaps the most formidable gathering of scientists ever, the international physics conference convened in Brussels in 1911

Marie and Pierre Curie sit with their eldest daughter, Irène in 1902. A second daughter, Eve, was born in 1904

Tragic death of Pierre Curie

On a rainy 19 April 1906, Pierre Curie had just finished lunch with a few professional associates in Paris, and was walking to another appointment nearby. When he reached the intersection of the Quai des Grands Augustins with the Rue Dauphine near the Pont Neuf, he attempted to quickly cross one of the most dangerous intersections in the city. Reportedly, two police officers were stationed at the intersection at all times to direct traffic. However, if they were present on this day there was little that could have been done to prevent the tragic accident that occurred. One of the world's foremost physicists stepped into the path of a horse-drawn cart and was immediately struck, apparently falling beneath the wheels of the cart and fracturing his skull. He died swiftly.

When she received the news of her husband's death, Marie was heartbroken, but maintained her composure. Others attributed the cause of the accident, at least in part, to Pierre's carelessness and hurried pace. When his father learned of the tragedy, he responded: "What was he dreaming of this time?" A lab assistant had reportedly observed that Pierre was often inattentive while walking and riding his bicycle, "...thinking of other things."

Marie named the newly discovered form of energy 'radioactivity', and began researching other minerals that exhibited similar properties. She found that the mineral pitchblende, now known as uraninite, was ideal for continued research. Pierre discontinued his work on other projects and joined Marie. In the summer of 1898, the husband and wife team discovered the element polonium, which Marie named after her homeland of Poland. Later that year, they discovered a second element and called it radium. Pierre concentrated on the physical properties of radioactivity, while Marie worked to isolate radium in its metallic state.

Meanwhile, the Curies and Becquerel were jointly awarded the Nobel Prize in Physics in December 1903, in recognition of their collective research on 'the radiation phenomena' discovered by Becquerel. Although the initial nomination was intended for Pierre Curie and Becquerel only, Pierre's complaint to the Royal Swedish Academy of Sciences resulted in the addition of Marie to the award as the first woman to receive the Nobel Prize. The Curies also received the prestigious Davy Medal from the Royal Society of London that year.

In 1906, Pierre was killed in an accident on a Paris street. Marie was devastated, but pursued her research with renewed vigour, succeeding her late husband as chair of the physics department at the University of Paris. Four years later, she successfully isolated radium as a pure metal. Even as her personal life became embroiled in scandal during a period of French xenophobia because of her foreign birth, right-wing criticism of her apparent atheistic perspective on religion, and speculation that she was Jewish amid a rising tide of anti-Semitism, her scientific contributions were undeniable. In 1911, it was revealed that she had been involved in an affair with a former student of her husband who was separated from his wife. Nevertheless, in that same year she received the Nobel Prize in Chemistry for the discovery of polonium and radium and the isolation of radium.

As the first person to receive the Nobel Prize twice, and to be so recognised in two separate fields (physics in 1903 and chemistry in 1911), Marie Curie's prestige made a convincing argument for government support of the establishment of the Radium Institute in 1914 at the University of Paris, which continues to this day as a leading research institution in medicine, chemistry and physics. With the outbreak of World War I, Curie worked to establish mobile x-ray units using equipment adapted to automotive chassis. Eventually, 20 of these units were completed. With the help of her daughter, Irène, the mobile units dubbed 'Little Curies' saved many lives with their proximity to the battlefield.

After the war, Marie continued her research in radioactive materials and chemistry. In 1921, she travelled to America to raise funds for the Radium

Pierre Curie contributed to the successes in the early study of radiation, and died an untimely death

"The couple married on 26 July 1895, and a pivotal scientific partnership was poised for great achievement"

Marie Curie pictured here in her laboratory c.1900

Institute. She was hailed upon arrival in New York City, and attended a luncheon at the home of Mrs Andrew Carnegie and receptions at the Waldorf Astoria hotel and Carnegie Hall. In Washington, DC, President Warren G Harding presented her with a gram of radium and praised her "great attainments in the realms of science and intellect."

Marie gave lectures and became a member of the International Commission on Intellectual Cooperation under the auspices of the League of Nations. She authored a biography of her late husband, and in 1925 returned to her homeland to assist with the establishment of the Radium Institute in Warsaw. She travelled to the US again in 1929, successfully raising funds to equip the new laboratory, which opened in 1932 with her sister, Bronislawa, as its first director. Prior to the development of the particle accelerator in the 1930s, continuing atomic research depended upon the availability of radioactive materials. Marie realised the importance of maintaining adequate stockpiles, and her advocacy facilitated discoveries by Irène and her husband, Frédéric Joliot-Curie.

Years of prolonged exposure to radioactive materials took their toll on Marie's health. Little was known of the effects of radiation exposure – she would carry test tubes of radioactive material in the pockets of her dress, and store them in her desk drawer. She was said to have commented on the soft glow emitted from the tubes, but never realised their potential lethality. During World War I, she had also been exposed to radiation while operating x-ray equipment. As early as 1912 she had been temporarily incapacitated with depression and undergone surgery for a kidney ailment. As a result of radiation exposure, she developed leukaemia and died in Paris at the age of 66 on 4 July 1934. She was buried beside her husband.

Marie Curie remains a towering figure in the fields of physics and chemistry. Her ground-breaking achievements were also empowering for succeeding generations of women.

A Daughter's Contribution

Irène Joliot-Curie, the oldest of two daughters of Pierre and Marie Curie, was an eminent scientist in her own right. Along with her husband, Frédéric Joliot-Curie, she received the 1935 Nobel Prize in Chemistry for her research into the properties of the atom.

The couple's greatest discovery resulted from the exposure of previously stable material to radiation, which in turn caused the material itself to become radioactive. The scientists made the discovery after bombarding a thin strip of aluminium with alpha particles, in this case helium atom nuclei. When the external source of radiation was removed, the aluminium continued to emit radiation because the aluminium atoms had been converted to an isotope of phosphorus. The discovery of artificial radiation served as a catalyst for further research into radiochemistry and the application of isotopes in medical therapies, and largely replaced the costly process of extracting radioactive isotopes from ore. The work of Irène and Frédéric also contributed to the discovery of the process of nuclear fission.

In later years, Irène became the director of the Radium Institute in Paris, and both were leaders in the development of atomic energy in France. She died of leukaemia in 1956 after years of exposure to radiation.

Irène Curie and her husband, Frédéric Joliot-Curie, conducted landmark experiments resulting in the discovery of artificial radiation

1937 – present

Valentina Tereshkova

As the first woman and first civilian to fly into space, Valentina Tereshkova is a true trailblazer

Valentina Tereshkova was not what you might call a typical cosmonaut. She wasn't a pilot nor was she in the military, but she was actually a textile worker with a passion for skydiving.

When Tereshkova learned that the Soviet government was seeking to assemble a female cosmonaut corps, she was one of 400 women who applied to join the programme. Just five were successful, and among these lucky five women was Valentina Tereshkova.

After undergoing months of physically and psychologically gruelling training to prepare her for the proposed trip to space, Tereshkova was inducted into the Soviet Air Force. This honorary rank allowed her to officially join the Cosmonaut Corps, a prerequisite for the job. On 21 May 1963 Nikita Khrushchev formally announced that Tereshkova had been selected from the five women in her group to become the first woman in space. She piloted Vostok 6 into orbit on 16 June 1963, going under the call sign, Chaika, or Seagull.

Tereshkova spent three days at the helm of Vostok 6 and orbited the earth 48 times. In doing so she logged more flight hours than the American astronauts – all men – who had flown in space up to June 1963 combined. When Tereshkova returned to earth, plans were already afoot for more women to follow her, but in fact it was nearly two decades before another woman went into space. None of the four candidates who had trained alongside Tereshkova ever made a space flight.

Highly decorated in her homeland, when Tereshkova was asked by the Soviet government if there was any gesture they could make in recognition of her efforts, she had just one request. She asked if they could identify the place where her father, a war hero, had died when fighting in the Finnish War. Her request was granted and today, a memorial can now be seen at the place where he perished.

After such an adventure, Valentina Tereshkova wasn't about to go back to the textile factory. She enrolled at the Zhukovsky Air Force Academy and began her formal education, eventually gaining a doctorate in engineering. Though she never returned to orbit, she became a Soviet celebrity and chose to turn her popularity to political advantage, beginning a new life in government. Tereshkova enjoyed a glittering political career within the Communist Party and was a popular international representative of Soviet interests, focusing on the issues facing Soviet women.

Though Tereshkova's political career shuddered to a halt with the fall of the Soviet Union, her celebrity and reputation as a national hero remained constant. She is considered one of the most important people in the history of Russian space exploration and continues to be celebrated within her homeland and the wider scientific community. Tereshkova returned to politics in 2011 and continues to serve in the Duma, but it is her role in the story of space travel that makes her such a remarkable figure. Fittingly, there is even a crater on the Moon that bears her name!

A life's work

1962
Tereshkova is picked from 400 applicants to join the Russian space programme.

1963
After months of training, Tereshkova is picked as the only one of her group to go into orbit.

1963
She successfully pilots the Vostok 6 into orbit as part of a duel mission with Vostok 5.

1966
Tereshkova begins her political career as a member of the Supreme Soviet of the Soviet Union.

1966
The World Peace Council welcomes Tereshkova as a member. She is a vocal Soviet supporter of peace.

Female cosmonaut

When Valentina Tereshkova piloted Vostok 6 into orbit in 1963, she became the first woman ever to go into space. She orbited the earth 48 times during the three days she spent on board Vostok 6 and joined an elite group of space explorers. When her capsule malfunctioned during landing and began to move further from Earth, she resolved the issue and landed in Altay as a heroine, where she joined locals for dinner before her debriefing. She never flew into space again, but she will forever be a pioneer not only for women, but for science too.

Valentina Tereshkova made history when she piloted the Vostok 6 capsule

"Fittingly, there is even a crater on the Moon that bears her name"

Two icons of space met when Tereshkova welcomed Neil Armstrong to the Gagarin Training Centre

Tereshkova joined Khrushchev and other cosmonauts to celebrate the Soviet space programme

Tereshkova trains aboard a Vostok spacecraft simulator

Five things to know about...
Valentina Tereshkova

1 A soviet skydiver

Valentina Tereshkova made her first skydive in 1959 and quickly fell in love with the thrilling sport. It was a later a major factor in her selection for the cosmonaut programme.

2 Flight postponed

Tereshkova was originally scheduled to pilot Vostok 5 but the position was eventually given to a man, Valery Bykovsky. Tereshkova and Bykovsky's flights orbited within three miles of each other.

3 Spreading the word for Soviet women

After her space flight, Tereshkova became a popular spokesperson for the Soviet Union. She travelled internationally as a representative of the country, attending official engagements across the globe.

4 Cosmonaut to politics

Tereshkova was a member of the Presidium and the Central Committee of the Communist Party. The collapse of the Soviet Union slowed her political career, but it didn't end it.

5 Dreaming of Mars

While celebrating her 70th birthday with Vladimir Putin, Tereshkova revealed that she would love to fly to Mars, even if there was no chance that she could return to Earth.

1974
Appointed to the Presidium of the Supreme Soviet, she is a vocal supporter of women in science and technology.

1977
After nearly a decade of study, Tereshkova graduates with a doctorate in engineering.

1990
The University of Edinburgh honours her achievements with an honorary doctorate.

2008
When the Olympic torch passes through St Petersburg, she is chosen as a torchbearer.

2017
Tereshkova celebrates her 80th birthday at a gala event held in London's Science Museum.

1820 – 1910

Florence Nightingale

How one woman's intrepid determination changed the face of nursing across the world forever

Florence was not born to be a nurse – in fact, she was not born to be anyone remarkable at all. Born to a rich, upper-class family in the 1820s, her path was laid out neatly before her. She was to marry a similar rich, upper-class man and become a wife and mother. Fortunately for history, and us today, Florence developed a habit of straying from the path.

Named after the city of her birth in Florence, Italy, she moved to England in 1821 and was brought up in the family's various homes in Embley, Hampshire, and Lea Hurst in Derbyshire. Her father was an extremely wealthy landowner and the family associated with those in the very highest circles of British high society. However, her father defied traditions with his strong belief that women should be educated to be more than mothers and wives. He educated Florence and her sister in Latin, Greek, philosophy, history and, unusually, writing and mathematics – two pursuits that were regarded as exclusively male at the time. Florence particularly excelled in mathematics and science, developing a love of recording and organising information, as can be seen by her excessive documentation of her shell collection. These skills would prove essential in her later life.

When Florence turned 18, she accompanied her father on a tour of Europe during which she met Mary Clarke. The bond between the two women was instant and the effect Clarke had on Florence was immense. Clarke was a forthright, bold woman who didn't care for her appearance and had little respect for the upper-class women she believed led inconsequential lives. For Florence, it was her first encounter with a woman who showed her that females could be equal to men, which was far from the opinion of Florence's own conservative mother.

In fact, Florence's mother had very traditional aspirations for her oldest daughter, wishing her to marry and lead a life of domesticity. The girl was certainly eligible, striking and intelligent, but that was not the life that appealed to Florence. In 1837, Nightingale experienced what she believed was a call of God, imploring her to dedicate her life

AS A YOUNG CHILD, FLORENCE EXCELLED IN MATHS AND SCIENCE

to the service of others. Florence became convinced that her path in life was that of nursing – a revelation that her parents were not pleased about. At the time, nursing was viewed as a lowly profession performed only by the poor, widows and servants. Nightingale's parents refused to allow her to train in Salisbury, hoping the desire would fade away. Florence, however, was dedicated and stubborn. She even declined a proposal of marriage after a long courtship believing it would intervene with her nursing aspirations.

Defying her parents' wishes, she worked hard to train herself in the art and science of nursing, and she visited hospitals in London, Paris and Rome, learning everything she could along the way. Her travels took her as far as Greece and even Egypt, where she again professed to have experienced godly intervention saying that "God called me in the morning and asked me would I do good for him alone without reputation". By 1850, both parents finally yielded to Florence's iron determination and her father granted her permission to train as a nurse in Germany.

Three years later, and almost a decade after her crusade for independence began, Florence finally achieved her ambition of becoming a nurse when she accepted the post of superintendent at a women's hospital in Upper Harley Street. But Nightingale's work was far from over. In October 1853, the Crimean War had broken out and it became one of the first wars in history to become widely reported and photographed. When Florence read about the horrific conditions suffered by the wounded, she was motivated to spring into action. On 21 October 1854, Florence and a staff of volunteer nurses trained by herself, and 15 Catholic nuns were sent to the Ottoman Empire.

Florence wasn't prepared for what awaited her in the Selimiye Barracks in Scutari. Not only were the medical staff incredibly overworked, but the care they were delivering was poor, medicines were running dangerously low, hygiene standards were nonexistent and none of the officials seemed to care. The floor of the hospital was described as being an inch thick with human faeces. Appalled, Florence rapidly mobilised her staff to clean the hospital and ensure that the soldiers were properly fed and clothed.

Determined to implore the government to take action against the dreadful conditions the soldiers were nursed under, Nightingale sent a plea to *The Times* for the government to act – and act they did in the form of Renkioi Hospital. Built in England and shipped overseas, the new civilian facility had a death toll that was less than one-tenth of that suffered in Scutari.

It is estimated that Florence managed to reduce the death rate from 42 to two per cent thanks to her pioneering improvements and those she implored the Sanitary Commission to make. Some of these were things that we take for granted today such as implementing handwashing procedures and other neglected hygiene practices.

Mother Seacole

Florence was far from the only remarkable nurse working in the Crimean War – Mary Seacole was an incredibly significant woman who also rose to prominence thanks to her efforts towards the nursing efforts in the war. Born in Jamaica to a Jamaican mother and Scottish father, Seacole learned her nursing skills from her mother who ran a boarding house for invalid soldiers. Through her frequent travels, she combined traditional medicine ideas with European ones.

In 1854, her request to be sent to the frontline of the war effort was rejected. However, this enterprising woman wouldn't take no for an answer and funded her own trip, setting up the British Hotel to care for sick soldiers. Incredibly fearless, Seacole even visited the battlefield to care for the wounded and dying. She was beloved by the soldiers who referred to her as Mother Seacole, and at the time her reputation was on par with Nightingale's.

Unfortunately, after her death Seacole all but vanished from public consciousness, which many cite as an example of hidden black history. However, by the 21st century she became a much more prominent figure, being posthumously awarded honours and having many medical establishments named after her. Although some argue that her contributions to medicine have been exaggerated, she certainly did all within her power to ease the suffering of soldiers when no cures existed. The hot tea and lemonade she served may not have saved lives, but she remains a beacon of kindness to one's fellow man in the most trying of times.

Seacole was voted the greatest black Briton in 2004

> *"When Florence read about the horrific conditions suffered by the wounded, she was motivated to spring into action"*

Thanks to Florence's recommendation, the sewers of the hospital were also flushed out and the ventilation was improved. The death rates from illnesses such as typhus, typhoid, cholera and dysentery, which were killing more soldiers than battle wounds, were drastically reduced.

Although Florence herself never claimed credit for the improved conditions, her work had started to make a pioneering name for herself. To the soldiers under her care she was known as a figure of authority, with one British soldier writing: "It would be a brave man that dare insult her... I would not give a penny for his chance." However, when a portrait of Florence carrying a lamp, tending to patients, appeared in an article in *The Times*, she was given her famous nickname 'The Lady with the Lamp'. She instantly inspired an army of committed Nightingale fans. She was described as a "ministering angel... as her slender form glides quietly along each corridor, every poor fellow's face softens with gratitude." Her enterprising work in Crimean War hospitals was hailed by the press and her family had to endure a wave of poetry dropping on their doorstep from adoring fans. Florence's image was even printed on souvenirs and she achieved Victorian celebrity status. The lady herself, however, was not so keen on this attention, and she adopted a pseudonym, Miss Smith, to avoid being mobbed by the adoring masses.

Considering Florence had defied tradition to become a nurse, this newfound celebrity was surprising but immensely powerful. This was a power the Lady of the Lamp did not intend to squander and she sprang into action upon returning home from the war. Florence began collecting evidence and in league with her staunch supporter Queen Victoria, she persuaded the government to set up a Royal Commission to look into the health of the military. Florence and the commission concluded that poor living conditions were the main cause of death in the hospitals, with 16,000 of 18,000 deaths due to preventable diseases spread by poor sanitation. She focused on promoting sanitary living conditions in all hospitals and with immense support behind her, the Nightingale Fund was created to help train new nurses in her sanitation techniques.

With £45,000 raised through the Nightingale Fund, Florence set up a training school at St Thomas' Hospital and went on to work at the Liverpool Workhouse Infirmary by May 1865. Perhaps one of her most remarkable contributions to medicine, however, was her book, *Notes on Nursing*, which was published in 1859. This book was not only used in her school by her own students, but also by those nursing privately in their own homes. Florence was all about accessibility and she wanted to be sure that anyone, regardless of class or ability, could read the book and follow the practices set out within it. For the era, the simple rules of sanitation and health within were revolutionary and the volume is considered a classic in the history of nursing. It was designed to help those who were unable to pay for private healthcare and it meant that people could care for their sick relatives and friends.

But there was an even more impoverished people Florence was determined to help – those in the workhouses. For the entirety of the workhouse system up until this point, the sick paupers were being cared for by the able-bodied paupers. Nurses in general were regarded with some disdain and were characterised as former servants and widows who had to scrape together an income. Many of these 'nurses' were not actually interested in nursing and showed little compassion. The hospitals were even worse – places of no hope where the floor was lined with straw to soak up blood. Florence introduced trained nurses into the workhouse system from the 1860s in a monumental move. The poorest and most unfortunate in society were finally being offered real medical care and attention, and this move was seen as an important step towards establishing the National Health Service.

It is hard to overstate how monumental Florence's work was in the nursing profession, which had seldom been treated with respect previously. She was an educated, upper-class woman with friends in high places and an iron will to achieve change. Many of her contemporaries commented on her stubborn, opinionated nature, but these were the essential parts of her character that ensured she saw the change she had set out to achieve. This change was not only witnessed in Great Britain, but the United States was also taking notice of the Lady of the Lamp's impressive achievements. The Union government directly approached Florence for guidance and her advice inspired them to create the United States Sanitary Commission. Florence also went on to mentor Linda Richards who is today regarded as the United States' first trained nurse and she went on to establish many nursing schools of her own, spreading Florence's teachings as far as Japan. By the start of the 1880s, nurses trained by Florence were matrons at the leading hospitals of the country from St Mary's Hospital to the Edinburgh Royal Infirmary, and even so far as Sydney Hospital in Australia.

Another of Florence's key areas of achievements was her work

The politician Sidney Herbert became close friends with Nightingale and helped her achieve many of her aims in her career

Queen Victoria was a big fan of Nightingale and her work in Crimea, awarding her a special brooch as a thank you

The Order of Merit

The Order of Merit is an award that was created to acknowledge distinguished service in the armed services, science, art, literature or the promotion of culture. First established by Edward VII in 1902, the award can only be given out at the discretion of the reigning monarch, with a maximum of 24 living recipients permitted at any one time. The idea of an Order of Merit was discussed far before it was installed in 1805 following the battle of Trafalgar, and again later by Queen Victoria. Since its installation it has not been an easily won honour, with politicians lobbying for candidates, but the monarch usually remains guarded about their decision. In 1907, Florence Nightingale became the first woman to receive the honour.

However, it wasn't only the Order of Merit Florence received for her work – she also became the first recipient of the Royal Red Cross. This military honour for exceptional nursing was basically created for her by Queen Victoria in 1883. The award is still given today for exceptional devotion and competence over a long period of duty, or for a very exceptional act of bravery or devotion.

It was Victoria's son Edward VII who finally established the Order of Merit

It was the strong visual of Florence grasping a lamp in a dark hospital that captured the nation's sympathy and catapulted her to stardom

SHE WAS CONVINCED THAT GOD HAD CALLED HER TO WORK IN HIS SERVICE

Nightingale, the maths whizz

Although many remember Florence for her role as the saintly nurse, perhaps her most notable ability that helped save countless lives was not compassion but mathematical genius. From an early age, Florence naturally took to mathematics and she was especially skilled in recording and organising information.

Over her life, Florence became a pioneer in statistics, graphs and the visual presentation of information. She frequently utilised the pie chart, which was a relatively new concept at the time. Today she is credited as having developed the polar area diagram, also known as the Nightingale rose diagram. This graph helped her to represent sources of patient mortality in an easy to understand manner.

Her very visual representations of findings meant they could be understood by civil servants and members of parliament who would have struggled to understand the long, complex written reports. Her contribution was so significant that in 1859, the Royal Statistical Society admitted her as its first female member. She also later became an honorary member of the American Statistical Association. Without her natural mathematical ability and statistical pioneering, it is unlikely Florence would have been able to make the strides forward in medicine that she achieved.

Nightingale took it upon herself to train as many nurses as she could in her pioneering new techniques

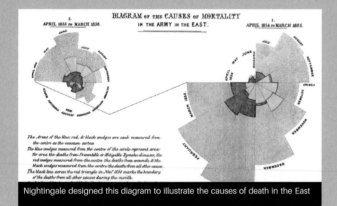
Nightingale designed this diagram to illustrate the causes of death in the East

towards improving the health of the British Army in India. Now a firm advocate of germ theory, she insisted on the importance of uncontaminated water supplies as well as warning about the dangers of overcrowding and poor ventilation. She believed that if the conditions of the people of India improved, so would those of the army and she campaigned to improve the conditions of the country as a whole. Her hard work and statistical gathering in India led to the establishment of a Royal Commission into the Indian situation, and the public health in the country improved dramatically. The death rate in soldiers posted there plummeted from 68 in every 1,000 to 18.

Outside of medicine, Florence also made some interesting contributions to theology and the role of God in her work ethic has often been examined. She believed she had been given a mission by God to dedicate her life in service to others, and she must have placed great importance upon this as she defied tradition and never married. Although she was a member of the Church of England, her views were unorthodox. She believed the purest manifestation of religion was to

show kindness and care for others. She was also a firm believer that all who died, regardless of their religion or lack thereof, would be admitted to heaven. We know this as it's a belief that she used to comfort those dying in her care, saying that God was "far more merciful than any human creature ever was or can ever imagine".

Although she was committed to Christianity, she was also a firm opponent of discrimination of non-Christian religions, believing that all religions encouraged its people to work hard. Her belief in the power of religion to encourage work was so strong she insisted all nurses she train attend religious services. On the other side of the coin, however, she was far from a blind believer, as she criticised the Church of England for often worsening the conditions of the poor, and she even said that secular hospitals usually provided better care than religious institutions. It is clear to see by her open-minded approach that she was not afraid to take a trail-blazing, different opinion, especially for her era, and ultimately her concern was not to further her own agenda, but to ensure the least fortunate in society were provided with the care and comfort they deserved.

However, as enterprising as she was, Florence was still mortal and from 1857 onwards she was bedridden and plagued by depression due to ill health, with modern sources claiming an extreme case of brucellosis was the source of her problems. Despite her bedridden state, Nightingale remained productive, continuing to carry out pioneering work in hospital planning across the world. Her work did gradually slow in the last decade of her life as she became steadily blind and with decreased mental capabilities. On 13 August 1910, at the impressive age of 90, Florence died in her sleep at her home in Mayfair, London. Due to her immense contributions to medicine, her family received an offer to bury her at Westminster Abbey, but this was declined by her relatives. She was instead buried in the graveyard of Saint Margaret's Church in Wellow, Hampshire.

Today, Florence's contribution to nursing cannot be overexaggerated. Regarded as the founder of modern nursing, she created a culture of compassion towards patients and a commitment to diligent hospital administration that continues to this day. The Florence Nightingale Medal was established in 1912 and it is regarded as the highest international distinction any nurse can achieve. Similar to the Hippocratic Oath recited by doctors, the Florence Nightingale Pledge is uttered by nurses at their pinning ceremony at the end of their training. Although the words were not written by Florence herself, it was her intrepid work and commitment to her cause that formed the basis for the pledge. Countless hospitals and monuments have been erected in her name, and plays, films and televisions shows focus on her life and work. Starting life as a headstrong girl who collected shells and defied tradition, Florence is truly a testament to the intrepid human spirit. Not only did her work change the perception of nurses forever, but she urged reluctant governments to act, and in the process she helped save thousands, if not more, from gruesome, painful deaths.

Lecabo. Faccupt atemporunt veliquo dipsaectorum sum exerfer ferisim ad

Nightingale, the feminist

Florence had some somewhat surprising views about women. She believed in general they were not as capable as men, and almost all of her friends were men, especially powerful ones. She believed males had done far more to help her attain her own goals than women and she even went as far to refer to herself as a "man of action".

Despite this less than flattering view, Nightingale's work did improve the situations of many women and she has become a central figure in English feminism. This is due to the immense number of works she penned and her ability to forgo the expectations of her gender to achieve her ambitions. Florence helped open up far more options for women in the workforce, expanding their horizons and offering a chance to escape a life of domestication.

Another important contribution made towards women's rights was Florence's work in abolishing overly harsh prostitution laws. Under the Contagious Diseases Act, policemen could arrest prostitutes and force them to undergo STD tests - any women found to be positive were locked in a hospital to 'protect men'. Florence campaigned to have the Act abolished and this finally happened in 1886.

In the 1920s and 30s especially, Florence was upheld as an icon for feminists across the country. Though she may not have thought particularly fondly of her own gender, her work towards bettering the lot of women everywhere cannot be ignored.

SHE RETURNED HOME AND LIVED UNDER THE PSEUDONYM MS SMITH

Today Nightingale's birthday, May 12, is celebrated worldwide as international nurses day

Nightingale would often write letters home on behalf of dying or dead soldiers to delicately break the news to their families

Nightingale avoided romantic relationships with men, preferring to focus on her work

Florence's interactions with Mary Clarke influenced her views on feminism from an early age

1934 – present

Jane Goodall

Through determination, perseverance and an all-consuming love, this woman defied society's expectations to become one of the world's leading scientists

In an age of education and experience, it's hard to imagine a situation where sheer passion is enough to make your dreams come true. But for Jane Goodall, that is exactly how her story begins. Born in London on 3 April 1934, she was always passionate about animals. Before she could talk, she was gifted a cuddly toy – a chimpanzee, which was sold to celebrate the birth of a new chimp at London Zoo. For Jane, it was love at first sight. She eventually named the chimp Jubilee and it accompanied her everywhere.

By five, Jane's passion for animals was evolving and the young girl was determined to understand the creatures she shared her environment with. Little Jane harboured dreams of travelling the world to write about animals, and rather than dissuade her daughter from such heady aspirations, Jane's mother encouraged her, stating: "If you really want something, and if you work hard, take advantage of the opportunities, and never give up, you will somehow find a way."

Sadly, the idyllic youth that Jane was so fond of came to a shattering close. World War II tore her parents apart and after her father returned in 1945, Jane's parents divorced. Despite her dreams, she couldn't afford to go to university and so instead went to secretarial college. She took on several jobs after college but in 1956, she received an offer that would change her life forever.

Invited to visit a friend's farm in Kenya, Jane leapt at the opportunity, boarding a boat to Africa on 2 April 1957. Upon arrival, she met the famous anthropologist Dr Louis Leakey, who was charmed by the passionate and intelligent Jane. He immediately hired her as his secretary, and Jane accompanied Leakey and his wife on their studies. In Jane, Leakey saw potential, and he allowed her to study primates.

In 1960, and with Leakey's recommendation, Jane (and her mother as a chaperone) was allowed to observe primates in Gombe National Park with six months of funding. Here, Jane made startling discoveries – chimps used tools, made tools and even ate meat. When she published her research, her work was met with incredulity. How could this "willowy blonde" (according to the Associated Press) with no scientific training understand what she saw? But over time, her findings were accepted, and by 1962 she was accepted onto a programme at Cambridge University. In 1966, she was awarded her PhD in ethnology.

Meanwhile, National Geographic had decided to support Jane's work, sending photographer Baron Hugo van Lawick to Gombe. For the first time, Jane's interactions with the chimpanzees were documented and published alongside her research in the magazine. Finally, Jane's vital work at Gombe was changing the way scientists thought about chimpanzees.

For Jane, her research on chimpanzees opened her eyes to another, more serious plight: protecting and conserving these animals and their environment. Today, Jane travels the world to enlighten and inform about her research and the need for conservation. Now in her mid-80s, Jane is a figure rallied around by many women scientists, having not only broken into science without prior education, but having turned the entire industry on its head.

A life's work

1935
Aged just one, Jane is given a stuffed chimpanzee toy called Jubilee.

1952
Jane goes to secretarial college after school, and she graduates in 1952.

1957
Jane leaves for Kenya. There she meets Dr Louis Leakey, who hires her as a secretary.

1960
Having proven her worth to Dr Leakey, Jane begins her research on chimpanzees.

1961
David Greybeard, a dominant chimp that Jane has been observing, accepts Jane by going to her camp to find her.

Roots and Shoots

With the hope of encouraging people to care about the world around them, Jane founded the Roots and Shoots mission in 1991. After decades of work, she recognised the importance of preserving not only the chimpanzees' habitats, but also those of local people, both of whose homes are all too often destroyed. In an effort to motivate others to act now to save the environment, Jane's Roots and Shoots is a youth organisation that hopes to build compassionate, considerate future leaders through online communities, campaigning and education.

Jane speaking at a Roots and Shoots event in Pennsylvania in 2003

Five things to know about...
Jane Goodall

"Jane's vital work… was changing the way scientists thought about chimpanzees"

National Geographic sent a photographer to capture not just her work, but the woman behind it too

1 Jane Doe
When Jane went to Cambridge in 1962, she was chastised for having given all of the chimpanzees names and talking about their personalities. According to scientists, they should've been given numbers, not names.

2 Eyes on the prize
Despite the claim that trophy hunting aids 'conservation' attempts, Jane is staunchly against it. Not only is there no reliable proof that the money paid for trophy hunting helps conservation, but the death of an animal hugely impacts its social circle.

3 Planet of the apes
When the reboot of Planet of the Apes was in production, Jane advised on human-chimp behaviour. Jane later claimed that she was "unexpectedly moved" by the film War for the Planet of the Apes, and especially Andy Serkis' performance.

4 Til death us do part
After her divorce with Hugo was finalised, Jane married Derek Bryceson, the director of Tanzania's national parks. Tragically, he died of cancer three years later, and Jane has not remarried since.

5 Rescuing an abandoned chimp
Back in 1992, Jane was part of a rescue mission for a chimp named Gregoire, who'd been left in a cage alone at Brazzaville Zoo in the Republic of the Congo since 1945. When Jane reached him, the door had rusted shut.

1961
Jane is accepted onto a special program at Cambridge University to study for a doctorate.

1962
Baron Hugo van Lawick goes to photograph Jane with the chimps. The pair marry two years later.

1974
Despite her divorce, Jane observes warring tribes of chimps. Some even turn cannibalistic.

1977
The Jane Goodall Institute is established to help people understand the forest preservation.

2002
After tirelessly working, Jane is awarded the title of the United Nations' Messenger of Peace.

NASA's
forgotten geniuses

**How 'female computers' helped the USA reach for the
stars and beat the Soviet Union to the Moon**

Hidden Figures tells the story of NASA's 'women computers'

Katherine Johnson, pictured at NASA in 1966

Dorothy Vaughan (far left), pictured with two other computers at NACA

When Katherine Johnson left university in 1937, her career options were limited. Despite being an extremely gifted mathematician, she was a woman and an African American, two qualities that made her quite unemployable. So she became a teacher, one of the few professions she could enter. Two decades later, however, she found herself at the centre of the Space Race between the world's two biggest superpowers. Ultimately, her talents – and those of many other women like her – helped send humans to the Moon.

In a time before women's suffrage, and before the civil rights movement gave African Americans a voice, women like Johnson faced not only discrimination but also segregation in the workplace. The state of Virginia, in particular, was fiercely intolerant to African Americans in the early 1900s, and one of the least progressive states in the nation. Although the Nineteenth Amendment to the US Constitution had been passed by Congress in 1919, giving women the right to vote, the Virginia General Assembly delayed its ratification until 1952. By that point, women had been voting and even holding public office for more than 30 years.

At the Langley Research Centre (LaRC) in Virginia, however, things were different. The nation's first aeronautics laboratory was established in 1917 and would go on to become the birthplace of the US space programme in the 1950s. It would be here that the original NASA astronauts would undertake their training, and where African-American women like Johnson would help launch man into orbit. The LaRC represented an island of rationality within Virginia, where forward thinking was not only allowed and encouraged, but also absolutely essential.

A consequence was that the LaRC operated in defiance of Virginia laws, and that included policies towards women and African Americans. In the 1930s, with only a few hundred engineers on its books and needing extra resources, the National Advisory Committee for Aeronautics (NACA) – which would become NASA in 1958 – started hiring women to sift through data and perform calculations. Using so-called 'women computers' was not unprecedented; in astronomy, the practice had been carried out for decades, and had led to some ground-breaking research. Notably, in 1912, an astronomer called Henrietta Swan Leavitt at Harvard had found that certain types of pulsating stars could be used as distance markers in the universe. Her amazing discovery ultimately led to the revelation that our galaxy is not alone in the vast cosmos.

At the LaRC, this programme benefited both parties. For the centre itself, women became a key part of the organisation, measuring and calculating the results of wind-tunnel tests. A memo dated 1942 stated: "The engineers admit themselves that the girl computers do the work more rapidly and accurately than they would." For the women involved, it was welcome work that was more financially rewarding than other professions, such as teaching. The first female to break the gender barrier was Pearl Young, who was hired to work at the LaRC in 1922 as a physicist. Later, she would play a vital role in making the work carried out by NACA more accessible to the public, in the form of readable technical reports, and go on to become chief technical editor.

When World War II struck and able-bodied men were summoned to fight, Langley began hiring black female mathematicians, too. President Roosevelt played a big part in this, as his issuing of Executive Order 8802 prohibited racial, religious and ethnic discrimination in the country's vital defence industry. Due to segregation laws, however, the new recruits were kept separate from their white female colleagues and counterparts and assigned to the 'West Area Computers' unit. At its peak, it's thought that there were about 200 women doing computing work for NACA, about 70 of who were African-American. The centre was so

"Due to segregation laws, however, the new recruits were kept separate from their white female counterparts"

The first American to orbit Earth, John Glenn, launches on Friendship 7 on 20 February 1962

Melba Roy, a female computer at NASA in 1964

The history of 'female computers'

Before modern electronic computers, the term denoted someone who computed something, and was used as far back as the 17th century. The work was often tedious, generally sifting through data and performing calculations, and it was generally carried out by men. In the late-19th century, however, astronomer Edward Charles Pickering at Harvard began employing women for the roles, dubbed 'Pickering's Harem'. This undoubtedly reflected the status of women at the time and they were paid half of what the men were, and yet they helped to map the universe.

The positive effect was that many agencies – including NASA – started employing female mathematicians to perform this type of work. Although not wholly prestigious, it provided a welcome career path for women in the early-20th century. Many went on to be programmers or engineers with the advent or electronic computers. During World War II, with a drastic shortage of manpower, the practice was greatly expanded. It opened doors for a huge number of people.

Grace Hopper, for example, is generally regarded as one of the first computer programmers ever in 1944, and was posthumously awarded the Presidential Medal of Freedom by President Obama on 22 November 2016, along with Margaret Hamilton, a computer scientist who played a key role in landing humans on the Moon. Katherine Johnson, one of the three main characters in Hidden Figures, also received the award in 2015.

From left to right, Vaughan, Johnson and Jackson in *Hidden Figures*

Katherine Johnson in *Hidden Figures*, played by Taraji P Henson

A group of computers (front row) at NACA in the 1950s. Mary Jackson is on the far right

President Barack Obama presents Katherine Johnson with the Presidential Medal of Freedom

impressed by these workers that, after the war ended, it continued in the employment of its women computers.

In the 1950s, the LaRC found itself becoming involved in rocket research, as the Space Race between Cold War rivals the US and the Soviet Union began. Langley's research took on a whole new meaning – they would be helping to send Americans to space in the bid for supremacy. The research was slow and steady at first, until 4 October 1957. That was the day the Soviet Union made history and launched the world's first artificial satellite, Sputnik 1, into orbit. Spurred on by the challenge, NACA was re-purposed into the National Aeronautics and Space Administration (NASA) and the race was on.

Three remarkable African-American women were working at the LaRC during this time, and their achievements are finally getting the recognition they deserve in the biographical blockbuster Hidden Figures. While only one was directly involved in sending people to space, each had their part to play in making the agency the world leader in space exploration, and changing attitudes there for good.

Dorothy Vaughan was hired by NACA in 1943, and it quickly became apparent that she was a very capable manager of people and a good judge of skill. When a white woman in charge of the West Area Computers became sick, Vaughan stepped in as acting head, and ended up in the role for three years – held in limbo – before being given the job officially. "Dorothy was the first black woman supervisor for NACA and NASA, and she was exceptional in a wide number of things, such as a sense of justice and willingness to go that extra step," said Bill Barry, NASA's Chief Historian and a consultant on the Hidden Figures film. Vaughan would often put her own position on the line in order to protect her team.

Mary Jackson, who came in to the LaRC as a computer, also had a degree in maths and physics, and was very mechanically inclined. She would end up becoming the first black female engineer and,

Barry said, possibly the first female engineer in the whole agency. "That was pretty exceptional at the time," he added.

But perhaps the most outstanding of the three was Katherine Johnson, at least in terms of her "raw intellectual ability," according to Barry. She had a mind wrapped around numbers, and could see things others couldn't. "I counted everything," she once said, "The steps to the road, the steps up to the church, the number of dishes and silverware I washed… anything that could be counted, I did." On her lunch breaks, she would pore over space technology manuals to figure out what her superiors were doing, and how her work fit in.

A pivotal moment in the women's lives was the sending of astronaut John Glenn into space. On 12 April 1961, the Soviet Union and Yuri Gagarin shocked the world by beating the USA to putting a man in to orbit. He was followed three weeks later by American Alan Shepard as part of Project Mercury on 5 May 1961, but the Americans were playing catch-up, and they knew it. First after first was going to the Soviets, and they looked ever more likely to send a human to the Moon – the arbitrary 'end goal' of the Space Race.

Shepard's flight was suborbital, meaning that his spacecraft had

"She was the expert on calculating the geometry of trajectories, namely how you got from one place to another in space"

A human computer at work with a microscope, collecting data at Langley Research Center

entered space and returned to Earth without entering orbit, whereas Gagarin's had been orbital. After another American suborbital flight, made by Gus Grissom, the aim was to send Glenn on an orbital flight in 1962 and match the Soviets. This was where Katherine Johnson came in. She was the expert on calculating the geometry of trajectories, namely how you got from one place to another in space by firing retro-rockets. She had done these calculations for Shepard's flight, but they were getting more and more complex, leading NASA to start using actual mechanical computers. However, they weren't considered reliable, and the software wasn't as robust as it needed to be.

"When it was time for Glenn's flight, the critical question was whether the computers work and give the answers they wanted," Barry explained. Glenn's solution? "Get the girl to check the numbers." It was now up to Johnson to manually work out the computer's calculations, and make sure they were correct. It took Johnson a day and a half to plough through the millions of calculations. In the end, her data matched the computers, and the mission went ahead. Glenn's flight was a success and, eight years later, men – Americans – would walk on the Moon, winning the Space Race.

Johnson's work proved crucial to later Apollo missions too, including solving issues with the rendezvous and docking techniques required to link two spacecraft. This would be crucial to getting the men on the Moon back to Earth – by docking their lunar module with the command module in orbit. "If you ask her, she'll tell you that's her most important work, making sure those calculations happened so they could rendezvous in lunar orbit," said Barry. Johnson's work even provided the backbone of modern spaceflight, as much of the maths used today can be traced back to her. She also wrote a technical report on the subject, with the somewhat unwieldy title of 'Determination Of Azimuth Angle For Placing A Satellite Over A Selected Earth Position'.

Perhaps one of the most remarkable things about all this, though, is just how much of a microcosm the LaRC was. Inside, the women were allowed to chat freely, regardless of race. Outside, they weren't even allowed to sit and talk to each other in a restaurant. Barry told of a story of a NASA engineer in downtown Hampton, Virginia, one night in the late 1950s, who saw people harassing an African-American man who worked at Langley. The engineer went over to intervene, and found himself thrown in jail. "I think that tells you something about the environment there," added Barry.

These three women have been overlooked until now, but the impacts made by these early NASA pioneers were far reaching. Mary Jackson, later in her career, for example, used her mathematical

Five key NASA women

MARGARET HAMILTON

Margaret Hamilton was a computer scientist working with NASA in the 1960s, leading the team that developed the software for Apollo and Skylab. She was awarded the Presidential Medal of Freedom in 2016 for her work.

SALLY RIDE

Trailblazer Dr Sally Ride was the first American woman to go to space, aboard Space Shuttle Challenger in 1983, and she flew again in 1984. She was completing her PhD in physics when she discovered that, for the first time, women could apply to become astronauts.

KALPANA CHAWLA

In 1997, Kalpana made history by becoming the first Indian-American to go to space, aboard Space Shuttle Columbia. She flew again on Columbia in 2003, but died tragically, along with her crewmembers, when the shuttle broke up on re-entry.

Katherine Johnson worked on calculating trajectories, launch windows and return paths for spacecraft at NASA

Astronaut John Glenn, the first American in space, entering his spacecraft Friendship 7 prior to launch, 1962

skills to show there was a bias against promoting women. She helped other women advance their careers, and ultimately became the federal women's programme manager at Langley. Now we live in an era when NASA is directed by an African-American man, Administrator Charles Bolden, and a woman, Deputy Administrator Dava Newman, and it's commonplace for women to lead technical projects at NASA in Langley. The LaRC serves as a reminder that, in sometimes the most unexpected places, rationality can prevail. "They were a group of engineers, not used to fitting in, and they found each other," said Barry. "I think it shows humanity at its best. It shows what we can be like when we act like decent human beings."

SHANA DALE
In 2005, Shana Dale became the first female deputy administrator of NASA. She held the position until 2009, and has been succeeded by two more women – Lori Garver and Dava Newman. At the time of writing, no woman has yet become NASA administrator.

PEGGY WHITSON
The American biochemistry researcher became the first woman to command the ISS in 2007. She has been to space three times, including most recently on Expedition 50 and 51, and is NASA's most experienced female astronaut.

1799 – 1847

Mary Anning

A trailblazer for palaeontology who excavated prehistoric fossils and helped broaden scientific study

Born into poverty on 21 May 1799, Mary Anning had to work hard from a young age. She didn't have a formal education and was only taught to read at Sunday school. Raised in the seaside resort of Lyme Regis in Dorset, Mary and her older brother Joseph made a living selling ammonoid fossils to holidaymakers at their father's waterfront stall.

Her life changed in 1811 when Joseph noticed a skull embedded in rock. Curious, the siblings chipped away until an entire skeleton was uncovered. Unbeknown to them, this was the first ever discovery of an ichthyosaurus, a marine reptile from the Triassic period.

There was a huge fanfare over the find, which only escalated when famous surgeon Everard Home wrote a scientific paper on the ichthyosaurus three years later. The fossil was found at an area now known as the Jurassic Coast, a part of Dorset that was underwater when dinosaurs roamed the Earth. The cliffs where Anning grew up were filled with fossils from the Jurassic period, and she would often scour the beach after storms when rocks had been eroded or dislodged by the weather.

Anning noted down every find she made, and after failing to find any new fossils for over a year, in 1821 she made her next discovery, unearthing three more ichthyosaur skeletons. This was followed two years later by an even more impressive find – a complete plesiosaur skeleton. This was so extraordinary that many leading scientists declared it a fake, unwilling to believe that an uneducated 24-year-old could find such remarkable remains. Additionally, society at the time was highly religious and many rejected these discoveries as they conflicted with the teachings of the Bible.

Despite the setback, Anning continued to make more startling revelations. She uncovered belemnoidea fossils, squid-like creatures that were among the first prehistoric animals discovered that had the ability to squirt ink as a defence mechanism. Anning also dug up fossilised faeces, known as coprolite, which helped experts understand the diets of prehistoric creatures. But her biggest finding of all was the first complete skeleton of a pterosaur in 1828.

All of Mary Anning's discoveries helped influence the study of palaeontology as scientists began to take an increased interest in fossilised animals and plants. Her work also prompted people to question the history of the Earth in more detail as well as encouraging girls and those from poorer backgrounds by proving that they could succeed in scientific study, a profession dominated by wealthy upper-class men. She died in her hometown in 1847 from breast cancer, aged just 47. A stained glass window in a local church was made in her memory and is still there today.

> *"The biggest finding of all was the first complete skeleton of a pterosaur in 1829"*

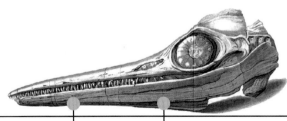

A life's work

1799
Mary Anning is born into poverty on 21 May in Lyme Regis in Dorset, England.

1811
Her brother Joseph finds an ichthyosaur skull and Mary, aged 12, helps dig up the rest of the skeleton.

1814
A scientific paper on the discovery is written and published by the famous surgeon Everard Home.

1819
The skeleton is put on display at the British Museum, giving the Jurassic Coast national coverage.

1820
After not finding any fossils for over a year, the Annings are forced to sell furniture to pay rent.

Groundbreaker

Mary Anning's discovery of the pterosaur Dimorphodon macronyx was a turning point. For the first time there was hard proof that many different species of flying reptile had existed in the prehistoric era. It lived 200 million years ago and had shorter wings and a larger head than previous species found in Germany. The fully intact skeleton provided scientists with a physical specimen to study. Additionally, her finding of a squaloraja fossil helped bridge the gap between the evolution of rays and sharks, decades before Darwin's On The Origin Of Species was released.

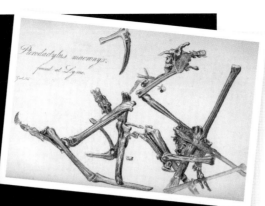

The specimen was the first pterosaur uncovered outside of Germany and the first complete pterosaur fossil found

Five things to know about...
Mary Anning

1 Immortalised in song
Mary Anning's life was thought to be the inspiration for a song written in 1908, which included the tongue-twister 'she sells sea shells on the sea shore'.

2 She could speak French
Anning was a keen reader of the works of Georges Cuvier, a prominent French palaeontologist. To help understand his writing, she learned to read French herself.

3 Two fish are named after her
In recognition for her achievements, Acrodus anningiae and Belenstomus anningiae are named in her honour. The two fish species were found by Louis Agaasiz, who visited the Jurassic Coast in 1834.

4 She was very nearly killed by lightning
A popular story claims that Anning nearly died aged just 15 months. Caught in a sudden thunderstorm with her babysitter and two other children, a lightning strike killed the other three but somehow she survived the ordeal.

5 Her discoveries were painted
Geologist Henry De la Beche was inspired by Anning's discoveries to paint a picture of what prehistoric life may have been like. The painting encouraged many people to speculate about the distant past.

Anning's unearthing of the Dimorphodon was the first pterosaur found outside of continental Europe

Anning is thought to have inspired the 'she sells sea shells on the sea shore' tongue-twister

Anning helped put the Jurassic Coast on the map as a hotbed for prehistoric excavation

1821
Three more fossilised ichthyosaurs are found, which are up to six metres in length.

1823
Anning finds her biggest discovery yet in December – the complete skeleton of a plesiosaur.

1824
Coprolite is dug up, helping experts understand the diets of prehistoric animals.

1828
Anning finds the first ever pterosaur fossil outside of Germany.

2010
The Royal Society recognises her as one of ten British women who have contributed to science.

Heroines of science & ingenuity

Over the centuries, women have been scientific pioneers against the odds

Gertrude B Elion
American 1918 – 1999

Gertrude B Elion was determined to battle cancer. She overcame gender discrimination to pursue a glittering scientific career and became a pioneering researcher, developing new drugs and research methods to identify and combat the spread of cancers, AIDS and other diseases. Her extraordinary achievements were recognised in 1988, when she was jointly awarded the Nobel Prize in Physiology or Medicine with her colleague, George H Hitchings, and Sir James Black. As well as a host of other awards, Elion received the honour of becoming the first woman to be inducted into the National Inventors Hall of Fame.

Dian Fossey
American 1932 – 1985

Dian Fossey achieved fame as one of the world's most recognised primatologists and, as a foremost expert on gorillas, she spent time studying them in their natural Rwandan habitat. Fossey became a vocal opponent of poaching in Rwanda and of the encroachment of tourism on the habitat of the gorillas. She set up a research centre to promote conservation too, urging governments to do all they could to preserve their natural habitat. Fossey was murdered in 1985. She was laid to rest at the Karisoke Research Center, beside the gorillas that she had studied and who had been killed by the poachers she had fought against.

Sofia Kovalevskaya
Russian 1850 – 1891

Denied admission to university because of her gender, Sofia Kovalevskaya sought private tuition and was awarded the doctorate that the establishment had sought to deny her. She became a celebrated mathematician in Europe and was the first woman to gain a modern doctorate in mathematics, the first to sit on the editorial board of a science journal and, with her appointment to the University of Stockholm in 1889, the first to become a professor of mathematics. A keen writer and advocate for the rights of women, Kovalevskaya is honoured to this day on the surface of the Moon itself, with a crater that shares her name.

Mae Carol Jemison
American 1956 – now

When she entered orbit aboard the Space Shuttle Endeavour in 1992, Mae Carol Jemison became the first African American woman to fly into space. She was one of 2,000 applicants for the position and had been inspired by watching Star Trek as a child. Jemison went on to pursue an academic career and founded her own technology company. A recipient of multiple awards and honours, the year after her space flight she even secured a guest appearance in Star Trek: The Next Generation, a modern companion to the programme that had inspired her love of space travel all those years ago.

Clara Barton
American 1821 – 1912

When Clara Barton was 10 years old, her brother was badly injured in a fall. Though doctors gave him up as a lost cause, Clara nursed him herself and under her care, he made a full recovery. Barton became a schoolteacher, but when the American Civil War broke out, she returned to nursing. She became a famous figure thanks to her battlefield endeavours and when fighting ceased, Lincoln granted her request to do all she could to locate and identify the remains of more than 20,000 dead. Barton established the American Red Cross in 1881 and served as its president until her retirement in 1904.

Hypatia
Alexandrian c.370 – 417 CE

Although none of her writings survive, Hypatia was renowned as a mathematician, philosopher and educator. She was a keen philosophical commentator and the only piece of surviving work attributed to her is the text of Ptolemy's Almagest, which it is believed that she edited. Hypatia was murdered by a mob who believed that she was purposefully meddling in a power struggle between Bishop Cyril of Alexandria and Orestes, the Roman governor of Egypt, whom she advised. Her death sent shockwaves though the empire and saw her hailed as a martyr for the cause of philosophy and learning.

Caroline Herschel
German 1750 – 1848

Though her name has been eclipsed by that of her brother, William, Caroline Herschel was an accomplished astronomer. Employed as her brother's assistant, he built a telescope for her sole use and she discovered several comets, including one named in her honour. She was the first woman to be awarded a Gold Medal of the Royal Astronomical Society and the first to be admitted to the society. Today Caroline's name lives on in the comet, as well as an asteroid and a crater of the Moon - fitting tributes for a woman who dedicated her life to astronomy.

Dorothy Hodgkin
British 1910 – 1994

Biochemist Dorothy Hodgkin was awarded the 1964 Nobel Prize for Chemistry thanks to her pioneering research into protein crystallography, a technique that used X-rays to map the 3D structures of molecules. This discovery led her to confirm the structure of insulin and penicillin. Hodgkin's research into insulin led to new breakthroughs in diabetes research, a subject about which she was passionate. Highly decorated and honoured across the globe, she is remembered today by the Royal Society's Dorothy Hodgkin Fellowship.

Émilie du Châtelet
French 1706 – 1749

Émilie, Marquise du Châtelet, was a French philosopher, mathematician and physicist who translated Isaac Newton's Principia. In fact, her translation was so seminal that it is still the standard French text today. Although her translation wasn't published until after her death, Châtelet achieved recognition in her lifetime for Foundations of Physics, as well as her willingness to engage her critics in debate. She was a vocal supporter of education for women, arguing that her gender was deliberately held back by a lack of proper learning.

ROYALTY & RULERS

126

98

142

138

大清國當今慈禧端佑康頤昭豫莊誠壽恭欽獻崇聖母皇太后
光緒癸卯年

108

120

1533 – 1603

Elizabeth I

She fought off foreign invasions and domestic rebellions but did she really preside over a golden age?

In 1588, against the advice of her most trusted aides, Elizabeth I rode out on her grey gelding to address her troops gathered at Tilbury in Essex in preparation of repelling the expected invasion force of the Spanish Armada. Looking out at the assembled faces before her, she delivered a speech that would go down in history and for many would forever define her: "I know I have the body of a weak, feeble woman; but I have the heart and stomach of a king – and of a king of England too."

The speech would have to be transcribed and redistributed for the soldiers who were unable to hear the queen but they had all seen their monarch, armoured and on her steed, ready to stand by them to repel the Catholic invasion. This image of Elizabeth has been the key to our popular perception of her for centuries, but there's much more to her. Elizabeth was cunning and capricious, but she could be blinded by affection, if only temporarily. She was tremendously clever, with an almost unfailing sense of what her people wanted or needed from her, but had to see off foreign invasion attempts and homegrown rebellions. While she was sitting on the throne of England the country became acquainted with some of its greatest triumphs and darkest hours.

When Elizabeth came to the throne in November 1558, the whole of Europe was on tenterhooks. How would the new Protestant queen follow the reign of her Catholic sister Mary? With an unstable nation and conspiracies at home and abroad, the situation required diplomacy, intelligence and bravery; three qualities which Elizabeth had always had in ample supply. In fact, the unstable situation was nothing new to her; Elizabeth's position had been precarious from the moment she was born. The daughter of Henry VIII's second wife, Anne Boleyn, she was immediately deemed as illegitimate by any Catholic nations, who regarded the king's divorce of Catherine of Aragon as illegal. In their eyes, Catherine's daughter Mary was the only rightful heir to the throne.

Although both parents had been desperate for a boy, Anne would be a doting mother to her child, but she was sent to the executioner's block in 1536 after failing to produce a male heir for her king. Although Henry's third wife Jane Seymour was kind to Elizabeth and Mary, she had her own child to attend to with the birth of her son and Henry's heir, Edward. Henry himself would not see much of Elizabeth until 1542, when he decided the time had come to reacquaint himself

with his daughter. He found her to be intelligent and charming, and decided that he would reinstate both Mary and Elizabeth back into his lineage.

In 1543, Henry married Catherine Parr, his last wife, and relations within the royal family warmed, as Mary took a maternal interest in young Edward, while Elizabeth enjoyed a sisterly relationship with both. However, when Edward took the throne upon their father's death, cracks started to form. First, Elizabeth had to contend with the amorous attentions of Catherine's new husband Thomas Seymour, which caused a scandal at court in 1548. Seymour's intentions were seen as treasonous, and Elizabeth was reported to be pregnant. The young princess denied these rumours, confounding her interrogator. "She hath a very good wit and nothing is gotten of her but by great policy," he wrote. This practice would serve her well once Mary took the throne but not all players were as skilled in the game of thrones; Seymour was executed the following year.

When the staunchly Catholic Mary refused to convert, Edward began proceedings to remove both his sisters from the line to the throne, fixing his hopes on his cousin, Lady Jane Grey, instead. However, the prince was seldom in good health during his short life, so it was no surprise that he died before the contract could be finalised and Mary became the new Queen of England. Just as Edward had asked Mary to change her faith, the new queen was determined that her sister should convert. She acquiesced without enthusiasm, but it was clear to both Protestants and Catholics that her true allegiance still lay with her father's Church of England rather than the Pope's Catholic Church. Over the course of Mary's reign, many conspiracy plots were designed to get Elizabeth onto the throne. None of them succeeded, but they did almost manage to get her killed.

In 1554, Thomas Wyatt attempted a rebellion following the announcement that Mary would marry the Spanish king Philip. The queen's reprisal was brutal and swift, executing not only the ringleaders, but Jane Grey as well. Elizabeth claimed ignorance, a trick she managed to successfully repeat a year later after another attempted rebellion in 1555, but her sister's patience was wearing thin and Elizabeth was placed in the Tower of London, with some Catholic supporters clamouring for her execution. Elizabeth's future prospects were looking anything but golden, and the next few months saw

ELIZABETH'S LONG REIGN PROVIDED WELCOME STABILITY FOR HER KINGDOM

her walking a political tightrope. Mary, desperate to provide her husband and her country with a Catholic heir to end the uncertainty surrounding the throne, announced that she was pregnant, but by 1558, it became clear that Mary's condition was not pregnancy, but a devastating illness. Her health broke quickly, and she died on 17 November of that year after begging Elizabeth to keep England Catholic once she took the throne. Her wishes would not be fulfilled.

Elizabeth's coronation was a stunning balancing act. With countless eyes waiting for any hint of an overtly Protestant or Catholic gestures, Elizabeth managed to confound them all. Instead, the emphasis was elsewhere: Elizabeth's intention to restore England to a state of prosperity. The new queen knew that if she was to have any chance of surviving her early years she would need trusted and astute advisors, and chose William Cecil and Robert Dudley. Cecil had worked for Edward, survived the reign of Mary and was fiercely loyal to Elizabeth. In contrast, Dudley's appointment and favour with the queen had nothing to do with his abilities as a politician. He had known Elizabeth since childhood and her affection for him had only grown stronger, and rumours abounded that she spent the nights as well as the days with him.

Cecil disapproved of Dudley and agreed with the majority of Parliament that Elizabeth should marry as soon as possible. The eyes of France and Spain were fixed on England and it made sense for the queen to create a marriage alliance with one of these major powers for her and the country's safety. King Philip II made no secret of his desire to marry Elizabeth, but she had no interest in marrying Mary's former husband. Henry of Anjou was suggested as a match, but he was still a child. Elizabeth spoke instead of being married to her nation, but scandal struck when Dudley's wife Amy died suddenly after apparently falling down the stairs in 1560. It was rumoured that Dudley had

How good was Elizabeth at balancing the books?

While the popular image is that Mary left England in a sorry state, Leanda de Lisle explains that Elizabeth's fiscal behaviour was far from immaculate. Mary left England £227,000 in debt, while her sister produced debts of £350,000. "Mary's reign was not a 'disaster'. The popular image of Mary - always 'Bloody Mary', rarely Mary I - has been greatly influenced by a combination of sexual and religious prejudice," explains De Lisle. "Mary I had named Elizabeth as her heir, despite her personal feelings towards her sister, and so allowed the crown to be inherited peacefully. Elizabeth continued to refuse to name anyone. In 1562, believing she was dying, she asked for Robert Dudley to be made Lord Protector with an income of £20,000." Elizabeth was notoriously reluctant to engage in warfare because of its costs and risk, but the Spanish conflict dragged on for years, while she awarded monopolies to her favourites at court and crops failed. "While we remember Elizabeth's success in repelling the Armada in 1588," says De Lisle, "We forget that the war continued and impoverished the country and the crown, a situation made worse by the corruption of court officials including notorious high-ranking figures such as Robert Cecil. People starved in the 1590s and the elite even began to fear possible revolution."

Verdict

Elizabeth was forced to deal with circumstances beyond her control, such as poor harvests and an ongoing conflict with Spain, but the fact is that she was not the financial marvel many believe her to be.

Borrowing money in the 16th century

Before the English merchant Thomas Gresham came to prominence, the Tudors had borrowed money from the great European banks such as the Antwerp Exchange. However, these banks charged a high interest rate and it was generally acknowledged that going around Europe borrowing money did nothing to improve England's image as a serious power. Money could also be borrowed from independent merchants, such as Horatio Palavicino, from whom Elizabeth was forced to borrow money late in her reign. Gresham had previously helped Edward VI rid himself of most of his debts and founded the Royal Exchange in 1571 to challenge the power of Antwerp.

Now that Elizabeth could seek loans from within her realm, she was able to exert greater pressure to get what she wanted, while Parliament could grant her more funds if they chose. Royal revenues were supposed to cover the basic expenses of governance, while Parliament could add to the war chest. Later in her reign, she began to use increasingly severe taxation, which contributed to her decreasing popularity.

Queen Elizabeth I opening the Royal Exchange

Picture depicting the coronation of Elizabeth I in 1558

Portrait of Mary, Queen of Scots, who was executed after being found guilty of plotting against Elizabeth I

Was a religious compromise met?

The Church of England was one of compromise and middle ground. While Elizabeth was a Protestant, she didn't hold the puritanical beliefs of some of her council members. She introduced the Act of Supremacy in 1558, which reaffirmed England's separation from Rome and established her as the head of the Church. Elizabeth understood the dangers of trying to impose religion and allowed Catholicism to continue, provided it took place in secret.

However, Leanda de Lisle reminds us that we should not forget Elizabeth's willingness to crack down when necessary. "Elizabeth's conservatism and pragmatism has seen her described as a religious moderate, in contrast to the 'fanatical' Mary," she explains. "But as the new Protestant Queen of a largely Catholic country Elizabeth was necessarily moderate, and as her reign grew longer, she proved that, like Mary, she could be utterly ruthless when faced by a threat. The hundreds of executions of villagers following the Northern Rebellion far exceeded anything her predecessors had done in similar circumstances; her later persecution of Catholics was also relentless and cruel. It is a little-known fact that she also burned heretics – namely Anabaptists – these were far fewer in number than Mary's victims, but then there weren't that many Anabaptists!" She executed both Protestants and Catholics for publicly disobeying the laws of the Church of England. However, events in Europe show the English Queen in a much more favourable light. Comparatively, Elizabeth was extremely tolerant. The St. Bartholomew's Day Massacre in Paris showed the fervour with which Catholic Europeans detested Protestants. She was also much more tolerant than many of her advisors.

Verdict

Elizabeth successfully found a moderate middle ground in a very turbulent time during her reign, but would crack down mercilessly if the rules she had laid down were broken.

VS

Catholic

1 The services were held in Latin, countermanding the reformation's ideal that everyone should be able to understand. The English prayer book was banned.

2 Church furnishings were restored to their former lavish state and the buildings were now decorated completely with Catholic artwork.

3 Catholic Mass was reintroduced, and Holy Communion was now banned by law.

4 The clergy were not allowed to marry. Priests who had married before the new law came into effect were given a choice of two options: leave their families or lose their job.

C of E

1 The image of the minister became much simpler. They were not allowed to wear Roman Catholic vestments, such as the surplice.

2 All rood lofts, a screen portraying the crucifixion, a common feature in Catholic churches, were removed. The Pope was not the head of the church.

3 The Bishop's Bible, which was in English rather than Latin, was restored, opening it up to a wider readership.

4 There was a general removal of 'superstition', such as making the sign of the cross during communion. Simplicity was what the Puritans strived for.

"The queen's reprisal was brutal and swift, executing not only the ringleaders, but also Jane Grey"

committed the deed for his queen, and Elizabeth was forced to expel him from her court.

In 1561, Elizabeth's cousin, Mary, Queen of Scots, returned to Scotland from France. For many Catholics, Mary was the true successor and she did little to downplay those clamouring for a Catholic monarch. Her arrival was perfectly timed, as Elizabeth was on the verge of death due to smallpox. However, she recovered and, with the scandal over Dudley dissipating, Elizabeth chose him to be Lord Protector, bringing him back into her court, before shocking everyone by suggesting a marriage between him and Mary. This was Elizabeth showing her political astuteness; she knew well that Scotland with a Catholic heir would have too much power, but an heir produced by her favourite and Mary, Queen of Scots could potentially unite the two countries. However, Dudley refused and Mary had no interest in marrying her cousin's paramour.

Instead, Mary married for love, choosing Lord Henry Darnley. Seeing this may have prompted Elizabeth to renew her interest in Dudley, which greatly upset the council, in particular the ambitious Lord Norfolk. When the tension between Norfolk and Dudley grew too great, Elizabeth understood that she needed to assert her authority. "I will have here but one mistress and no master," she told Dudley. It was

both a political statement and a personal one. The lack of a husband and heir was only made worse in 1566 when Mary gave birth to a son, James, but she was desperately unhappy. Darnley was a violent, drunken husband: many believed he brutally murdered her secret lover, David Rizzio. Darnley would meet his own nasty end a year later, when he was found strangled in the garden of a house. Mary quickly married the Earl of Bothwell, the man who had allegedly murdered Darnley, and Scottish forces rose against her. Imprisoned and forced to abdicate, she eventually fled to England. Elizabeth agreed to give Mary shelter, but her arrival in the north had given Catholics a figurehead and rebellion brewed.

The northern Earls suggested that Norfolk should marry Mary: soon, the Northern Rebellion had begun. As the rebel forces marched south, Elizabeth moved Mary to Coventry and mustered troops of her own. The southern Earls rallied to her cause, which stunned the rebel forces, who began to retreat. Elizabeth's victory was quick and decisive, with 700 men being executed in a brutal display of power. Norfolk was placed under arrest, but a lack of concrete evidence postponed his execution, until he was implicated in the Ridolfi plot, which aimed to make Spain's Philip II king. Elizabeth ordered and rescinded Norfolk's execution three times – a prime example of how

Did Elizabeth have a genuine thirst for new worlds?

Although the expansion of trade into India occurred during Elizabeth's reign, in terms of exploration she is best remembered for England's attempt to colonise North America. The Spanish and Portuguese had already laid claim to much of South America, establishing lucrative trade routes, but North America was relatively unexplored. Elizabeth was reluctant to fund exploratory voyages for much the same reasons that she was reluctant to fund wars: they were expensive and risky. However, she could be won around with the promise of riches from one of her favourites and, when sailor Davy Ingram returned to England with alluring tales of riches and simple inhabitants, geographer Richard Hakluyt began plotting a serious expedition to be led by Walter Raleigh.

With the promise of fortune and the flattery of Raleigh, she agreed to a trip to form a colony named after her: Virginia. The first party launched, and Raleigh would follow. When the nobleman arrived, he saw the settlement had failed. The English were desperate to leave. Raleigh's second attempt was intended for Chesapeake Bay, but the first group, led by John White, returned to Roanoke. Raleigh arrived with his second group and found no trace of survivors. Elizabeth was disappointed that these costly ventures yielded no results. There was one purpose to these expeditions, as de Lisle explains very simply: "Making money."

Verdict

The Elizabethan era's reputation for exploration is largely due to the fact that there was money to be made from it. Piratical ventures were profitable; colonisation was not.

2. 1585
Following a positive report, Raleigh dispatches colonists to settle at Roanoke in Virginia. By the time he arrives on a later ship, the crops have failed and the English are desperate to leave.

3. 1587
Raleigh tries again to establish a colony at Chesapeake Bay, but instead the settlers travel to Roanoke. When Raleigh arrives, all 150 colonists have disappeared, with only a single skeleton remaining.

1. 1584
Walter Raleigh and Richard Hakluyt convince Elizabeth to fund an expedition to explore the possibility that a colony could be founded on America's east coast.

indecisive she could be at times – before finally deciding that he simply had to die.

If Elizabeth's position at home appeared shaky it was positively stable compared to how she was viewed abroad. The Pope decreed that anyone who murdered the heretical English queen would be forgiven, a statement King Philip took to heart. Not wanting to risk open war, Elizabeth found other ways to aggravate her enemies. She quietly patronised the piratical exploits of John Hawkins and later his cousin Francis Drake. In 1577, when he planned to travel to South America to raid Spanish gold, Elizabeth met Drake with Francis Walsingham, one of her ambassadors to France.

The cautious Cecil had to be kept in the dark, but she told Drake explicitly that she supported him: "I would gladly be revenged on the King of Spain for diverse injuries I have received." Having sailed through the Straits of Magellan and captured a Spanish ship carrying up to £200,000 in gold, Drake decided to sail across the Pacific, becoming the first Englishman to circumnavigate the globe. Elizabeth gloried in his achievement, and when she met the Spanish ambassador in 1581, she pointedly wore a crucifix Drake had given to her from the loot. She dined with Drake on the Golden Hind and knighted him. He had done her proud.

These piratical exploits stood in sharp contrast to the events of 1572. The St. Bartholomew's Day Massacre in Paris – the assassination of a number of French Calvinist Protestants – shocked England and the ambassador Sir Francis Walsingham was forced to take refuge. Elizabeth brought him back to London to become her spymaster, where he advised that Mary, Queen of Scots was a real danger. The uprising was not only a shocking scene for English Protestants; it was also a sign that the Protestant Netherlands and their booming wool trade would soon be in danger.

The return of Mary, Queen of Scots to Edinburgh

When William the Silent asked Elizabeth for military assistance, she did not want to be seen to intervene and give Philip of Spain an excuse to attack. Walsingham counselled war, while Cecil continued to preach marriage. So Elizabeth entertained the idea of marrying the Duke of Anjou, roughly ten years after it had first been suggested. Then, he had been an ugly youth and she had been a beautiful queen. Now, she was visibly older and the flattery of the French ambassador and Anjou's letters began to win her over. When they finally met, it appeared that Elizabeth really was in love, but there were genuine concerns over how the English people would react.

"The anxieties Elizabeth expressed to the emissary of Mary, Queen of Scots in 1561, that she too could not marry anyone without triggering unrest in one group or another, only deepened following Mary, Queen of Scots's disastrous marriages to Darnley and then Bothwell – which ended in her overthrow," explains Leanda de Lisle, author of Tudor: The Family Story. "Elizabeth continued to look publicly for a husband to fulfil national expectations that she would provide them with an undisputed heir, and surely she hoped it was not impossible. She was married to her kingdom – a phrase she had learned from Mary Tudor. But while Mary had married, Elizabeth did not because she feared revolt by those who disapproved of her choice."

"The Queen rallied troops by declaring that she would fight by their side to repel anyone who dare set foot on their land"

Although she clearly wanted to marry the man that she had nicknamed her "frog," the English people found the idea of their Virgin Queen marrying a French Catholic absolutely repulsive. When a pamphlet appeared that condemned the union, Elizabeth decreed that both the author and his printer should have their right hands cut off. Her Privy Council was split in half, with the jealous Robert Dudley vehemently opposed. Elizabeth was heartbroken, but she agreed to abstain. She gave Anjou £10,000 to continue his war against Philip in the Netherlands, but did not see him again. He tried to take power for himself but failed and died a year later. When William the Silent was assassinated in his own house in 1584 by a Catholic fanatic, it was clear that military intervention could not be put off any longer and so in 1585, to the relief of her impatient councillors, she agreed to send a small force of men. Dudley took command in the Netherlands but proved to be incompetent, losing territory to Philip's general, the Duke of Parma. Mary was now more dangerous than ever. Elizabeth ordered her imprisonment at the urging of Francis Walsingham, who had no intention of allowing her to live much longer. He arranged for a servant, one of his own spies, to suggest that Mary smuggle letters in beer barrels, allowing Walsingham to read everything. When Thomas Babingdon wrote to Mary with a plan to assassinate Elizabeth and give her the crown Mary wrote back with her approval; the spymaster's trap had worked perfectly, and he had ensnared his unwitting prey.

Walsingham leapt into action and ordered the conspirators' execution. Elizabeth had always been reluctant to execute her cousin, but she agreed she would have to stand trial. It was no surprise when the court decided that Mary should be put to death. Elizabeth grieved for Mary, or at least lamented her death. The man who had delivered

Queen Elizabeth I knighting Francis Drake in 1581

the warrant was imprisoned and stripped of his title.

Elizabeth was always reluctant to sign a death warrant – or at least she was reluctant to be seen to sign it. We can't know how much of Elizabeth's grief was genuine, but she bitterly resented the circumstances of Mary's execution.

"Elizabeth was reluctant to be seen to execute first the senior nobleman in England, in Norfolk, and then a fellow queen, in Mary," says de Lisle: "That is not to say she regretted their deaths. She would have preferred to have Mary murdered, for example, as she made very clear.

It is also notable that she was quite ruthless in ordering the deaths of traitors of humble birth – the 900 or so executed after the Northern Rebellion testifies to that. This was three times the numbers Henry VIII had executed after the far more serious Pilgrimage of Grace, and ten times the numbers Mary executed after Wyatt's revolt."

Mary's execution provided Philip II with the reason he needed to declare war and his Spanish Armada co-ordinated with the Duke of Parma's forces in the Netherlands, with the two forces meeting before sailing on England.

They launched on 12 July 1588, their forces possessing more than twice the number of English ships, but the English ships did have some advantages; they were smaller, faster, and designed to carry guns rather than men. The English ships could outmanoeuvre the Spanish fleet in open water and began to engage them in small skirmishes. It was at this point that Elizabeth rode out to meet her troops. With the threat of a Catholic force at their doorstep, the queen rallied the spirit of the English troops by declaring that she would fight by their side to repel anyone who dared to set foot on their land.

This grandstanding was impressive and may have gone down in history's annals but was ultimately unnecessary. The Spanish Armada failed and Elizabeth's victory was the seal on her status. 'The Golden Age' had begun, where art and literature flowered. With England a visibly powerful state, the aristocracy began to patronise the arts with great abandon.

The famous playwrights of the age enjoyed patronage, albeit with some caveats. When Shakespeare wrote Richard II he was encouraged to remove a scene suggesting the ageing monarch should step aside. "Elizabeth did not care for plays," confirms de Lisle: "All too often they wereW used to lecture her on this or that."

Her crown may have been safe for now, but she received devastating blows with the deaths of two of her most trusted

Mary, Queen of Scots being led to her death

Main play

Council and Government

William Cecil
1520-98
A canny political operator who understood the difficulties that were ahead, Cecil was Elizabeth's first appointment and was fiercely loyal, dedicating his life to helping her. Although he believed she should marry, Elizabeth knew Cecil was invaluable and pressured him into staying on, even when he was sickly and deaf.

Robert Dudley
1532-88
Dudley had known Elizabeth since childhood, and was her first love. His appointment to court had more to do with her affection for him than any outstanding abilities as a politician, however, and his presence at court proved to be a continual source of rumour and scandal. Their relationship was rocky and driven by passion.

Francis Walsingham
1532-90
The Protestant Walsingham was allowed to return to England after Mary's death, and quickly became one of Elizabeth's most invaluable assets. A brilliant spymaster and politician, he understood the threat that Mary, Queen of Scots posed, and engineered her downfall. He also supported Drake and Raleigh's explorations.

Explorers

John Hawkins
1532-95

Hawkins may have possessed a coat of arms, but he first managed to find favour with the Queen as a pirate. With Elizabeth's implicit permission, he planned and executed a series of daring raids on Spanish ports in the West Indies, but after a disastrous third voyage he returned to England, where he began working for the Queen in a more direct capacity.

Francis Drake
1540-96

Having sailed on his cousin John Hawkins' expeditions, Francis Drake had no love for the Spanish. He was willing to circumnavigate the globe in order to rob them of their riches and deliver them to Elizabeth, who was delighted with his exploits, and continued to commission him to undertake raids on Spanish ports.

Walter Raleigh
1554-1618

Raleigh gained Elizabeth's favour at court and quickly set his sights on expanding her empire. He decided he would establish Britain's first colony in North America, and told the Queen it would be named after her: Virginia. To his great dismay, the colony at Roanoke failed. He is often falsely credited with bringing potatoes and tobacco to England.

Enemies

King Philip II
1527-1598

The main religious threat to Elizabeth for the majority of her realm came from the King of Spain. The Pope might have given the bull that deposed Elizabeth but the fiercely Catholic Philip was the man with the army that could enforce it. He had attempted to woo the princess while still married to her sister but, once rebuffed, relentlessly opposed her.

John Whitgift
1530-1604

As the issue of religious tolerance became increasingly difficult to manage, Elizabeth hand-picked her old chaplain for the role of Archbishop of Canterbury. He was a stubborn man, as evidenced by his refusal to leave England during Queen Mary's reign. Like Elizabeth, he was a Conformist and ruthlessly punished those who publicly strayed from the 'right' path.

Pope Pius V
1504-72

As the head of the Roman Catholic Church, Pope Pius V saw Elizabeth's status of Queen of England and head of its church not only as an affront to his religion, but as an act of heresy. He went as far as to issue a Papal Bull on 27 April 1570, which declared that her subjects no longer owed her any kind of allegiance.

Family

Henry VIII
1491-1547

Henry was desperate for a boy to carry on his family name, and was disappointed when Anne Boleyn gave him Elizabeth. He was absent for much of her childhood, but was kept informed of her progress nonetheless. When he finally met his daughter he was very impressed, so much so that he reinstated her and Mary into his legacy.

Mary Tudor
1516-58

Despite their differences, Mary, Elizabeth and their brother Edward had a relatively close relationship as children. When she became Queen, Mary was desperate for Elizabeth to convert and unable to understand why she wouldn't. She came close to executing her sister, but abstained, finally requesting that she keep England Catholic.

Catherine Parr
1512–48

Catherine and Elizabeth became close during her marriage to Henry, and Elizabeth lived with Catherine for some time after his death. However, Catherine's husband Thomas Seymour was more interested in their young charge than his wife, and she assisted in his attempts at seduction, dying soon after they failed.

The Spanish Armada is put to display by English ships

The gun-crew of an Elizabethan ship – she funded the journeys of numerous privateers

advisors, Dudley and Walsingham. Dudley was replaced at court by his handsome stepson, the Earl of Essex, and the young flatterer quickly became her favourite.

"Robert Dudley's death in 1588 signalled the passing of the old order, but Elizabeth still hoped she could continue ruling according to her motto, 'Semper Eadem' ('Always the same')" explains de Lisle. "As the years began to pass and her servants died she either did not replace them or find a near-equivalent to the servant she had lost." It's a sign of how much she leaned on her old guard that she continued to place her trust in William Cecil, even though he was almost entirely deaf and increasingly ill. It was only when he died in 1598 that Elizabeth finally agreed to appoint Robert Cecil to his father's old post. When it became known that the Spanish were attempting to rebuild their fleet, Essex led a fleet on Cadiz and decimated their forces in port. The success gave Essex fame, something Elizabeth was taken aback by. She tried to curb him, aware that her standing among the people was her greatest asset, but Essex continued to promote his own celebrity. She became more and more frustrated with his outrageous behaviour at court, which came to a dramatic head when he half-drew his sword on her in a fit of pique.

The arts and literature may have been flourishing, but those who subscribe to this being a golden age in England's history often forget that even after the defeat of the Spanish Armada, other uprisings, such as the 1598 Irish rebellion, occurred. Now, with a Spanish-backed uprising, Elizabeth needed to take decisive action.

She sent her army at the start of 1599, led by Essex, who was looking to prove himself once more. He was a disaster. Rather than confronting Tyrone on the battlefield, he met him in secret and returned to England having made a treaty without the queen's authority.

When Essex thought Cecil was plotting against him, he rushed to plead his case. Assuming he was still the queen's favourite, he burst into her chamber while she was preparing for the day. He had seen Elizabeth without her make-up and regal dress; not as a queen but as an old woman. She could not afford to be seen like this. She dismissed him before summoning him later to confront him with his failures and strip him of power. Rather than accepting his fate, Essex attempted rebellion. He assumed Londoners would back the popular war hero, but Elizabeth proclaimed him a traitor and sent her troops to meet him. The rebellion was a failure and Essex was executed.

Although the later years of Elizabeth's reign were far from golden, she could still rally her people when needed. The war in Ireland was expensive and unsuccessful, while overcrowding and failed harvests caused agitation. When Parliament publicly condemned her for granting monopolies to her favourite courtiers, which had led to price-fixing, Elizabeth was forced to address them in 1601. She agreed to put a stop to the monopolies and she reaffirmed her love for England. She won over Parliament, there was a good harvest, and a truce was reached in Ireland and Spain. "Elizabeth, old and ill, did lose some of her former grip, but never entirely," states de Lisle. "She had followed Mary I's example in wooing the common people from the beginning of her reign, and they continued to support her."

Having seen off another uprising, the 50-year-old monarch's health was failing and after an all-too-rare period of good health, Elizabeth grew sickly. She was desperately frustrated by Cecil's growing power over her. Elizabeth finally died on 23 March 1603. Although she had struggled to change with the times in the face of younger, ambitious advisors, she had been a formidable political operator. She had still shown the cunning and cleverness to understand her situation, and had never lost the image of a queen loved by her people.

"That image was not created for her," explains de Lisle. "Elizabeth never forgot the events of 1553 when the ordinary people had backed the Tudor sisters, while the political elite had supported Jane Grey." Nor did she forget how in 1554, Mary had made a speech at the Guildhall that roused London in her defence against the Wyatt rebellion. Mary had spoken of her marriage to her kingdom, describing her coronation ring as a wedding band, and her love of her subjects as that of a mother for her children. These were the phrases and motifs Elizabeth would use repeatedly.

In addition, Elizabeth also had an instinct for the crowd's demands. Even her enemies would admit she had 'the power of enchantment'. She wooed her people with smiles, words of love and great showmanship, and so won their hearts. Elizabeth's people would never forget her.

Elizabeth's reign was not the golden age that legend so often depicts; she faced serious uprisings, both internal and external, during her reign. She was capable of heartlessness and ruthlessness, and could be indecisive and impetuous. During the course of her rule, England saw famine, rebellion and war. However, there's no mistaking her dedication to her country and her determination to listen to what the people wanted from her – and then give it to them. She walked a political tightrope for most of her life, and the fact that she died peacefully in her bed as queen was a major triumph in itself. The English loved her, and she, in turn, loved them. In the hearts and minds of many of her subjects, she was – and will always be – Britain's golden monarch.

Why did the Armada fail?

King Philip amassed his Armada and sent them to the Netherlands to join up with his ground troops, led by the Duke of Parma. The English outposts saw the ships coming and alerted the admiralty. The weather was against the Spanish, as they were blown off course. While they outnumbered the British fleet by two to one, the Spanish ships were enormous, built to carry troops that could board enemy vessels. Their crescent formation was famous, but it did little against the smaller English ships. When the English sent fireships into the Spanish fleet, the enemy panicked and scattered. They managed to regroup for one confrontation, and lost. The Spanish retreated, with many ships crashing on the rocks of the English and Irish coastline.

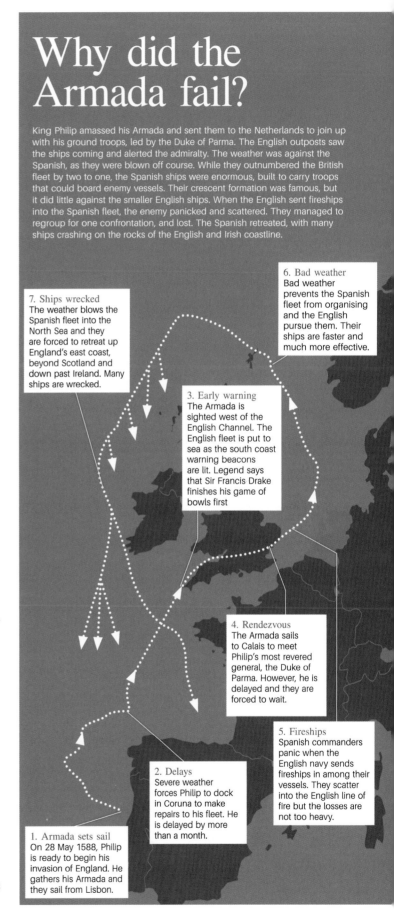

7. Ships wrecked
The weather blows the Spanish fleet into the North Sea and they are forced to retreat up England's east coast, beyond Scotland and down past Ireland. Many ships are wrecked.

6. Bad weather
Bad weather prevents the Spanish fleet from organising and the English pursue them. Their ships are faster and much more effective.

3. Early warning
The Armada is sighted west of the English Channel. The English fleet is put to sea as the south coast warning beacons are lit. Legend says that Sir Francis Drake finishes his game of bowls first

4. Rendezvous
The Armada sails to Calais to meet Philip's most revered general, the Duke of Parma. However, he is delayed and they are forced to wait.

5. Fireships
Spanish commanders panic when the English navy sends fireships in among their vessels. They scatter into the English line of fire but the losses are not too heavy.

2. Delays
Severe weather forces Philip to dock in Coruna to make repairs to his fleet. He is delayed by more than a month.

1. Armada sets sail
On 28 May 1588, Philip is ready to begin his invasion of England. He gathers his Armada and they sail from Lisbon.

1835 – 1908

Empress Dowager Cixi

From concubine to conqueror, was China's last empress a shrewd moderniser or a pivotal player in imperial collapse?

From the rumour mills of Medieval courts to modern-day gossip magazines, humanity has throughout its history been fixated with rumour and hearsay, and many historians would argue there are few leaders in Chinese history who have fallen prey to such intense speculation as Empress Dowager Cixi.

Born in the winter of 1835 when the Chinese empire was still strong, Cixi was the daughter of an ordinary official from the Manchu Yehenara clan. She was well educated and able to read and write – an unusual skill for Manchu women of the time – and in 1851, she participated in the selection of consorts for the Xianfeng Emperor alongside 60 other candidates.

Contrary to modern-day interpretations of the Chinese concubine tradition, being chosen as a royal consort was a huge honour, and Cixi, one of the few candidates chosen, was placed in the sixth rank of the emperor's nocturnal companions, rising to fifth rank in just a few years.

Thanks to her ability to read and write Chinese, Cixi had many opportunities to help the emperor with the daily business of government. As the emperor aged, he'd ask Cixi to read palace memorials and write down his wishes. This meant that Cixi quickly became very well informed about state affairs and benefited from a valuable lesson in the art of governance under the ailing emperor's tutelage. This already put her in an advantageous position, but her starring role in Chinese history was cemented when she gave birth to Zaichun, the Xianfeng Emperor's only surviving son, in 1856. By Zaichun's first birthday, Cixi was elevated to the third rank of consorts, putting her second only to the Empress Ci'an within the Xianfeng Emperor's household.

In September 1860, tension erupted between Britain, France and China, and troops attacked Beijing, destroying the Imperial Summer Palace. It's said that on hearing this news, the Xianfeng Emperor – who had fled the city with his royal household – fell into a deep depression and, turning to alcohol and drugs, never recovered. He died in 1861

CIXI WAS CHOSEN TO ENTER THE FORBIDDEN CITY AS A FOURTH-RANK CONCUBINE

having named eight regents for his five-year-old son, the new emperor, and expressing his hope that Ci'an and Cixi would continue to play a pivotal role in the boy's royal career. While historians largely agree that Xianfeng never intended Cixi to wield direct political power, his passing marked the beginning of the end for Chinese Imperialism, and Cixi, as the new emperor's politically shrewd mother, was at the helm.

However, as the emperor's mother, Cixi's position had no power attached to it, so it was necessary for her to ally herself with other strong figures. Cixi had formed a close friendship with the late emperor's wife Ci'an, and suggested to her that the pair become co-reigning empresses with powers surpassing the eight regents. The two women enjoyed a harmonious partnership; Ci'an had little interest in politics and preferred to take care of household matters, leaving Cixi free to rule as she saw fit. But the eight regents did not take kindly to Cixi's interference in politics, and constant confrontation with the empress dowagers meant Ci'an frequently refused to attend court audiences, leaving Cixi to fend for herself – no small feat as, because she was a woman, she was forced to govern from behind a screen, battling to make herself heard amid a sea of male voices.

Ever the shrewd political player, Cixi began to assemble support from talented ministers and soldiers who had great ambitions but had been ostracised by the regents for political or personal reasons. Two individuals, Prince Gong and Prince Chun, the late emperor's sixth and seventh brothers, would go on to play a pivotal role in Cixi's story.

With Prince Gong's help, Cixi brought about a number of charges against the regents, deeming them 'incompetent' for the way they handled the invasion of Beijing that ultimately led to the Xianfeng Emperor's death. Three of the regents were executed, and in a move that further demonstrated her apparent grace and benevolence, Cixi refused to have the regents' family members killed, as would have been tradition. In a single stroke – known as the Xinyou Coup – Cixi had removed her challengers and emerged as a merciful yet powerful ruler.

The Boxer Rebellion was arguably the beginning of the end for Imperial China

Prince Gong was a pivotal player in Cixi's rise to rule

The issue of succession sparked widespread global interest, as demonstrated by this German caricature

"In a move that demonstrated her apparent grace and benevolence, Cixi refused to have the regents' family killed"

In the following years, Cixi turned her attention to cleaning up national bureaucracies, which had become infested with corruption, and even had two prominent officials executed to serve as an example to others. Worryingly for Cixi, a number of reports accused her trusted confidant Prince Gong of corruption and so, fearing his growing influence, the prince was dismissed from his offices and appointments, but allowed to keep his status as nobility. The move once again highlighted Cixi's refusal to give up absolute power to anyone, even one of her most important friends – and, as it would soon emerge, even her son, the rightful emperor of China.

In 1872, the Tongzhi Emperor turned 17, and under the guidance of Ci'an, married the Jiashun Empress. Both her ancestry and zodiac symbol of tiger were cause for concern for the superstitious Cixi. Unhappy with the union, Cixi ordered the couple to separate. The Tongzhi Emperor, who proved to be an incompetent ruler anyway, fell

into a deep despair and turned to a life of debauchery and hedonism outside the Forbidden City. His escapades led him to smallpox and ultimately death. By 1875, Cixi was back at the helm of total power.

The Tongzhi Emperor died without a male heir, leaving China in an unprecedented succession crisis: members of the generation above were ruled out as they could not succeed their nephew. After disagreement between Cixi and Ci'an, the four-year-old son of Prince Chun and Cixi's sister, Zaitain, was chosen to be the new Guangxu Emperor.

Soon after, Ci'an died and Cixi fell seriously ill. For some years the empress dowager had only written contact with her ministers, but she continued to wield ultimate power. When the Guangxu Emperor gained the right to rule in 1887, court officials encouraged Cixi to maintain her position until a later date. Court officials would put more effort into impressing Cixi than the emperor, and the young man was often

This opulent ceremonial headdress was likely worn by the Empress Dowager Cixi

The Xianfeng Emperor never recovered from the destruction of the Old Summer Palace in 1860

Empress Dowager Cixi's final resting place is one of the most impressive imperial tombs of China

overlooked entirely when it came to official government business. This decision, which Cixi had no issue accepting, arguably marks the start of Imperial China's unravelling, as behind the scenes, the Guangxu Emperor paid increasing attention to liberal ideas of reformation, and when he acceded to the throne, he implemented a series of political, legal and social changes in his empire.

These changes proved too sudden for China, and displeased the conservatively minded Cixi, who brought allegations of treason against the emperor, and subsequently resumed her previous role of regent.

By this time, China was increasingly facing pressure from foreign influences. Cixi, frustrated with foreign interference, allied with an anti-Christian, anti-foreign cult known as The Boxers. This was to be her most disastrous failure. The Boxers launched widespread attacks on missionaries and diplomats, ultimately resulting in another foreign occupancy of Beijing. Court officials encouraged her to continue the fight against allied forces, but she knew she'd been bested. Cixi was able to negotiate a treaty that meant China would not have to give up any further

territories, and – crucially – she would be permitted to continue her reign when the war was concluded.

She uncharacteristically accepted responsibility for the Boxer Rebellion, issuing a decree of 'self-reproach', and upon her return to Beijing, set about implementing sweeping political reforms that drew upon foreign policies in a bid to rectify internal issues within China. She even sponsored the implementation of a reform programme more radical than the one suggested by the reformers she'd previously had beheaded.

This was a marked step-change for the conservative Cixi, who had historically distrusted foreigners, and historians debate whether she truly envisioned a bold new China, or if, after a lifetime of fighting for power, she'd simply grown tired of resistance. She died on 15 November 1908, and on her death bed said she'd "never had a moment in life without anxiety."

IT'S THOUGHT THAT THE COST OF RUNNING HER COURT WAS $6.5 MILLION A YEAR

© Alamy.

1729 – 1796
Catherine the Great

How the unstoppable Russian ruler enthralled an empire with sex, lies and military might

She has gone down in history as 'Catherine the Great' thanks to her dedication and devotion to her adopted country. One of the Russian Empire's greatest leaders, Catherine oversaw its unprecedented expansion, a series of military successes and the arrival of the Russian Enlightenment. Her reign is considered the Golden Age of Russia but her time on the throne was full of salacious scandal, intrigue and hidden truths that others used to tarnish her legacy. So, what really happened during her reign?

Catherine was born in 1729 as Princess Sophie of Anhalt-Zerbst, an impoverished German royal. Her prospects were dim until Elizabeth, empress of Russia, wrote to Sophie's mother proposing a match with her nephew and heir, Grand Duke Peter of Holstein. It was keenly accepted and Sophie was determined to seize her destiny, learning to speak Russian fluently, which greatly impressed Elizabeth. She was a perfect fit for the Russian throne.

In contrast, her betrothed was a terrible choice for an emperor. Born and raised in Germany, Peter was brought to Russia aged 14 and he hated it. He refused to convert to the Russian Orthodox Church — unlike Sophie, who converted and adopted a new name, Catherine, in 1744. A year later, the couple married in Saint Petersburg. Recalling the wedding in her memoirs, Catherine stated that her "heart predicted but little happiness; ambition alone sustained me."

Catherine thought greatness awaited her. Instead, her husband turned out to be a drunk who played with toy soldiers like a child. They despised each other and their marriage went unconsummated for several years. But Catherine didn't want to waste her life and she told herself that she would become "the sovereign Empress of Russia in [her] own right."

Feeling isolated and unloved, Catherine was getting desperate. After years of marriage, there was no heir, Elizabeth was breathing down her neck and the court was watching her every move. She

THE PERIOD OF CATHERINE'S RULE IS KNOWN AS THE CATHERINIAN ERA

started a series of affairs, firstly with Sergei Saltykov, a handsome rake and court member. Elizabeth actually encouraged their relationship, hoping it would result in a pregnancy.

Catherine finally gave birth to a long-awaited heir, Paul, in 1754. The paternity is still debated today but Catherine implied in her memoirs that it was Saltykov, though possibly only to spite Peter. Regardless, she succeeded in her purpose and stabilised her position at court as the mother of the future emperor.

However, Catherine barely saw her baby as Elizabeth whisked him away and raised him herself. Catherine was devastated and her affair with Saltykov ended when he was sent away, too. Meanwhile, Peter's behaviour became foolish, worrying those around him. His wife, having fulfilled her duty, couldn't bear Russia crumbling in his insipid hands because he had failed to do his. She began to mastermind his downfall.

Elizabeth died in 1761 and Peter became Peter III. Catherine was now empress consort but it wasn't enough — she wanted sole power. Support for her grew after Peter's childish behaviour at Elizabeth's funeral, where he created a game to alleviate his boredom. Taking advantage of this, Catherine openly grieved for the deceased empress, winning many admirers in the process.

Peter's behaviour was inexcusable. He skipped his own coronation and withdrew from the Seven Years' War — despite the fact Russia was winning — returning all the land that they had conquered from Prussia. His actions disrespected those killed or injured during the conflict, alienating the army. Peter's contempt for the Church and his desire to wage war against Russia's long-time ally of Denmark exacerbated growing hatred towards him. He flaunted his mistress, Elizaveta Vorontsova, stating his desire to divorce Catherine and disinherit their son.

By April 1762, the situation was unbearable. Peter publicly

humiliated Catherine at a state banquet by denouncing her as a fool, leaving her in tears. Whispers circulated that night that the emperor, incensed and drunk, had ordered his wife's arrest. Fortunately, Prince Georg Ludwig of Holstein, Catherine's uncle, managed to dissuade him from committing such an impulsive act. It was the final straw and Catherine knew that she and her son were now in grave danger.

The empress knew that if her coup was to succeed, she needed someone with influence and power by her side. She started an affair with Grigory Orlov, a lieutenant of the Izmailovsky Guards who had caught her eye the year before. Catherine had chosen her new lover wisely. Alongside his brother and fellow guard, Alexei, he had the political influence that she needed to sway the imperial guardsmen to her faction.

Aside from the political benefits, the couple also fell deeply in love and Orlov was determined to see his beloved on the Russian throne.

However, there was one obstacle that stopped Catherine from seizing power: she fell pregnant with Orlov's child. Previously, Catherine and Peter had been sleeping together infrequently and she could have claimed that he was the baby's father, however unlikely

it may have seemed. But as communication between the two had practically stopped, there was no denying a secret liaison. Nobody could uncover the truth, lest it risk Catherine losing her valuable supporters. She managed to hide her pregnancy under voluminous dresses for months, fooling everyone around her. In April 1762, she secretly gave birth to a little boy, who ended up being raised far away from court.

Peter soon left for Oranienbaum, in preparation for his fight against Denmark, while Catherine stayed at the nearby palace of Monplaisir. Her supporters prepared themselves and among them were the Orlov brothers, a number of guardsmen and Princess Dashkova, Elizaveta's sister. Even Nikita Panin, the politician entrusted as Paul's governor by Elizabeth, supported Catherine. With his control over her heir, Panin's backing was vital for the empress if she wanted the takeover to be seen as legitimate.

Peter ignored rumours of an impending coup but a conspirator was arrested on 27 June. Fearing that she would be exposed, Catherine, barely dressed, climbed into a waiting carriage and rode straight to Saint Petersburg in the early hours of 28 June. She headed to the

> *"The seriousness of the situation sank in as he arrived at Monplaisir to find it abandoned, with Catherine long gone"*

Nakaz, or Instruction, outlined Catherine's vision for Russia's future

Catherine wore military dress when she deposed Peter III

Date for an Empress

Who is the perfect lover for Catherine the Great?

DO YOU WANT A YOUNGER MAN?
— YES → — NO →

DO YOU WANT TO GET MARRIED?

DO YOU NEED A MAN WHO IS GOOD AT POLITICS?

WOULD YOU PREFER A RUSSIAN?

WOULD YOU LIKE TO HAVE A FAMILY TOGETHER?

DO YOU WANT A WEAK-WILLED MAN?

DOES HE HAVE TO BE DASHINGLY HANDSOME?

DO YOU WANT TO FALL IN LOVE?

DO YOU WANT A MILITARY MAN?

DO YOU WANT SOMEONE WHO CAN ALWAYS BE BY YOUR SIDE?

DO YOU WANT someone WITH POWER?

DO YOU WANT TO CONTROL HIM LIKE A PUPPET?

DO YOU WANT A FAITHFUL MAN?

DOES IT MATTER IF HE only HAS ONE EYE?

Peter and Catherine as grand duke and duchess of Holstein

Peter III of Russia

Catherine's cold and childish husband hated his adopted country of Russia, managing to upset the army, the Church and the nobility just a few months into his reign. Catherine and Peter despised each other and he even threatened to divorce his wife and replace her with his mistress. Catherine deposed her husband in 1762 and he soon died under suspicious circumstances.

Stanistaw Poniatowski

Catherine fell in love with Poniatowski while she was still a grand duchess and together they had an illegitimate daughter, Anna. Poniatowski was forced to leave the Russian court during the Seven Years' War and his affair with Catherine ended. They kept in contact and with Catherine's support, Poniatowski was elected king of Poland, although she used him as puppet.

Count Grigory Orlov

Orlov was Catherine's foremost supporter in her plot to overthrow her husband and played an instrumental role in the coup in 1762. He remained Catherine's favourite for over a decade and together they had an illegitimate son, Alexey. Orlov's downfall was guaranteed once she discovered his affairs with other women and she banished him from the court.

Prince Grigory Potemkin

Catherine and Potemkin had an extremely passionate, if short-lived, love affair. Just like Orlov, Potemkin supported Catherine during the coup and eventually succeeded him as her favourite. After their physical relationship ended, Potemkin remained by Catherine's side and was the most powerful man in her court for two decades before his early death aged 52.

Expansion of an Empire
How Catherine extended Russian territory

01 Alaska Colonisation, 1766

Catherine wrote to the governor of Siberia, declaring the indigenous people of the Aleutian Islands and the Alaska Peninsula to be Russian subjects. She instructed the Russian fur-traders to treat their new fellow subjects well. After this, tax collectors accompanied Russian fur-hunters on their voyages to Alaska and the government licensed fur-hunting expeditions.

02 First Russo-Turkish War, 1768-74

The first in a series of wars between Russia and the Ottoman Empire was sparked by a conflict over borders. Catherine's victory led to Russia expanding its influence in Europe and gaining territory in modern-day Ukraine. The Turks were forced to accept the Crimean Khanate's independence, giving an opportunity for Catherine to annex it later on.

RUSSIAN EMPIRE 1700 - 1796

05 Polish-Russian War, 1792

War broke out in Poland between the anti-Russian, pro-reform Polish-Lithuanian Commonwealth and the anti-reform Targowica Confederation. The latter was supported by Catherine, who was angered by a new alliance between the Commonwealth and Prussia. Poniatowski believed Russia would eventually win and sought a ceasefire, to the anger of his allies.

06 Russo-Swedish War, 1788-90

The Ottoman Empire formed an alliance with Gustav III of Sweden against Catherine, his cousin. Gustav wanted to depose her, hoping that it would bolster his popularity in Sweden, but despite some success, the war racked up some serious debt. As for Catherine, she gained nothing from the conflict and wanted to reach peace deal, which was concluded in 1790.

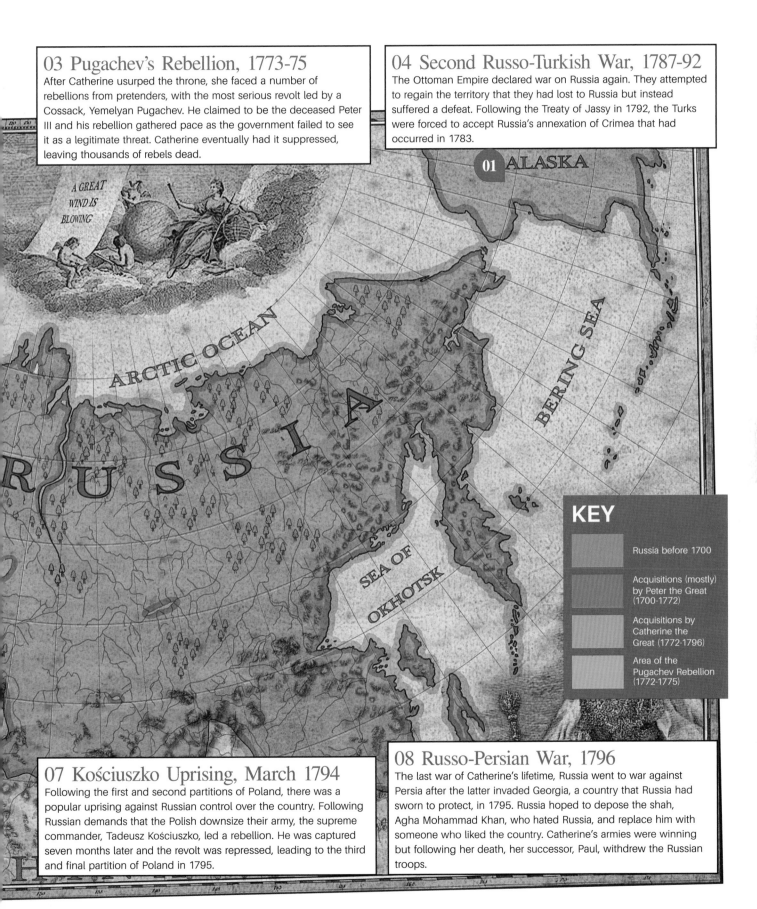

03 Pugachev's Rebellion, 1773-75

After Catherine usurped the throne, she faced a number of rebellions from pretenders, with the most serious revolt led by a Cossack, Yemelyan Pugachev. He claimed to be the deceased Peter III and his rebellion gathered pace as the government failed to see it as a legitimate threat. Catherine eventually had it suppressed, leaving thousands of rebels dead.

04 Second Russo-Turkish War, 1787-92

The Ottoman Empire declared war on Russia again. They attempted to regain the territory that they had lost to Russia but instead suffered a defeat. Following the Treaty of Jassy in 1792, the Turks were forced to accept Russia's annexation of Crimea that had occurred in 1783.

A GREAT WIND IS BLOWING

01 ALASKA

ARCTIC OCEAN

BERING SEA

R U S S I A

SEA OF OKHOTSK

KEY

Russia before 1700

Acquisitions (mostly) by Peter the Great (1700-1772)

Acquisitions by Catherine the Great (1772-1796)

Area of the Pugachev Rebellion (1772-1775)

07 Kościuszko Uprising, March 1794

Following the first and second partitions of Poland, there was a popular uprising against Russian control over the country. Following Russian demands that the Polish downsize their army, the supreme commander, Tadeusz Kościuszko, led a rebellion. He was captured seven months later and the revolt was repressed, leading to the third and final partition of Poland in 1795.

08 Russo-Persian War, 1796

The last war of Catherine's lifetime, Russia went to war against Persia after the latter invaded Georgia, a country that Russia had sworn to protect, in 1795. Russia hoped to depose the shah, Agha Mohammad Khan, who hated Russia, and replace him with someone who liked the country. Catherine's armies were winning but following her death, her successor, Paul, withdrew the Russian troops.

barracks of her loyal guardsmen, visiting the Izmailovsky regiment first. The colonel of the regiment, Krill Razumovsky, had loved Catherine for years. They pledged their allegiance to her and those who resisted were arrested. The usurper made her way to the Winter Palace to be sworn in as Russia's new ruler, to the exclamation of the crowd there.

As for Peter, the seriousness of the situation sank in as he arrived at Monplaisir to find it abandoned, with Catherine long gone. Despairing, he begged with his estranged wife, hoping to negotiate an escape to his native duchy of Holstein with Elizaveta. The answer was no. Peter fell into a drunken stupor, while Catherine readied herself outside the Winter Palace, wearing the uniform of a male guard. Climbing onto her horse, it was time to arrest her husband.

Word arrived of Peter's arrest and Catherine sent him a document of abdication, which he was forced to sign. Just over a week later, Peter was killed at Ropsha while in the custody of Alexei Orlov. Catherine waited a day before issuing a statement, claiming that Peter died of "a haemorrhoidal colic." But as Peter's body lay in state, it was bloody and bruised, the hallmarks of strangulation likely committed by

Alexei himself. When Alexei wrote to Catherine to inform her of Peter's illness, he stated ominously, "I fear that he might die tonight, but I fear even more that he might live through it."

As suspicions arose that Catherine had committed regicide, she became nervous that her reign was already tainted. Was she involved in Peter's death? It couldn't be proven, but the fact that her position was now more secure is beyond certain. Catherine wanted sole, autocratic power, yet some of her co-conspirators, namely Panin and Dashkova, expected her to assume the regency on behalf of her young son. Catherine remained stubborn and was finally crowned in a sumptuous coronation in September 1762. Her message that she was in control came across loud and clear.

Catherine discovered the Enlightenment movement as a young girl and dreamed of modernising Russia. Conversing with some of the most famous French philosophers of the day, such as Voltaire and Diderot, Catherine had the opportunity to become the enlightened leader she craved to be. However, Russia was a mess. With a poor administrative system and a backwards economy, the country languished in the shadows

CATHERINE'S CROWN WAS INSPIRED BY THE BYZANTINE EMPIRE

Enlightenment pen pals
Catherine corresponded with many of the great minds of her day

Voltaire

Catherine and the French philosopher Voltaire never met but wrote to each other for years. While Voltaire is famous for savaging the French monarchy for its extravagance, he approved of Catherine's role as an 'enlightened despot', nicknaming her the 'Star of the North'. Some have interpreted Catherine's side of the correspondence as a public relations exercise, casting her in a more positive light in Europe, but she had been an enthusiastic reader of Voltaire since she was a princess, so no doubt she was flattered to chat with one of her adolescent idols.

Baron von Grimm

Frederich Melchior, Baron von Grimm, hung out in Paris' progressive literary circle thanks to his acquaintance with Jean-Jacque Rousseau. He wrote a cultural newsletter for foreign sovereigns and nobility that were keen to keep up with 18th-century French fashions. However, Catherine and Grimm also kept up a personal correspondence for 26 years. Grimm fed her tidbits about what was going on in European courts while she patronised some of Grimm's preferred architects. Despite both being of German descent, the pair always wrote to one another in fluent French.

Denis Diderot

Another French thinker, Denis Diderot, is best known for co-founding and heavily contributing to the Encyclopédie, the definite work of Enlightenment thought. When the empress heard that he was in need of money, she offered to buy his library. She also appointed him caretaker of it until he died and paid him a 25-year salary in advance. Diderot felt obliged thank her in person in 1773, but the trip was mired when he tried to lecture her on the best way to govern Russia. Though Catherine dressed him down for this, she continued to patronise Diderot until his death in 1784.

Allegory of Catherine's victory over the Turks, 1772

Catherine fought for her power and refused to let it go

The Siege of Ochakov was a key battle in the Second Russo-Turkish War, led by Potemkin

69 – 30 BCE

Cleopatra

How the middle daughter of a despised pharaoh fought and schemed her way to becoming the most famous of all Egyptian rulers

CLEOPATRA IS RUMOURED TO HAVE BEEN ABLE TO SPEAK A DOZEN LANGUAGES

Egypt was in turmoil. In the year 81 BCE Ptolemy IX, the pharaoh who had dared to melt down the gold coffin of Alexander the Great, was dead. A series of bloody and violent family feuds had robbed his dynasty of any legitimate male heirs, so his popular and beloved daughter, Bernice III became queen. Following the family tradition, she married her half-brother, Plotemy XI, but just 19 days after the ceremony, the groom had his new bride murdered and claimed the throne as his own. The citizens of Alexandria were furious, and an angry mob quickly seized the new pharaoh and lynched him. This left Egypt leaderless and seemingly out of control.

As the commander of the army and the personification of god on Earth, a pharaoh's presence was essential to prevent mass unrest in Egypt and anyone, absolutely anyone, was better than no pharaoh at all. So the throne was offered to the illegitimate sons of Ptolemy IX, and Ptolemy XII stepped forward to claim it. A notorious womanizer with a fondness for drink and excess, he was hardly the shining beacon the struggling country needed to guide it through the darkness of the pit it had fallen into. A nickname for the illegitimate pharaoh quickly became popular – Nothos, or 'the bastard.' Ptolemy XII had at least five legitimate children, and Cleopatra VII was the second oldest after her sister, Berenice IV.

The young princess was clever and quick-witted, with an eager and curious mind driven by a near-insatiable thirst for knowledge. She easily excelled at her studies and even her esteemed scholars were amazed by her aptitude for languages, readily conversing with any foreign visitors whether they were Ethiopians, Hebrews, Troglodytes, Arabs, Syrians, Medes or Parthians. While she surrounded herself with the wonders of the academic world in the riches and luxury of the royal residence, outside her palace the real one was being stretched at the seams, in danger of being ripped apart.

Pharaoh Ptolemy XII was in a troublesome position. His father had promised Egypt to Rome, a promise the Roman Senate had chosen not to act on – not yet, at least. Still, Ptolemy XII was smart enough to understand that to keep the Romans happy was to ensure Egypt's survival. He sent masses of money and bribes to Julius Caesar (at that time one of Rome's most important figures), which secured the Romans' support, but dammed him in the eyes of his tax-burdened

citizens. In 58 BCE he was forced into exile, taking his talented younger daughter with him. When he finally returned three years later, with the backing of a Roman army courtesy of the statesman Aulus Gabinius, he discovered his oldest daughter Berenice sitting on the throne. Displaying the brutal and uncompromising ferocity that ran through his entire family, he had his daughter summarily executed. He then proceeded to reclaim the throne, from which he ruled until his death in 51 BCE. The crown and all the debts he had amassed became the property of his oldest surviving daughter, Cleopatra.

The 18-year-old was not – as some expected – a naïve, wide-eyed child torn from her books to rule a kingdom on the brink of war. She had served as consort to her father for the final few years of his reign and all her education since birth had been designed to mould her into a capable queen. Queen, that was; not king, not pharaoh. Cleopatra was cursed by the requirement of all Egyptian queens to serve alongside a dominant male co-ruler and so found herself burdened with the task of being a subordinate co-regent to her ten-year-old brother, Ptolemy XIII.

Faced with a regency council full of ambitious men who ruled in her brother's stead and led by her own ruthless, impatient and intelligent nature, Cleopatra pushed her brother-husband into the background and established herself as sole monarch of the country. This was dangerous; the Alexandrian courtiers swarmed over the young, impressionable king, filling his head with whispers of sole rule and the dangers of his older sister. If Cleopatra had been more patient and attentive, she could perhaps have trained a capable and obedient co-ruler in him, one who would have aided her rule, instead of bringing it crashing down. But that was simply not the Ptolemy way, and she was a Ptolemy in every sense of the word – daring, ambitious and deadly. She dropped her brother's image from coins and erased his name from official documents. With her skill, drive and cunning she was perfect for rule; in her mind she deserved Egypt and wasn't prepared to share it.

The early years of her reign would be testing, as not only was the country still struggling under the father's debts, but years of infrequent floods of the Nile had led to widespread famine. Over her shoulder Cleopatra could feel the ever-looming and rapidly expanding threat of Rome, and with a weak Egyptian army, her fertile land was ripe for

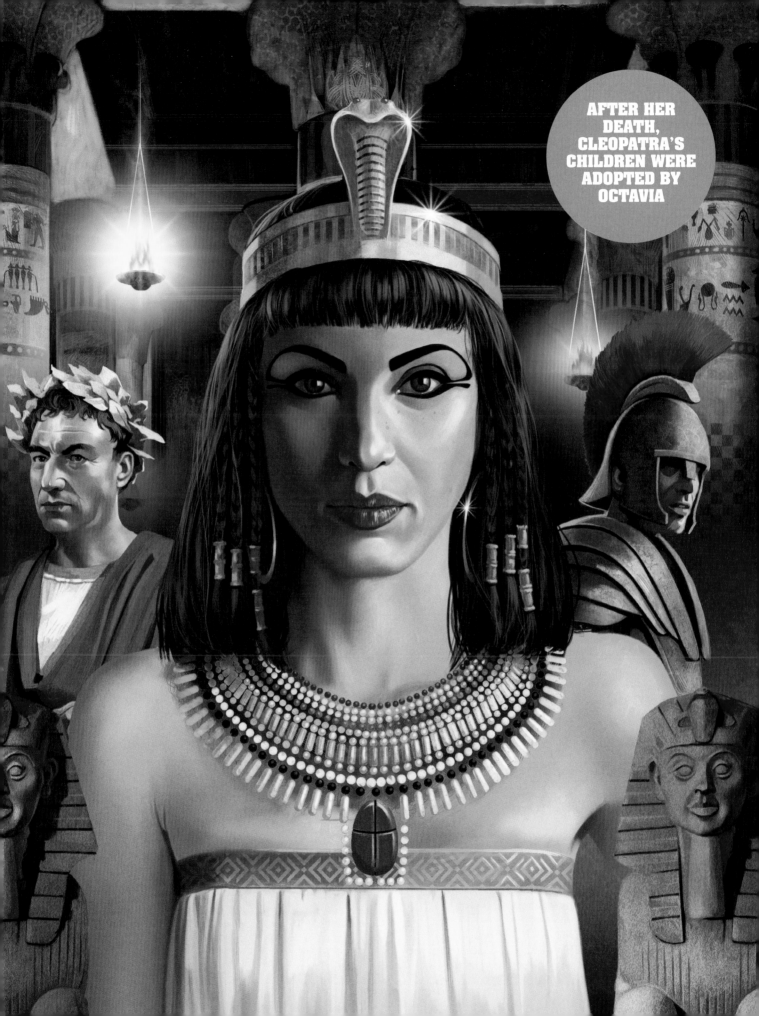

AFTER HER DEATH, CLEOPATRA'S CHILDREN WERE ADOPTED BY OCTAVIA

SHE HAD FOUR CHILDREN BY TWO FATHERS – CAESAR AND MARK ANTONY

the picking. As hungry peasants flooded into the cities, Cleopatra's popularity plummeted, and her repeated decisions that seemed designed to please Rome at Egypt's expense reminded the bitter population of her despised father.

In the middle of this political turmoil, Cleopatra found herself facing a familiar rival. Her brother was back and, aided by his many guardians and regents, was now a vicious and ruthless king who was not afraid to wipe her from the land and from history. He completely erased his sister's name from all official documents and backdated his monarchy, claiming sole rule since his father's death. With her popularity and reputation already in tatters, the disgraced queen fled the city of her birth before an angry mob could storm the palace and inflict upon her the same grisly fate as so many of her greedy and ill-fated predecessors.

Having lost not only the support of her people but also the land she so strongly believed was hers to rule, Cleopatra escaped to Syria with a small band of loyal supporters. Fuelled by outrage at her brother, and even more so at the advisors who had crafted him into a vicious enemy, Cleopatra did not abandon her ambitions, but set about building the army she would need to reclaim her throne. As the female pharaoh amassed her forces in Syria, her young brother, barely 13 years old, became distracted by the ever-pressing Roman civil war. After a humiliating defeat to Caesar in Pharsalus, the Roman military leader Pompey the Great fled to the one place he was assured he could find refuge; his old ally, Egypt.

With his wife and children watching nervously from afar, Pompey disembarked his grand ship to board a small fishing boat to the shore. The Egyptian boy pharaoh, Ptolemy, sat on the shore in a throne

A husband & two lovers

Ptolemy XIII Theos Philopator
Macedonian, 62-47 BCE

How did they get together?
The marriage between Ptolemy and his sister was arranged, as was the tradition with Egyptian royalty.

Was it true love?
Considering their joint rule erupted into a brutal civil war, we can assume there was little love lost between the siblings. There is no evidence they consummated their marriage.

How did it end?
Ptolemy was forced to flee Alexandria when the forces of Caesar and his sister-wife Cleopatra claimed victory. He reportedly drowned attempting to cross the Nile when fleeing.

Julius Caesar
Roman, 100-44 BCE

How did they get together?
Cleopatra and her brother both needed Caesar's support. Cleopatra met with Caesar before their scheduled meeting and managed to sway his vote. Her methods can be left to the imagination.

Was it true love?
Although the union was initially spawned from mutual political gain and the two were forbidden by Roman law to marry, Cleopatra seemed to stay loyal to Caesar and had his child.

How did it end?
This love affair was cut short when Caesar was assassinated on the Ides of March.

Mark Antony
Roman, 83-30 BCE

How did they get together?
Antony summoned Cleopatra to see if she would hold true in her promised support during the war against the Parthians. She reportedly charmed him during this meeting, perhaps much the same way she had Caesar.

Was it true love?
Although it may have been borne out of political agendas, the two had three children together, and Antony risked everything to be with his Egyptian queen.

How did it end?
After the ill-fated Battle of Actium, Antony committed suicide upon mistakenly hearing Cleopatra was dead, and she quickly followed suit.

fashioned specifically for the occasion. He watched Pompey closely, his face guarded and unreadable, but the men around him threw their arms open and, with wide smiles, cried, "Hail, commander!" It was not until the ship reached the shore that Pompey realised the murderous web in which he was entangled. Before he could cry out he was ran through with a sword and stabbed over and over again in the back. While the once-great consul was decapitated and his mutilated corpse thrown into the sea, Ptolemy did not rise from his throne. The ceremony had been a ruse; a rival of Caesar's was more valuable dead than alive.

When Caesar arrived in the harbour of Alexandria four days later, he was presented with the head of his rival. However, in mere moments Ptolemy's advisors realised their mistake, for the Roman general was completely and utterly appalled. He wept loudly and openly before leading his forces to the royal palace in Alexandria. As he observed the local resentment and civil war threatening to break the land in two he made a decision; he needed the wealth that Alexandrian taxes would give him, and the only way of increasing taxes was to establish stability in the city. The sibling rivalry had to end. He summoned Cleopatra and Ptolemy to appear before him. This was easy for Ptolemy who swiftly journeyed to Alexandria, but Cleopatra would have to use all her cunning just to make it into the city alive.

With the harbour blocked by her brother's ships, she slipped away from her troops and travelled in a small boat along the coast in the dead of night. Her journey had been completely and utterly unfitting for a pharaoh of Egypt, a Ptolemy queen; but victory demanded sacrifice and she was confident the streets and waters she was being smuggled down would soon be hers again. It had been a challenge

SHE SET ABOUT BUILDING THE ARMY SHE WOULD NEED TO RECLAIM HER THRONE

Five things to know about...
Cleopatra

1 She was smuggled in a rug

The image of a dishevelled Cleopatra being unrolled from a Persian rug at Caesar's feet after being smuggled into the palace comes from the pen of Greek biographer Plutarch, but it's difficult to prove this happened. It seems unlikely that Caesar would have welcomed a suspicious package into his room.

2 She was a femme fatale

The idea that Cleopatra flittered between powerful men, wooing and manipulating with no idea of who fathered her children, is the result of a smear campaign run against her by Roman officials. In fact, there's only evidence of her having been with two men: Julius Caesar and Mark Antony.

3 She was Egyptian

One of the most famous Egyptian pharaohs of all time wasn't Egyptian – she was Greek. Her family line is that of Ptolemy, a general of Alexander the Great, and despite her family living in Egypt for 300 years, she would have been regarded as Greek.

4 She wore a fake beard

The concept of female Egyptian queens sporting fake beards comes from the Egyptian belief that the god Osiris had a grand beard, prompting Egyptian pharaohs to do the same to establish themselves as divine beings. But by the time of Cleopatra this tradition had all but died out.

5 She died from an asp bite

This myth gained momentum due to paintings of Cleopatra holding a snake to her bosom as she dies. However, the accounts of this event are in some doubt, mainly because an asp will not cause a quick death as Cleopatra's was reported to be. It is more likely she drank poison.

All in the family

Follow Cleopatra's family tree and discover just how close-knit the Ptolemies really were...

The Ptolemies of Egypt could trace their ancestry to Ptolemy I Soter, a Greek general of Alexander the Great who became ruler of Egypt in 323 BCE. After Alexander's death, his most senior generals divided his vast territory between themselves. Completely oblivious to the dangers of interbreeding, it became customary for the Ptolemies to marry their brothers and sisters. It was convenient for them as not only did it ensure queens could be trained for their role from birth, but also established them as an elite, untouchable class far removed from the masses, similar to the revered Egyptian gods who married their sisters.

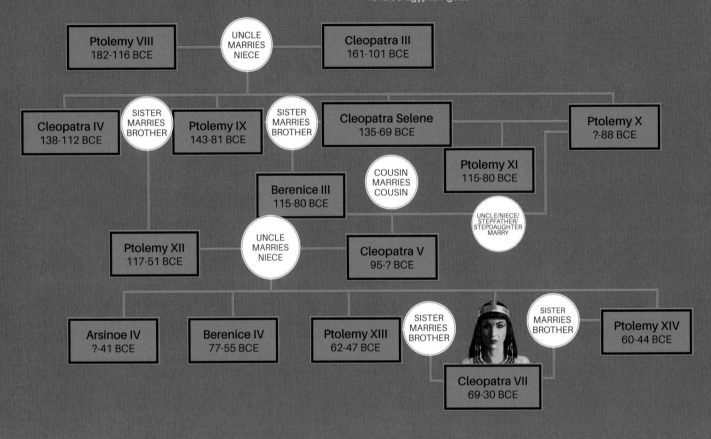

to make it into the palace district, but the real night's work was about to begin – she was about to go face to face with arguably the most powerful man in the known world.

Her brother would bend over backwards, slay Caesar's enemies and kiss his feet for his support, but he was quick to panic, eager to please and terrified of angering Rome. In short, her brother was a fool. Caesar needed Egypt as much as Egypt needed Rome and she would use that fact to her advantage. She would not wait to bow and plead her case alongside a scared child, she was going to speak to the Roman general that night. She sneaked into the palace and managed to find her way into Caesar's private chamber for a private audience.

The 'dictator in perpetuity', as he would come to be known in Rome, towered over the small woman; she would have to crane her head to look him in the eye, she realised instantly. He was far older than the young, bold Egyptian queen and his receding hairline was poorly disguised. The general was past his physical prime, but he had just won his greatest victory. This was her first time gazing upon the Roman celebrity known the world over, but this was also the first time he was facing her. Her brother was a child, a mere puppet pharaoh on strings, dancing to the pulls of his corrupt advisors, but she had been

granted all the charm, intelligence and ambition of her forefathers. She would steal Caesar and Rome's support while her brother slept; her charisma would succeed where her brother's sword had failed.

The young Ptolemy XIII awoke the next day, not expecting his dangerous older sister to have even made it to the palace. When he discovered that not only was she there, but had also seduced Caesar overnight into joining her cause, it was the final straw. Screaming in desperation, he fled from the palace, tore his crown from his head and fell to his knees. His sister had done it again. She was completely and utterly impossible to get rid off and, even as the crowd surged forward in protest, Caesar could not be swayed. The siblings would rule Egypt together, just as their father had intended. Rome had spoken.

The apparent peace did not last long. Already poisoned by the ambitious whispers that had fed his youth, Ptolemy joined with his rebellious sister Arsinoe IV. Between them they amassed an army large enough to challenge Cleopatra and Caesar's forces in Egypt. The country they fought for would pay the price, and in December of 48 BCE the famous city of Alexandria was set alight, destroying not only the lives of hundreds of citizens, but also the world-famous library that housed countless priceless manuscripts. When Caesar's

Cleopatra was as much an intellectual and scholar as a passionate fighter

End of an Era

Cleopatra's surviving children were adopted by Octavia. They became Roman citizens and faded quickly into obscurity. Egypt, now a Roman province, was ruled by a prefect. Greek remained the official language. While Alexandria continued to flourish, it became a site of many religious and military uprisings.

In 269 CE, Alexandria was claimed by another woman, when Zenobia, the warrior queen of Palmyra, conquered Egypt. Zenobia, who was an admirer of Cleopatra, was quick to behead her Roman foes. She ruled Egypt until 274, before she herself was taken hostage by the Roman Emperor Aurelian. In an ironic twist of fate, Zenobia appeared in golden chains during Aurelian's Triumph in Rome.

The legacy of Greco-Roman Egypt still survives. It can be seen in a series of magnificent temples that were built along the River Nile. These include the Temple of Hathor at Dendera, where fabulous images of Cleopatra and Caesarion still dominate the walls therein.

The delicate amalgamation of the Egyptian and Roman cultures can also be seen on many mummy portrait panels from the Greco-Roman period. Contrasts are visible in paintings and sculptures where traditional Egyptian iconography is paired with Roman symbolism. The result – a hybrid blend of the ancient and even more ancient – is now all that remains of the former bond between Rome and Egypt, Antony and Cleopatra.

reinforcements poured into the city from Pergamum, Ptolemy's forces were finally defeated. The impetuous king tried to flee across the Nile in an overcrowded boat, but his vessel sank, dragging him and his heavy golden armour down with it.

One Ptolemy was dead, but another still lived. Ptolemy XIV, Cleopatra's 13-year-old brother, became her husband and co-ruler immediately after her brother's death. She might have had Caesar's support, but tradition was still tradition and a lone woman could not rule Egypt. As for Caesar, he had put in place a reliable partnership and Egypt was, for all intents and purposes, a Roman territory. In a lavish display of the new union, a fleet of Roman and Egyptian ships sailed down the Nile accompanied by the grand royal barge where Cleopatra and Caesar sat together.

Egypt and Rome were united, but Cleopatra still found herself co-ruler to another Ptolemy who would inevitably grow up to be ambitious and treacherous. She could not allow another brother to be swayed by advisors and driven to take up arms against her. As long as Ptolemy XIV lived, her rule was under threat. She wasn't a fool, she knew that Egypt would never accept a solitary female queen, but there was a technicality that would ensure her effective sole rule. Her partnership with Caesar had provided more than his political support; she was pregnant and in 47 BCE she gave birth. The gods' will was in her favour – the child was a boy. She named him Caesarion, or 'Little Caesar', and now had an heir. For three years Cleopatra tightened her grip on the Egyptian throne, slowly winning the love of the Alexandrian mobs that had previously screamed for her head. She travelled to Rome with her son and resided in Caesar's country house as heated rumours about the paternity of her son gained speed. She

did little to squash them; a possible heir of Caesar was a very powerful tool to have.

When Caesar was assassinated by his Senators on 15 March 44 BCE, Cleopatra left Rome and returned to Alexandria. If there was ever a time to act, it was now. Without her powerful Roman lover by her side she needed an ally who could assure her rule, one who wasn't going to lead a rebellion against her. Brothers, she had learned, could not be trusted. Later that year the youngest Ptolemy was found dead, seemingly poisoned. The people's grief was muted; the death of Ptolemies, however young, was not so uncommon in Egypt, and the people had a new pharaoh to replace him: the young Caesarion. Cleopatra had finally done it, she was Egypt's pharaoh, and with her son an infant she was ruling alone in all but name. The power of Egypt was finally hers.

1926 – present

Elizabeth II

From happy and glorious to annus horribilis, Queen Elizabeth II has seen changes to the monarchy, her country and the world that 90 years ago would have seemed unimaginable

IN 2007, ELIZABETH II BECAME THE LONGEST-SERVING MONARCH

"… I declare before you all that my whole life, whether it be long or short, shall be devoted to your service."

Perhaps the most recognisable face in the world, the queen's enduring popularity is showing no signs of waning after over 90 years. And after 65 years on the throne, she's provided Great Britain and the Commonwealth with a welcome sense of stability. Unexpectedly thrust into the royal line of succession as a child after the abdication of Edward VIII, her life has been wrought not only with the tragedies of loss and war, but with the joys of marriage and family, as well as her success as one of Britain's most popular monarchs.

Over the next few pages, discover the key moments in the life of Queen Elizabeth II, from her carefree youth in the 1930s to her regal coronation in the 1950s and all the years up to now, where she celebrates the birth of her great-grandchildren. Queen Elizabeth II became the longest reigning British monarch in 2015, surpassing her Queen Victoria, who reigned for 63 years, seven months and two days.

90 years is an achievement by anyone's standards, but the occasion was a momentous one for Queen Elizabeth II in particular – so here's to plenty more years ahead, and a happy and glorious reign!

The 1930s

The decade of three kings

Princess Elizabeth Alexandra Mary Windsor was never meant to be queen. As daughter of the second in line to the throne, she spent her childhood enjoying relative freedom, living not in a palace, but in a house at 145 Piccadilly, playing with her father's corgis, singing, dancing and taking part in pantomimes.

Then at the age of ten, her whole life was turned upside down, and her fate was sealed forever. Her uncle Edward was first in line to the throne and had always been a busy and charismatic member of the royal family, as well as a key figure in 1920s society. When Edward entered into a relationship with the married US socialite Wallis Simpson in 1934, his parents King George V and Queen Mary were angered and dismayed, while the Conservative government was horrified. At that time, the Church of England did not permit the remarriage of those with living ex-spouses, and as future king, he would one day hold the title supreme governor of the Church of England. Edward could not be allowed to marry Wallis.

King George V died on 20 January 1936, and Edward acceded to the throne. However, three months later, when Princess Elizabeth turned ten, her future – as well as that of her father and uncle – still hung in the balance. Wallis Simpson's divorce was finalised in October, but the following month, Edward was still trying to find a way to accede to the throne with Wallis by his side. He met with the Prime Minister Stanley Baldwin and proposed a morganatic marriage, in which the spouse of a monarch has no royal title, but his suggestion was dismissed. Unwilling to give Wallis up, he brought an end to his ten-month reign by signing the Instrument of Abdication on 10 December 1936, and in a radio broadcast the following day, stated: "I have found it impossible to carry the heavy burden of responsibility, and to discharge my duties as king as I would wish to do, without the help and support of the woman I love."

His younger brother immediately acceded to the throne, becoming King George VI. Fortunately, the turbulent royal year came after over a century of stable monarchy, paving the way for a flourishing relationship that would be inherited by his daughter Elizabeth.

The young Princess Elizabeth, as photographed in the 1930s, poses in a frilly dress

21 APRIL 1926

A queen is born
Princess Elizabeth is born at 17 Brunton Street, Mayfair, in London, England, at 2.40am. Named after her mother, she will later be christened Elizabeth Alexandra Mary.

21 AUGUST 1930

The royal sister
Four years after the young princess had been born, a second daughter follows. Named Margaret Rose, the two sisters and their parents will become a very close family.

10 DECEMBER 1936

King Edward VIII abdicates
Choosing love over power, King Edward VIII abdicates. The next day, his younger brother, Bertie, is named king, becoming King George VI. Elizabeth becomes first in line to the throne after her father.

22 JULY 1939

Elizabeth meets Philip
As a naval officer, Philip is asked to escort the two young princesses around HMS Dartmouth base. Here, 13-year-old Elizabeth takes an immediate liking to the 18-year-old Philip of Greece and Denmark.

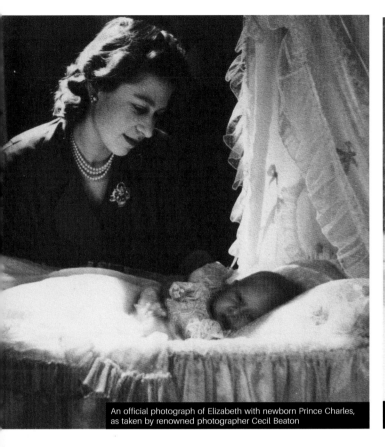

An official photograph of Elizabeth with newborn Prince Charles, as taken by renowned photographer Cecil Beaton

Here, photographed in her Auxiliary Territorial Service uniform, Elizabeth poses in front of one of the force's ambulances

The 1940s

The sun sets

In the decade that Princess Elizabeth passed many happy personal milestones – including falling in love, getting married and having her first baby – the world was in turmoil. When World War II ended in 1945, the waves of change it brought continued for decades, washing from King George VI's reign long into that of his daughter Queen Elizabeth II. One of the most significant was the fall of the British Empire, and the subsequent cementing of the Commonwealth – and the young Princess Elizabeth was paying attention. After the devastating impact of World War II, Britain's authority and wealth had been depleted. Resistance to British rule in India had always been quashed, but after increased opposition, Britain withdrew, and on 15 August 1947, India – along with Pakistan – achieved independence,

followed by Burma and Ceylon. Kenya was not to achieve its own independence until 1963, Rhodesia until 1980, and finally Hong Kong in 1997, but this was the decade when the empire began to crumble.

The Commonwealth, however, went from strength to strength. The organisation had first been set up in 1931 to champion democracy, human rights, racial equality and the rule of law, while membership also brought economic benefits including cheaper trading costs. One by one, as former British colonies achieved independence, the Commonwealth grew, and in 1949 it was formalised with the London Declaration. It now has 53 member states, almost all of whom were formerly ruled by Britain. Princess Elizabeth had entered the decade aged 13, but she was already preparing for her future role. She and Prince Philip of Greece and Denmark had recently met for the first time, and the princess was instantly taken with the athletic 18-year-old. They started courting in the mid 1940s, and married on 20 November 1947, but throughout the whirl of first love, Elizabeth's eye was already very much on doing her duty. She had been undertaking royal engagements since she was 16, and in a radio broadcast from Cape Town on her 21st birthday, she said: "This is a happy day for me, but also one that brings serious thoughts, thoughts of life looming ahead with all its challenges and with all its opportunity... I declare before you all that my whole life, whether it be long or short, shall be devoted to your service."

---

13 OCTOBER 1940

First public speech
As WWII breaks out, the young princess makes her first public speech to British children who face evacuation. Princess Margaret joins in at the end of the broadcast to wish the children goodbye.

4 MARCH 1945

Joins the ATS
Determined to do her bit in the war, Princess Elizabeth joins the Auxiliary Territorial Service. She remains the only female royal to have ever joined the armed forces.

20 NOVEMBER 1947

A royal wedding
As soon as Elizabeth reaches 21, she marries Philip in Westminster Abbey. As their wedding is held in the post-war recovery years, the young bride saves up and pays for her wedding dress using ration coupons.

14 NOVEMBER 1948

Prince Charles is born
Almost exactly a year after their wedding, the happy couple welcomes their first child into the family. Prince Charles is born at 9.14pm at Buckingham Palace.

The 1950s

Standing up to Churchill

On the evening of 5 February 1952, a young woman went up a tree a princess, and the following morning she came back down a queen. Princess Elizabeth and husband Prince Philip were just six days into a tour of Kenya, New Zealand and Australia, and after a busy first few days around Nairobi, they had a night to themselves at Treetops Hotel, near Nyeri in Kenya. After climbing a rickety ladder to tree house, the princess spent a few hours filming elephants at dusk. She rose again before dawn the next morning to resume watching the wildlife, and unknown to her, more than 4,000 miles away, her father passed away. She spent her last few hours of blissful unknowing filming rhinos at a watering hole before descending at 10am to hit the road again. She wasn't to find out about her father's passing until that afternoon. The news was eventually confirmed to Elizabeth's private secretary Martin Charteris, who informed Prince Philip. It was his job to inform his wife of the news.

King George VI had been a heavy smoker, and after being diagnosed with lung cancer the previous year he had a lung removed, and was deemed unfit to embark on a royal tour. His daughter took his place, accompanied by her husband, and when she waved goodbye to her father at London Airport, he had seemed in good spirits. However, his health deteriorated fast, and he passed away in his sleep in the early hours of 6 February 1952 at Sandringham House. Prince Philip broke the news to his wife on a walk through the foothills of Mount Kenya, and the two of them spent some time talking and walking together. On the plane home she was given a telegram

from her mother, reading: "To: Her Majesty The Queen. All my thoughts and prayers are with you. Mummie, Buckingham Palace." Queen Elizabeth II was met straight off the plane in London by her prime minister, Winston Churchill, along with fellow officers of state. She was 25 years old and had two young children. Not only was she dealing with the death of her beloved father, but her life had changed forever. Gone was her existence as a young military wife, full-time mother and monarch in training.

In the years since her wedding she had lived in Malta where Prince Philip was stationed as a Royal Navy officer, and she would drive herself around, go to the cinema and attend dances. Now Prince Philip's naval career would be over, and Elizabeth was queen of the United Kingdom of Great Britain and Northern Ireland, head of the Commonwealth, Defender of the Faith and supreme governor of the Church of England, and head of the Armed Forces. She was plunged very much into a man's world.

Heads of the military and church, politicians and heads of state were all male, but she was already a formidable young woman. Her coronation was planned for the following year, and Winston Churchill did not want the event to be televised. But the fledgling queen understood the importance of including the people – as well as embracing the advancements of the modern age – and insisted that it was. Queen Elizabeth II's coronation was held on 2 June 1953 at Westminster Abbey. She inherited a robustly royalist nation that would remain with her throughout her life.

Elizabeth II passes the coronation chair, first used in the 1761 coronation of King George III and Queen Charlotte

The queen and her husband pose proudly with their children, Prince Charles and Princess Anne, in October 1957

---

15 AUGUST 1950

Princess Anne is born
Only two years after the young Prince Charles's birth, a princess is born to Elizabeth and Philip. Birthed at Clarence House, the child will later be christened Anne Elizabeth Alice Louise.

6 FEBRUARY 1952

King George VI dies
The princess learns of her father's peaceful death while on tour in Kenya. The rest of the visit is cancelled and the new queen flies back to Britain to take her place as monarch.

2 MAY 1953

First football match
As the new queen of England, Elizabeth II attends her first football match. It is the 1953 FA Cup Final between Blackpool and Bolton Wanderers, with the former team boasting a win.

Queen Elizabeth, the Queen Mother and her daughter and namesake Queen Elizabeth II, pictured together in 1967

The 1960s

Keeping up with the Windsors

The easy-breezy spirit of the 1960s didn't blow quite as strongly down the corridors of Buckingham Palace as through the rest of the world, but to some extent, times they were a changin'. For many years royalty had succeeded quite well in keeping to themselves. Royal babies were born in palaces not hospitals, and children were educated by governesses at home, rather than in the public system.

Prince Charles was the first heir to the throne to go to school, and in 1965 he was the first to sit GCE O Levels (passing five), followed by A Levels a couple of years later. Not only were members of the family going forth and mixing with the public, but the public themselves were also invited inside palace doors for the first time. At the suggestion of Prince Philip, Buckingham Palace was opened to the public in 1962 with the forming of the The Queen's Gallery – which displays items from the royal collection, the one that is held in trust for the nation rather than Her Majesty's private collection. Up until then, the closest anyone would have come was peering through the railings at the front of the palace, while a very select few would be invited to the annual garden parties. No one without an invitation would have been able to pass onto the forecourt of the palace and walk through its doors.

Six years later, there were also changes at the queen's Norfolk property, when Sandringham Country Park became open, free of charge, to the public. The opening up of both properties chipped away at the wall between the family and their public, and paved the way for a more modern relationship between the two, but the most ground-breaking move was yet to come.

To commemorate Prince Charles becoming the Prince of Wales, the queen agreed to the 1969 fly-on-the-wall documentary called Royal Family, which was filmed over the course of a year, and gave an amazing insight into life behind palace doors. The BBC aired the programme on 21 June 1969, and it was watched by 68 per cent of the population – while 350 million people tuned in around the world. It has not been shown since, for fears it made the family seem too 'ordinary'.

---

2 JUNE 1953

Queen Elizabeth's coronation
A respectable 18 months after her father's death, Elizabeth II is crowned at Westminster Abbey. An estimated 27 million people watch the event on TV, while 11 million listen on the radio.

24 NOVEMBER 1953

Commonwealth tour begins
With the coronation behind her, Queen Elizabeth II sets off on a tour of the Commonwealth. It is a continuation of the tour she had been on when her father died.

25 DECEMBER 1957

First televised Christmas speech
Queen Elizabeth II continues her father's tradition of a speech on Christmas Day, but in 1957, she gives her speech on television - live.

Revellers in Seaham, County Durham enjoy a street party to celebrate the queen's Silver Jubilee on 7 June 1977

Prime Minister Edward Heath joins Her Majesty in escorting US President Richard Nixon and his wife on their visit to the UK

The 1970s

Let's talk

If advancements in the 1960s were about inviting the people closer, moves in the 1970s were about the royal family edging closer themselves. First Princess Diana, and later the Duke and Duchess of Cambridge and Prince Harry, have all been credited with breaking down barriers and creating a new more 'touchy-feely' monarchy, but it was the queen who made the initial strides in 1970 – breaking centuries of royal protocol when she introduced 'the royal walkabout' while on a tour of New Zealand and Australia. In Wellington, New Zealand, she encountered a group of children, and after stopping to chat with them, ended up spending some time shaking their hands and receiving posies of flowers. It was a simple gesture, but it changed the face of royal tours forever. Before walkabouts were introduced, the family would wave remotely from a motorcade as it made its way through crowded streets, or there may be a wave and a smile as they left a building. Processing before the people, and being visible – rather than accessible – were the order of the day, while those deemed fit to meet the monarch would have been approved by courtiers, and the atmosphere would be formal.

However, as the starchy environs of the 1950s gave way to a more relaxed society, the reverence for the monarchy was evolving into a more emotional connection. The walkabouts sat perfectly in this evolution – a ground-breaking and canny move because it meant that the family no longer seemed quite so remote. Princess Diana built on this blueprint in the 1980s and 1990s as she waded into crowds with hand outstretched. A large part of the princess's popularity was the way she made people feel when she came face to face with them, and this would not have been so easy if she didn't have the opportunity to actually greet, hug or laugh with the masses. Now, the younger members of the family – William, Kate and Harry – do the same, revealing little tit-bits of information along the way, such as the Cambridges' dog's name. On the downside, both Prince Philip and Princess Anne got in trouble on the first tour that walkabouts were introduced, as Philip was said to have said a rude word in Greek, while Anne shocked the crowd when she exclaimed on a particularly breezy day, "This bloody wind!"

The 1980s

International relations

In the decade that the world was scrutinising Princess Diana's wardrobe, the queen was quietly showing how a role that wielded no political power could still do its bit for diplomacy. Ever since Henry VIII told Catherine of Aragon, "This isn't working out," and in 1536 changed his country's religion forever, relations between Great Britain and the Vatican were turbulent to say the least. During the reign of Elizabeth I, English law prohibited any official relations with the Papal States, and in 1801, the formation of the United Kingdom of Great Britain and Ireland caused further friction. However, in 1829, legal obstacles relating to the Papal States were removed, paving the way for a new age.

In 1980, Pope John Paul II sent a congratulatory message to the queen for her efforts in championing the peace process during the Troubles, and this paved the way for his historic visit in 1982 – the first papal visit to Britain in 450 years. During the trip, His Holiness met with the queen at Buckingham Palace, became the first pope to visit Canterbury Cathedral, and celebrated mass with 80,000 people in Wembley Stadium. His visit was not the only momentous event in international relations in this decade, as four years later, the queen was heading east on one of the most important overseas tours she has ever undertaken. The rocky and turbulent history between Britain and China had spanned centuries. During the 1960s there had been rioting in Hong Kong against British rule, and in December 1984 there were talks between the Prime Minister of China Zhao Ziyang and Margaret Thatcher, which resulted in them signing the Sino-British Joint Declaration – meaning that Hong Kong would be given back to China on 1 July 1997. Hot on the heels of these high-profile, high-stakes talks, the queen and Prince Philip visited less than two years later, making Her Majesty the first reigning monarch to make a state visit to China. Important new bonds were forged as she walked among the newly excavated army of Terracotta Warriors in Xi'an. Such highly visible trips have been invaluable in forging and maintaining strong relationships with other states and countries, and will prove a fitting legacy to a reign filled with unprecedented change.

The queen in a less guarded moment, laughing with veterans at Stirling Castle, July 1986

Prince Charles and his fiancée, Lady Diana Spencer, pictured on the eve of their 1981 'fairy tale' wedding

---

1970

The royal walkabout
On a trip to Australia and New Zealand the first royal walkabout takes place, with the queen and her husband greeting as many people in the

28 MAY 1972

Edward VIII dies
Having lived most of his post-monarch life in Paris, Edward VIII passes away. He will be buried at Windsor Castle. When Wallis Simpson dies 14 years later, she will be buried alongside him.

29 MARCH 1976

The first email
While at an army base, Elizabeth becomes one of the first heads of state to send an email. Given the username HME2 – Her Majesty Elizabeth II – in a few clicks, she sends her first email.

7 JUNE 1977

Silver Jubilee
After 25 years on the throne, the queen celebrates her Silver Jubilee. In the summer months, she takes part in a tour, intending to meet as many of her people as possible.

The 1990s

Reality bites

The golden age of public goodwill that the queen had experienced from her coronation and into the 1980s was beginning to dull. Three royal divorces, affairs, and acrimonious words from those who had lived behind palace walls diminished the family's popularity. Recorded private phone conversations were sold to newspapers, tell-all books were published and the public picked sides. The institution of a royal family was accused of being outmoded and a waste of money. Polls in the 1990s showed support for the family had dropped, and that many people did not believe the monarchy would last another 100 years. The family was out of sync with the rest of the country.

The difference between life inside and outside palace walls had always been marked. There was little royal interaction with the public, and the family's daily lives, their concerns and interests were very different from that of their people. While the world modernised throughout the 20th century, moves were made to lessen this divide, but it wasn't enough. The royal family gradually lost their power, but retained their privilege, and one of these privileges was reassessed after a fire caused almost £40 million of damage to Windsor Castle at the end of 1992 – the queen's 'annus horribilis'.

Because the castle is not a private residence, but owned by the state, restoration was due to be funded by the tax-payer, however, after the public debate reached the House of Commons, it spilled into a bigger discussion about the queen not paying taxes. The queen subsequently volunteered to start paying tax, and the Memorandum of Understanding on Royal Taxation was published in February 1993. From April 1994, the queen has paid income tax and capital gains tax. Additionally, instead of the Windsor Castle restoration being funded by the tax-payer, the queen made the decision to open up the Buckingham Palace state rooms to the public when she wasn't in residence over the summer months. This meant that the money raised for the Windsor Castle restoration came predominantly from those ticket sales.

The funeral procession of Princess Diana

Windsor Castle, the largest inhabited castle in the world, burned for 12 hours, causing damage worth millions of pounds

Windsor Castle fire
A devastating fire sweeps through Windsor Castle, ravaging anything in its path. More than £36 million worth of damage is done. The year becomes known as the queen's 'annus horribilis'.

Charles & Diana divorce
The people's princess and Prince Charles have been separated for years by this time, but at last their marriage is officially dissolved.

Diana dies
Just over a year after her divorce with Prince Charles, Diana tragically dies in a car accident in Paris. Her sudden death will send Great Britain into a state of national mourning.

Golden wedding anniversary
Queen Elizabeth II and Prince Philip celebrate their Golden wedding anniversary. They held a garden party at Buckingham Palace for other couples celebrating the same anniversary.

The 2000s

Behind closed doors

Following the constitutional crisis after the abdication of Edward VIII, the relationship between divorcees Prince Charles and Camilla Parker Bowles needed to be handled very carefully. Historically, the Church of England did not permit the re-marriage of people with living ex-spouses. However, this rule was changed in 2002 when the Church voted that, dependent on the decision of the vicar in question, divorcees could remarry. It now became possible for Charles to marry Camilla and still be king when the time eventually came. Things had started to go awry for Charles when he wasn't permitted to marry the woman he loved 30 years previously. The star-crossed couple were first in a relationship in 1971 when Charles was 23 and the then Camilla Shand was 24, but Charles felt too young to commit. While he spent time away in the navy, Camilla returned to her ex-boyfriend Andrew Parker Bowles and they married. Charles lamented in a letter to his godfather Lord Mountbatten: "I suppose the feeling of emptiness will pass eventually."

After his marriage to Diana broke down, he returned to the now-separated Camilla. Following their divorces, the couple were preparing to go public with their relationship when Diana died. Charles and Camilla made their first public appearance together two years later in 1999 at Camilla's sister's birthday party at The Ritz, but for many years they were both very unpopular in the public eye, and goodwill towards the royal family was the lowest it had been for decades. The couple married at Windsor Guildhall in 2005, with the blessing of the queen, and Camilla became Duchess or Cornwall.

In her religious position, the queen believed she shouldn't attend the civil ceremony, and so she stayed away. She did, however, attend the blessing held afterwards at St George's Chapel, Windsor Castle. After the disasters of the 1990s, the following decade was all about the family re-building, and making changes behind closed doors. During her reign, the queen has focused on the big issues, such as making the royal family more accessible to the public, going on ground-breaking international visits and paying tax like the rest of her people, but now the smaller changes needed to be made.

Her Majesty The Queen Mother pictured on a visit to Dover Castle in this photograph by Allan Warren

William marries Catherine
In a lavish ceremony at Westminster Abbey, Prince William marries his sweetheart Kate Middleton. The wedding is broadcast around the world, and the streets of Britain are lined with well wishers.

Diamond Jubilee
To mark the queen's 60-year reign, a weekend of celebrations take place across the country. Over the course of the year, she travels the length of the country to mark the occasion.

Longest-serving monarch
Having overtaken Victoria as the longest living monarch, Elizabeth overtakes her as the longest-serving monarch, too. Victoria managed 63 years, seven months and two days on the throne.

The 90th birthday
While the queen's actual birthday is 21 April, and on it she was turning 90, she also celebrated an official birthday on a Saturday in June with the Trooping the Colour.

The 2010s

A new generation

Prince William and Catherine Middleton were launched onto the world's stage as a couple in an explosion of flashbulbs, and following the announcement of their engagement in November 2010, they reaped the rewards of lessons learned. Kate was edged slowly into royal life, and given access to a battery of advisers. The queen advised William to tear up his official wedding guest list suggested by courtiers, and start with his friends. Then as the years passed, Kate's family became the first Windsor in-laws not to be 'left at the door' when they walked out of the church on the wedding day.

While for many the queen's defining moment of the decade is her cameo alongside James Bond in the London 2012 Olympics opening ceremony, perhaps the most significant move she made was her historic trip to Ireland in 2011, at the age of 85. For nearly 500 years the relationship between Britain and Ireland had been complicated and dangerous, but 13 years after the Troubles officially ended, the queen arrived in May 2011. It was the first time a British monarch had visited Ireland since the Troubles, and so the city centre was turned into a car-free zone to prevent terrorist bombs. More than 100 armed British police were on the streets, with 8,000 local police and 2,000 soldiers drafted in as additional security. Among other events, the queen gave a speech at Dublin Castle, the former centre of British rule, saying: "So much of this visit reminds us of the complexity of our history, its many layers and tradition, but also the importance of forbearance and conciliation. Of being able to bow to the past, but not be bound by it."

"Catherine Middleton was edged slowly into royal life"

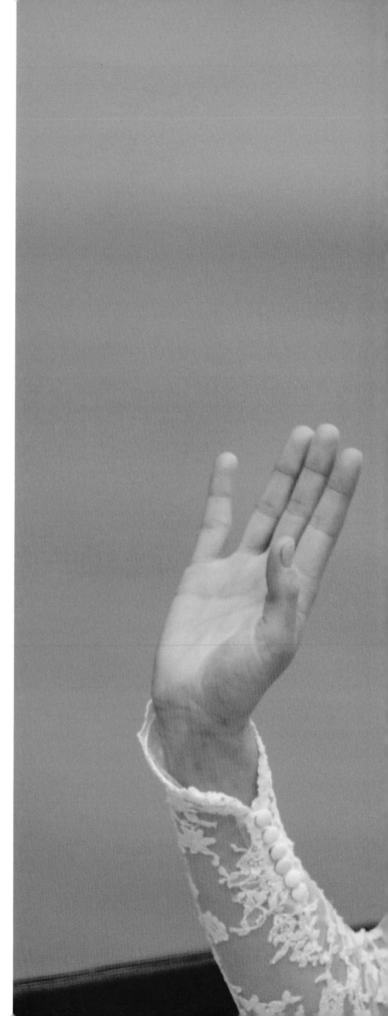

c.240 – c.274 CE

Zenobia

Armed with the bravery and beauty of her ancestor Cleopatra, Zenobia defied the Romans to rule her own empire

Blame William Shakespeare — or Elizabeth Taylor — for the fact that Cleopatra has overshadowed all other strong, cunning and comely queens of antiquity. Three centuries after the legendary Cleopatra ruled from the Pharaoh's throne in Egypt, her blood heiress, as well as equal in courage and beauty, rose to power in the eastern oasis of Palmyra, part of the Palmyrene Empire in modern-day Syria. After the assassination of her war-hero husband, Zenobia assumed confident control of this wealthy city state on the fringes of the fading Roman Empire in the 3rd century CE. Claiming independence from Rome, she would drive her loyal armies across Egypt and Palestine, briefly ruling a large and stable empire of her own. But her kingdom, and life, would ultimately be cut short by the sword of the conquering Roman Emperor Aurelian.

The true story of Zenobia is shrouded in centuries of legend. The earliest historical source is the wildly unreliable *Historia Augusta*, a colourful work of fiction posing as fact from the 4th century CE. The 18th century historian Edward Gibbon, in his monumental work *The Decline and Fall of the Roman Empire*, relied heavily on descriptions of Zenobia found in the *Historia Augusta* to paint his own romanticised portrait of the Palmyrene queen.

"Modern Europe has produced several illustrious women who have sustained with glory the weight of empire," wrote Gibbon. "But... Zenobia is perhaps the only female whose superior genius broke through the servile indolence imposed on her sex by the climate and manners of Asia. She claimed her descent from the Macedonian kings of Egypt, equalled in beauty her ancestor Cleopatra and far surpassed that princess in chastity and valour. Zenobia was esteemed the most lovely as well as the most heroic of her sex."

Modern historians have pieced together a more reliable biography of Zenobia from early Christian sources, archaeological inscriptions and ancient coins, but much of her life story is still up for debate, starting with her lineage and ethnicity. Much is made of Zenobia's claimed relation to Cleopatra along the famed Seleucid bloodline on her mother's side. Her father also ruled Palmyra and was descended from a long line of Roman citizens, as well as royalty dating back to Julia Domna, the influential empress wife of Roman Emperor Lucius Septimus Severus.

Whether or not either of these genealogies are true, it's clear that Zenobia was born into a wealthy and powerful family in a city state at the height of its own wealth and power. Palmyra is located in the

HISTORIANS NOW BELIEVE THAT ZENOBIA MAY HAVE HAD ARAMAEAN OR EVEN JEWISH ORIGIN

middle of the desert halfway between the Euphrates River valley and the Mediterranean Sea. Underground springs transformed the land into a fertile oasis and a critical stop on the Silk Road trade route that brought spices and textiles from the exotic East to the bustling markets of Rome. Palmyra's security forces offered protection to passing caravans while the government exacted an import tax — 25 per cent of every camel load — to fill Palmyra's substantial coffers.

Zenobia, as described by Gibbon, was an olive-skinned beauty who spoke Aramaic, Greek, Latin, Arabic and Ancient Egyptian. Unlike the delicate noblewomen of Rome — who wouldn't leave the house without a protective veil and covered carriage — Zenobia was a capable camel and horse rider who enjoyed wild lion and panther hunts as much as her husband.

Zenobia was the second wife of Odaenathus, the ruler of Palmyra and a critical ally of Rome in the east. During Odaenathus' rule, Palmyra was an important buffer state between the Romans and the Persian Sasanian Empire. Rome allowed Palmyra to remain independent in exchange for its strategic neutrality in the region. In 260 CE, the Persians captured the Roman Emperor Valerian and conquered the eastern Roman stronghold of Antioch. Fearing a Persian expansion towards Palmyra, Odaenathus struck first, decimating the Persian army as it returned victorious from Antioch. Later Palmyrene campaigns pushed the Persians all the way back to their capital. These victories won Odaenathus praise and titles from Rome and may have triggered visions of his own future rise to be Emperor himself.

Odaenathus would not live long enough to find out. He was murdered by a nephew along with his son Hairan, from his first wife, over a hunting argument. Odaenathus' death left Zenobia's young son Vaballathus as heir to the throne. Since the boy was too young to rule — between five and ten years old — Zenobia assumed the role of regent, a position that quickly evolved into the undisputed political and military leader of Palmyra. On coins recovered from the years after Odaenathus' murder, archaeologists first find them with Vaballathus' face on the front and Zenobia's on the back. Very quickly these positions are reversed.

As the de facto ruler of Palmyra, Zenobia picked up exactly where her husband left off, with her own dreams of a Palmyrene Empire. Historians argue about Zenobia's specific motivations and political calculations. During the 3rd century, the Roman Empire suffered an extended period of great tribulation known as the Imperial Crisis. The

Aurelian the unstoppable

After the Imperial Crisis of the 3rd century, the Roman Empire owed its survival to the hard-nosed military mastermind Aurelian. Born into a family of humble peasant farmers in the Danubian provinces of the Roman Empire near the Balkans, he joined a long line of tough and disciplined military men. Aurelian rose to prominence as a strict and stalwart army officer during one of the messiest periods in Imperial history. In 268, the Emperor Gallienus was under fire from the so-called Thirty Tyrants, Roman military and political leaders who aimed to topple the throne. Aurelian, along with his compatriot Claudius, put down the rebellion, but may have played a role in Gallienus' assassination. Claudius succeeded as Emperor, but died after only 18 months, making room for no-nonsense Aurelian to assume the crown. He whipped the Roman legions into shape and marched them on the barbarian marauders — groups such as the Goths, Vandals, Alemanni and Juthungi — threatening Roman sovereignty in northern Italy. By this point, Zenobia had established herself as the Queen of the East and ruler of the independent Palmyrene Empire. If Aurelian had any hesitation about crushing a woman, he didn't show it, and brought the full force of his best legions against Zenobia, finally offering her a measure of mercy if she would surrender her empire at the gates of Palmyra. When she refused, Aurelian dragged her captive to Rome and had her entire inner circle executed. He returned two years later during a short-lived revolt.

Empire had gone through 19 emperors in 30 years, most of them killed by ambitious generals or their own Praetorian Guard. Britain and Gaul had split from the Empire, the Goths were invading from the north, there was a smallpox epidemic in the provinces and pirates were disrupting trade along the Libyan coast. In Rome's moment of weakness, Zenobia saw an opportunity, but did she see herself as Rome's partner in empire, or its conqueror?

What happens next is undisputed. In the year 269 CE, with the support of her husband's battle-tested General Zabdas, Zenobia marched the Palmyrene army into Egypt, what she called her ancestral homeland. When the Roman prefect of Egypt objected to Zenobia's occupation, she swiftly had him beheaded. Zenobia bestowed upon herself the title of Queen of Egypt and commissioned a ten-volume history of Cleopatra to commemorate the victory. If the Roman Emperor Claudius had his own objections, he was too busy fighting off the Goths to worry about the upstart empress in Egypt.

Without Roman resistance, Zenobia the warrior queen was given free rein to extend her territory into Syria, Lebanon and Palestine. At its greatest extent, Zenobia's empire stretched from the Nile River in the south up through the Sinai Peninsula and Palestine, north to the Black Sea and west to modern-day Ankara, Turkey. Around this time, Zenobia changed her coins yet again to add the title Augustus, or empress, alongside her own portrait.

In 270, a new face appeared on the scene in the form of Aurelian, a lifelong military man who rose to the ranks to become Emperor of Rome and Restitutor Orbis, or restorer of the world. Aurelian brought order and discipline back to the Roman military. He pushed out invading Germanic tribes such as the Vandals from northern Italy and erected the fortress-like Aurelian Walls around Rome. Next he marched against the Goths in the Balkans and crushed them. By 272, Aurelian had dealt with Rome's most pressing problems and was ready to turn his attention east to the so-called Palmyrene Empire and its warrior empress. The *Historia Augusta* relates Zenobia writing a letter to Aurelian proposing that they rule the Mediterranean as co-emperors. If that letter ever actually existed, then Aurelian likely ignored it.

> *"When the Roman prefect of Egypt objected to Zenobia's occupation, she swiftly had him beheaded"*

Defining moment
Assassination of Odaenathus 266 CE

Zenobia's husband, Odaenathus, died far from the battlefield. One story sees him going on a hunting trip with a rude nephew, Maeonius, who Odaenathus punished by taking away his horse and locking him up for a few nights. Insulted, young Maeonius killed the Palmyrene king at a party. Other accounts implicate Rome in the murder. Another story puts Zenobia herself at the centre of the plot. Odaenathus was killed along with his eldest son, putting the throne in the hands of Zenobia's son Vaballathus and under her capable control.

Timeline

A Queen is born
Cleopatra claimed to be descended from Isis and Zenobia hitched her own star to Cleopatra's. She was born into the ruling family of Palmyra and schooled in language, philosophy, horse riding and hunting.
240 CE

Her match in marriage
Zenobia became the second wife of Odaenathus, whose bravery and cunning on the battlefield were a perfect match for his ambitious young warrior bride.
258 CE

An heir in waiting
Zenobia bore Odaenathus a son, Vaballathus, but the direct heir to the Palmyrene throne was Hairan, a child by Odaenathus' first wife. In Zenobia's day, it was common for competing wives to jostle — or even kill — to get their son on the throne.
259 CE

Taking Egypt
Zenobia and her trusted general marched uncontested into Egypt while Rome's military was busy fighting off Goth invaders and Libyan pirates. The Egyptian people embraced Zenobia as the rightful heir to Cleopatra's greatness.
269 CE

Aurelian and Zenobia first met in battle at Antioch. Zenobia's forces were anchored by heavily armoured cavalry called clibanarii, using a style of warfare borrowed from the Persians. Both horses and riders were covered with thick armoured plates to withstand a line of Roman archers known as sagittariorum. The clibanarii had a weakness, though, and Aurelian exploited it brilliantly. In Latin, clibanarii means the camp oven-bearers, because the armoured suits heat up like a furnace in the midday Sun. Aurelian feinted retreat and lead the cavalry on lengthy chases, timing his greatest offensive to coincide with the greatest heat of the day. Zenobia's overheated cavalry were no match for Aurelian's well-trained legions and Zenobia retreated to Emissa, modern-day Homs.

Aurelian attacked Zenobia again at Emissa, using Palestinian slingers armed with rocks and slings, like young David who fought Goliath to disrupt and confuse the Palmyrene cavalry. At one point, the 70,000-strong cavalry turned in on itself, trampling its own horsemen in the chaos. Zenobia was right there alongside her troops. "In both [battles] the Queen of Palmyra animated the armies by her presence," Gibbon writes. Facing defeat at Emissa, however, Zenobia decided to flee to the stronghold of Palmyra on her speediest camel.

Back in Palmyra, Zenobia failed to gather enough forces to engage in conventional warfare. Aurelian laid siege to the city for months, which, according to Gibbon, drew criticism from Rome.

In *The Decline and Fall of the Roman Empire*, Gibbon quotes a letter from Aurelian: "The Roman people speak with contempt of the war that I am waging against a woman. They're ignorant both of the character and of the power of Zenobia. It's impossible to enumerate her warlike preparations, of stones, of arrows and every species of missile weapons. Every part of the wall is provided with two or three ballistae and artificial fires are thrown from her military engines. The fear of punishment has armed her with courage."

In the end, the gods favoured Rome, Palmyra swiftly fell and Zenobia, along with her son and heir, was captured. The *Historia Augusta* recalls Zenobia being paraded through the streets of Rome in golden chains. Other accounts say she died on the journey from Palmyra, while others still claim she committed suicide — like her tragic heroine Cleopatra — rather than suffer the indignity of submitting to the Emperor or facing the jeering Roman crowds.

Life in the time of
Zenobia

Stealing from Rome's own breadbasket
Rome supplied free rations of wheat to its citizens to win their political loyalty, but much of the wheat was imported from Egypt. When Zenobia conquered Egypt, she allegedly cut off the wheat supply, a tactic not unlike kicking a hornet's nest.

By name only
The wealthy city state of Palmyra held a unique position in the Roman Empire. It functioned as an independent colony, free to collect its own taxes, but privy to the protection of the emperor. Palmyra grew fat off the taxes levied on caravans travelling the Silk Road to the west.

Spice security
As a critical stop on the Silk Road, Palmyra was responsible for protecting the silk and spice caravans along the stretch of road within its boundaries. The task fell to private armies of swift horsemen that earned a reputation for their prowess at repelling bandits.

Lost in translation
Zenobia's full name in Greek was Septimia Zenobia, but was most likely a Latinisation of the Arabic al-Zabba, which was itself a translation of Zenobia's true Aramaic name, Bat-Zabbai, or 'daughter of Zabbai'. Zenobia's native language was Aramaic.

Roman triumph
Some sources claim that a captured and chained Zenobia was paraded through Rome as part of Aurelian's massive triumph in 274 CE, featuring 800 gladiators and conquered captives from every barbarian tribe.

ZENOBIA'S RULE OF PALMYRA LASTED LESS THAN A TOTAL OF FIVE YEARS

Defining moment
Siege of Palmyra 274 CE

According to exaggerated accounts in the *Historia Augusta*, Aurelian's final offensive against Zenobia at Palmyra was almost a failure. As the Roman legions marched from Emessa, they were hounded by Syrian robbers and target practise for Persian assassins. His troops exhausted from two massive battles, Aurelian attempted to strike a deal with Zenobia, promising her life and the freedom of her people in return for peaceful surrender. Zenobia said that she, like Cleopatra, preferred death to dishonour. She threatened Aurelian with talk of reinforcements from Persia. Aurelian surrounded and starved out the city, bringing Palmyra to its knees.

274

l Face fit for a coin
Zenobia ordered the Alexandria mint to produce new coins featuring her silhouette and the presumptuous inscription, 'S. Zenobia Aug', shorthand for Septimia Zenobia Augusta, Empress of the East.
270 CE

l Bread baroness
Zenobia further provoked Rome by cutting off Egyptian wheat exports to the Imperial capital, where politicians assuaged the plebeians with free bread and circuses. If she was picking a fight, she would certainly get one.
271 CE

l Eastern empire
At its peak, Zenobia's Palmyrene Empire absorbed the entire eastern shore of the Mediterranean, stretching from the Nile to the Black Sea. Most of her conquered territory submitted to their new empress without resistance.
272 CE

l Aurelian strikes back
Emperor Aurelian follows his conquest of the Goths by turning his attention — and his armies — east to the Palmyrene Empire. In a rare move by the severe general, Aurelian spares the citizens of conquered Palmyrene cities, causing even more to surrender peacefully.
273 CE

1124 – 1204

Eleanor of Aquitaine

Loathed, adored, celebrated and damned, she defied her gender, waged war and became the most powerful woman in Europe

When Pope Eugene III requested that Louis VII, king of France, lead a Crusade to help rescue the Crusader states in the Middle East, he took up the sword with enthusiasm. However, Louis would not travel to the Holy Land alone. His wife, adored by him, despised by others, did not plan to sit back and wait at home for her husband to return. Eleanor of Aquitaine's launch and involvement in the Second Crusade would go down in myth and legend. It is said that the queen rode through the streets of Vézelay dressed in the costume of an Amazon upon a white steed, brandishing her sword and urging the people to join her. Whether it truly occurred or not, this image of the warrior queen has survived through the centuries, and her enduring connection with the Second Crusade would see Eleanor damned for its failure.

Eleanor was born to rule. The first child of William X, Duke of Aquitaine, her doting father bestowed upon his eldest daughter education fitting not a submissive queen, but one who would rule. Alongside general household skills and 'womanly' pursuits of embroidery and needlework, she also learned history and arithmetic, she could speak Latin, ride a horse proficiently and was a skilled hunter. She grew up in her grandfather William IX's court, surrounded by music, poetry, and most notably, courtly love. All this bred a girl who was lively, intelligent, confident and headstrong. These were not traits prized in ladies at the time, but they were essential for Eleanor, as she would soon become one of the most powerful heiresses in Europe.

Her only brother died in the spring of 1130, along with her mother. This left Eleanor as the heir presumptive of one of the largest domains in France, larger than those held even by the king. It would not take long for these kingdoms to fall into Eleanor's hands. In 1137, when Eleanor was aged approximately 15, her father went on pilgrimage and left his daughters in the care of the Archbishop of Bordeaux. However, on the journey home, he fell seriously ill and died. Poitou and Aquitaine were now clasped in the hands of a 15-year-old female heir.

All this control was a very dangerous thing for the young teenager to

WHEN ELEANOR FLED TO MARRY HENRY, SHE HAD TO AVOID BEING KIDNAPPED

bear. Power-hungry men of the period were not above kidnapping eligible heiresses to seize their lands and claim a title. Eleanor's father knew this, and placed his daughter under the guardianship of King Louis VI of France, also known as Louis the Fat. William's will stipulated that Louis take care of his daughter and her lands until a suitable husband was found. Mortally ill and so obese he was confined to his bed, Louis was very aware of his own impending mortality and did not intend to waste this opportunity. Within hours, Louis arranged for Eleanor to be married to his son, Prince Louis, bringing her ample lands under the control of the French crown.

Louis the Fat married Eleanor off to his son confident in her suitability as a wife. Not only did she come with lands that greatly strengthened the French crown, she was also stunningly beautiful, young, fertile and a lady of court. However, Eleanor was anything but a quiet, submissive wife. Prince Louis was a very pious, meek man, a younger son intended originally for a monastic life, but Eleanor had been trained to rule. She had knowledge beyond her husband's, she was strong where he was weak, forceful where he was relenting, and he was completely and utterly besotted with her. As expected, Louis the Fat shortly died, the prince became King Louis VII and Eleanor became queen of the Franks. Her colourful and high-spirited nature was not well liked in the royal court, and Louis's own mother loathed her daughter in law, believing her to be a bad influence on her son. However, as much as Eleanor's unusual behaviour confused and infuriated the king, he could not resist bending to her every desire.

Sensitive and pious he may have been, but Louis was a king, and a king in the Medieval era could not avoid war. An illicit affair involving Eleanor's younger sister, Petronella, with Raoul I of Vermandois – then married to the daughter of the powerful Stephen of Blois – caused war to break out. With Eleanor's encouragement, Louis supported Petronella and Raoul, and in the resulting conflict, the king was responsible for the burning of the town of Vitry. The terrified townspeople sought refuge in a church, but it also burned to the ground and more than 1,000 people

Guide to the Crusades

From 1096 to 1291, Jerusalem was at the epicentre of a war that killed millions

1st 1096-99
LEVANT, ANATOLIA
As Turkish forces gained control of the Holy Land, Pope Urban II called for a Crusade to eliminate the threat. Gradually the Christian forces reclaimed Jerusalem. They also began to set up Latin Christian states in the region.
Victors: Crusaders

2nd 1147-49
IBERIA, HOLY LAND, EGYPT
When Edessa, fell, Pope Eugene III encouraged the monarchies of France and Germany to wage war. However, both armies were defeated by the Turks amid claims the Byzantine emperor plotted against the Crusaders.
Victors: Muslims

3rd 1189-92
LEVANT, ANATOLIA
After Jerusalem was conquered by Saladin, Richard I of England and King Philip II of France united to claim it back. They enjoyed a string of successes, notably in the cities of Acre and Jaffa, but failed to capture Jerusalem.
Victors: Mostly Crusaders

4th 1202-04
BALKANS
With Jerusalem still under Muslim control, the Fourth Crusade was launched. Although the aim had been to claim Jerusalem, the Crusaders instead sacked Constantinople, beginning the decline of the Byzantine Empire.
Victors: Crusaders

5th 1213-21
LEVANT, EGYPT
With Hungarian and Austrian armies failing to conquer Jerusalem, Flemish and Frisian forces attempt to claim Ayyubid and prevent the Crusaders having to fight on two fronts. The attack was repelled with huge Crusader losses.
Victors: Muslims

6th 1228-29
CYPRUS, NEAR EAST
With the aim to reclaim Jerusalem, Holy Roman Emperor Frederick II used diplomacy and lies to obtain Jerusalem in exchange for a ten-year truce with the Sultan of Egypt. Jerusalem was in Crusader hands.
Victors: Crusaders

7th 1248-54
AL-MANSOURAH, EGYPT
In 1244, Jerusalem returned to Muslim control, so Louis IX of France led a Crusade to get it back. Although they enjoyed initial success, the Crusader forces were defeated and Louis himself captured and ransomed.
Victors: Muslims

8th 1270-72
TUNISIA, NEAR EAST
Louis IX launched a final attempt to reclaim the Holy Land, but became ill on the journey and died. This prompted Edward I to sail to Acre, where he enjoyed victories, but he was forced home to solve conflicts there.
Victors: Muslims

The Crusades

Feeling threatened by Muslim forces, the Christian Church sought to prove its dominance and gain control of the Holy Land. This unleashed a 200-year-long struggle for power.

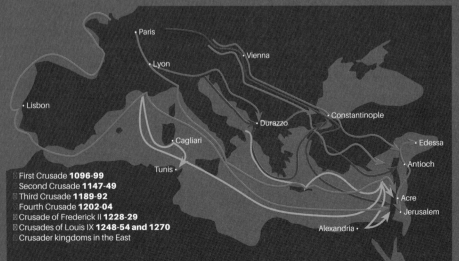

First Crusade **1096-99**
Second Crusade **1147-49**
Third Crusade **1189-92**
Fourth Crusade **1202-04**
Crusade of Frederick II **1228-29**
Crusades of Louis IX **1248-54 and 1270**
Crusader kingdoms in the East

The Second Crusade council: Conrad III, Louis VII & Baldwin III

"She had knowledge beyond her husband's, she was strong where he was weak"

were lost in the flames. The event would have a profound effect on the sensitive Louis, who was plagued by his guilty conscience and the eternal screams of the dying. What Louis needed was a pilgrimage to clear his conscience, and luckily for him, a trip to the Holy Land was just on the horizon, though it would not be quite as peaceful as he hoped. In the autumn of 1145, Pope Eugene III called upon Louis to lead a Crusade to protect the Crusader-owned kingdom of Jerusalem. The king obliged, but he would not be waging war alone.

Eleanor not only decided to join her husband on Crusade, but took up the Crusader cross with, likely, more enthusiasm than he himself. Aged 19, she offered the church the aid of her fighting vassals, which they were very happy to accept. However, they were less than pleased when she proclaimed that she, accompanied by 300 of her ladies in waiting, would join the Crusaders. Eleanor said that she and her ladies would help tend the wounded, but it is also likely that the headstrong queen was not so keen on her meek husband fighting a war without her. She appointed herself leader of her soldiers and departed with her husband.

The women were dressed in armour and carried lances, but did not fight. Nevertheless, the prospect of 300 women riding off with warriors was looked upon suspiciously by her contemporaries. However, Eleanor was not one to be swayed by criticism. Although the church may not have approved of her, when the army reached Constantinople, the warrior queen quickly impressed, and was compared to the mythical queen of the Amazons.

Unfortunately, the Crusade wasn't going quite so smoothly. The French had been informed by the Byzantine Emperor that their ally, the German King Conrad, had enjoyed a decisive victory against a Turkish army. However, as the French army continued their journey onwards, a dazed and ailing Conrad was found near their camp and revealed the truth. The Europeans hadn't won, in fact they had been massacred. It was with haste and some unease that the French and what remained of the German army headed to Antioch, where Eleanor's uncle ruled.

Little did the Crusaders know they were already being stalked by Turks. The French monarchs decided to split, with Louis at the rear of the column with the baggage trains and Eleanor at the front with her vassal, Geoffrey de Rancon. Although the vanguard was able to reach the summit where they planned to make camp, Rancon decided to continue onwards. The rear of the column, laden down with baggage, struggled to keep up and the Turks leapt on this opportunity. The French, including many unarmed pilgrims, were trapped and unprepared. Any who tried to escape were killed, and the king, disguised in simple pilgrim clothes, barely escaped the attack by scaling a rock.

The blame for the massacre was placed firlmy at de Rancon's feet, and, as he was Eleanor's vassal, so it was at her's. The fact that her own soldiers had marched in front and weren't involved did little to help her popularity, and it was even argued that the majority of the baggage was hers. Thus, despite having no involvement in the fight, the queen was blamed for the disaster. Tensions between the royal couple were reaching a fever pitch.

When the Crusaders reached the city of Antioch, it gave Eleanor an opportunity to renew her friendship with the lord of the city and her uncle, Raymond. Not only was Raymond close in age to Eleanor, but he was also tall, handsome and charming. In fact, she spent so

Growing up in Medieval Europe

Being born in the Middle Ages meant life was fated to follow a certain path

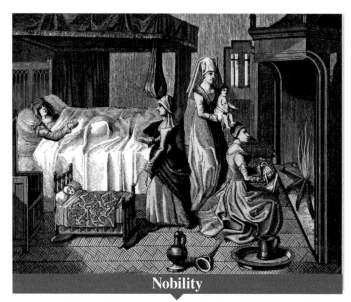

Nobility

Boys: Sons were sought after to continue the family name, and royal boys were especially prized. Noble boys began training to be a knight aged just seven, and those unsuitable were sent to monasteries. Popular boys' toys were wooden soldiers, toy horses and whips.

Girls: Daughters were seen as expensive, as a dowry had to be paid to the groom at marriage, which could occur as young as seven. Generally noble girls were sent to train as ladies at a young age, learning how to weave, sing, play instruments and how to care for children.

Peasants

Boys: In poorer households, boys helped tend the fields and care for animals. Work was so consuming that children as young as two could be left alone. Poor children did not receive education apart from in the church, and few peasant boys knew how to read.

Girls: Female peasant children were expected to help their mothers with household chores. As they were working hand to mouth, toys were scarce and often handmade. Like their noble counterparts, peasant girls were married off as soon as they reached maturity.

The marriage of Louis VII and Eleanor of Aquitaine ended in annulment in 1152

Eleanor was said to be "gracious, lovely, the embodiment of charm"

much time with her uncle that rumours quickly spread about an illicit affair between the two. Raymond suggested they first capture Edessa, a strategic stronghold in the Holy Land, but Louis was determined to focus solely on Jerusalem. When Eleanor supported her uncle, it was the final straw – the meek, adoring and abiding king had reached his limit.

Louis, likely for the first time in his marriage, demanded that Eleanor follow him. His queen, outraged, called into question the entire marriage, claiming that she and her husband were too closely related, and this was grounds for divorce. This didn't go down well with Louis, and in an effort to establish his authority, he took Eleanor away from her uncle and Antioch against her will and headed to Jerusalem. For the woman who was born to rule, to command and to control, this was humiliating beyond all measure. The remainder of the Crusade achieved little, Louis's subsequent assault on Damascus was a failure, and the royal couple returned to France in different ships.

A marriage where Eleanor was expected to be meek and obliging was not going to work. She could deal with her sensitive and generous husband, but the one that returned from the Crusade was as humiliated as her and increasingly suspicious of the growing relationship between niece and uncle. Although they had children, no male heirs were born, and Louis faced increasing opposition to Eleanor from his barons. The king was left with no option, and in 1152, the marriage was annulled. The lands that Louis's father had so slyly secured for his son were torn away from him, and aged about 30, Eleanor once again became one of the most eligible and desirable heiresses in Europe.

However, Eleanor was no longer a naive 15-year-old, she was a worldly and knowledgeable woman. She knew she would have to remarry, and she intended to do so on her own terms. Amid several attempts of kidnap and forced marriage, she manufactured her own union with Henry, Duke of Normandy and future king of England. Henry wasn't stupid either; he travelled immediately to visit Eleanor, and within

eight weeks of her annulment to Louis, she was married to a man even more closely related to her than Louis.

On paper the union was a powerful one. In 1154, Henry became Henry II, king of England, and his lands combined with Eleanor's. This united England, Normandy and the West of France into a hugely powerful and influential kingdom. However, both Henry and Eleanor were strong, dominating characters. Henry was the eldest child; he too had been born to rule. He was used to getting his way and had an explosive and at times terrifying temper. Eleanor was 11 years older than him, knew her worth, and wasn't prepared to obey the commands of a domineering husband. Despite their stormy relationship, the couple had five sons and three daughters, and ruled over an impressive Medieval empire.

However, a storm was brewing. Henry was ruled by passion, and this led to many illicit affairs and a number of mistresses. His affair with one mistress in particular, Rosamund Clifford, became public knowledge and drove his proud and headstrong wife to breaking point. Eleanor departed for her native land of Aquitaine and took several of her children, including Richard, her chosen heir, with her. The queen was tired of dealing with the wills of husbands; she wanted to rule Aquitaine, and she wanted to rule alone.

Eleanor wasn't the only one who had been pushed to the limit by

A painting of the 'Last Crusader' returning home after the failure of the Ninth Crusade

The Angevin Empire

When Henry, Count of Anjou and Duke of Normandy, married Eleanor in 1152, the regions of Normandy, Anjou, Maine, Touraine, Aquitaine, Gascony, Poitou and Auvergne were brought together. When their son, Geoffrey, brought Brittany into the mix, the concentration of fiefs held by one man became a very real threat to the French monarchy.

KINGDOM OF ENGLAND

DUCHY OF NORMANDY

DUCHY OF BRITTANY

DUCHY OF AQUITAINE

COUNTY OF TOULOUSE

- **Before 1144:** Maine, Anjou, Touraine
- **1144:** Normandy
- **1152:** Aquitaine, by Eleanor
- **1154:** England
- **1166:** Brittany, by a son of Henry II
- Kingdom of France
- Royal domain of the French King
- Possessions of the Count of Toulouse

Eleanor launched the Crusade from the rumoured location of Mary Magdalene's grave

10 most influential women in history

01 1533-1603
ELIZABETH I
QUEEN OF ENGLAND AND IRELAND

Crowning achievement:
Defeating the Spanish Armada, greatly boosting national pride and putting a stop to Spain's invasion of England.

Did you know?
Elizabeth's refusal to marry was so extraordinary for the period that many believed the only explanation was that she was secretly a man.

02 1729-96
CATHERINE II
EMPRESS AND AUTOCRAT OF ALL THE RUSSIAS

Crowning achievement:
Catherine ruled over Russia for longer than any other female ruler, during which time she expanded the Russian Empire to the Black Sea and defeated the Ottoman Empire twice.

Did you know?
Her name wasn't Catherine and she wasn't Russian. She was born as Sophia to an impoverished Prussian prince.

03 1370-1330 BCE
NEFERTITI
QUEEN CONSORT OF EGYPT

Crowning achievement:
In the male-dominated world of Ancient Egypt, Nefertiti achieved near equal status with her husband, Pharaoh Akhenaten, and received the title 'Priest of Aten'.

Did you know?
Nefertiti is known for the beautiful bust of her face, but CT scans have revealed that beneath lies a carving of a wrinkled woman with an uneven nose.

04 1835-1908
EMPRESS DOWAGER CIXI
EMPRESS DOWAGER OF QING CHINA

Crowning achievement:
One of the most powerful women in China's long history, she was regent for her son and nephew, but held the real power for nearly 50 years.

Did you know?
Her true nature is a mystery, with some painting her as a ruthless murderer and others an enlightened ruler.

05 1953-2007
BENAZIR BHUTTO
PRIME MINISTER OF PAKISTAN

Crowning achievement:
Not only the first woman to head a major political party, but the first elected head of an Islamic country.

Did you know?
She refused to change her name when she was married, stating: "Benazir Bhutto doesn't cease to exist the moment she gets married. I am not giving myself away. I belong to myself."

06 1954-PRESENT
OPRAH WINFREY
'QUEEN OF ALL MEDIA'

Crowning achievement:
Born into poverty, Winfrey is now the most successful black philanthropist in American history and is regarded by many as the most influential woman in the world.

Did you know?
Although she's one of the richest women in the world, growing up Oprah was bullied at school for wearing dresses made from potato sacks.

07 1451-1504
ISABELLA I OF CASTILE
QUEEN OF CASTILE AND LEÓN

Crowning achievement:
She not only set up the unification of Spain with her marriage, but also cleared her kingdom of the crippling debt left by her brother.

Did you know?
One of Isabella's daughters was Catherine of Aragon, none other than Henry VIII's first wife.

08 UNKNOWN- C. 61 CE
BOUDICA
QUEEN OF THE ICENI TRIBE

Crowning achievement:
Uniting many British tribes to revolt against the occupying Roman army, she led her force to defeat the Romans in three battles.

Did you know?
It wasn't until the Victorian Era that Boudica earned legendary status, as hers and Victoria's name were identical in meaning.

09 1954-PRESENT
ANGELA MERKEL
CHANCELLOR OF GERMANY

Crowning achievement:
As well as being the first woman to serve in her position, she is known as the 'decider' in her handling of the financial crisis and is also viewed as the de facto leader of the EU.

Did you know?
She has been named most powerful woman in the world by Forbes magazine nine years running.

10 1819-1901
QUEEN VICTORIA
QUEEN OF THE UNITED KINGDOM, EMPRESS OF INDIA

Crowning achievement:
Victoria ruled over the biggest empire in the history of the world, spanning six continents and 458 million people.

Did you know?
Despite her imposing presence, Victoria was barely five foot tall.

"A marriage where Eleanor was expected to be meek and obliging was not going to work"

Eleanor's effigy can still be seen in Fontevraud Abbey in France

Henry. Several of her sons had inherited her proud, stubborn nature and decided that enough was enough. Henry the younger secretly travelled to Aquitaine and, likely encouraged by Eleanor, joined with two of his brothers, Richard and Geoffrey. Together they decided to rebel against their father. For Eleanor the rebellion was the culmination of years of abiding his infidelities, bearing his children and a lifetime of sharing power; it was her chance to rule Aquitaine with her beloved son Richard. But, as always with Eleanor, fate did not run smoothly. The rebellion was quashed, and the woman born to rule was thrown in prison.

For the next 16 years Eleanor was imprisoned in England. If the

humiliation of imprisonment wasn't bad enough, the lack of contact with her sons over the years caused Eleanor to become distanced from them. Now aged 50, Eleanor hopelessly and powerlessly waited for her chance to rule again. It would take the death of her tempestuous husband for her to finally glimpse freedom once more.

When Henry died in 1189, Richard I became heir. Although Eleanor's favourite son had become more distant, one of his first acts was to release his mother from her prison. In the autumn of her life, Eleanor could finally fulfil the role she was born to play - ruler. While Richard, who would later become known as Richard the Lionheart, travelled and embarked on the Third Crusade in the Holy Land, she ruled England as his regent. She defended his lands, and even used her political acumen to negotiate Richard's release when he was captured by the enemy. Her citizens approved of their able, intelligent and strong queen, and, although it was likely no concern to her, Eleanor finally earned popularity.

The queen was not one to let old age stop her. She continually travelled across Europe, cementing powerful marriages for her brood of children, managing her army and building a strong and influential empire. At the age of 70, she rode over the Pyrenees to collect her choice of wife for Richard, then continued to traverse the Alps. She would outlive nearly all of her children, and survived long into the reign of her youngest son, John. However, determined as she was, Eleanor could not avoid time catching up with her. She retired to the religious house of Fontevraud where she became a nun. In 1204, aged 82, Eleanor died and was buried beside the son she most adored, Richard. Her legacy would continue not only in the children she bore, but in her lands, which remained loyal to England even after the loss of Normandy. Though many were quick to discount her for her frivolity in her youth, Eleanor had proved herself an intelligent, driven and wise ruler. As the nuns who spent her final years with her wrote, she was a queen "who surpassed almost all the queens of the world."

Heroines of royalty

For these royal heroines, life wasn't all about crown jewels and ermine

Diana, Princess of Wales
British 1961 – 1997

When Lady Diana Spencer married the Prince of Wales in 1981, she became a superstar. The shy, blushing young woman flourished, becoming a fashion icon and a hugely popular figure. More importantly, she was also an active patron of several charities. Diana was the first member of the royal family to become involved with AIDS charities, making efforts to destigmatise the disease. She also ventured into politics to raise awareness of land mines and was credited with helping to secure the international ban on their use. She championed cancer and homelessness charities, as well as other causes. Her death in 1997 left the globe in grieving.

Hatshepsut
Egyptian 2507 – 1458 BCE

As the second female pharaoh and the longest- reigning indigenous woman in Egyptian history, Hatshepsut blazed a trail through Egypt. She established a far-reaching trade network that brought wealth to her dynasty and was an enthusiastic builder of monuments. Under Hatshepsut's rule the country echoed to the sound of industry as she commissioned an enormous number of buildings and statues, including the monumental obelisk that still stands at the entrance to the Temple of Karnak. When death ended Hatshepsut's long reign, she left behind a legacy of peace and prosperity, as well as her famed structures.

Boudicca
British Celtic Unknown – 61 CE

When her husband Prasutagus died, Boudicca expected to inherit his Iceni kingdom in modern-day Norfolk. Instead, his land was annexed by Rome and his wife and daughters flogged and raped. Boudicca rallied her forces against the Romans and revolted against their occupation of England. Her armies killed more than 70,000 people and for a time Emperor Nero considered withdrawing altogether. Ultimately, Rome fought back against Boudicca's rebellion and crushed the Iceni uprising. The exact manner of Boudicca's death and the place of her defeat are still debated, but she has become a legend, celebrated as a warrior queen.

Theodora of Byzantium
Roman 500 – 548 CE

From humble beginnings, Theodora rose to become the most powerful empress of the Eastern Roman Empire by her marriage to Emperor Justinian. As co-ruler, Theodora held equal sway in all political matters but her moment of glory came when, during the Nika riots, her husband prepared to flee the public uprising. Theodora urged him not to run, but to fight and their resulting triumph confirmed the couple as one to be reckoned with. Their empire was one of the richest the world had ever seen and following Theodora's death, Justinian continued to work on her projects.

Wu Zetian
China 624 – 705 CE

As concubine of Emperor Taizong and then wife of his son, Emperor Gaozong, Wu Zetian wielded enormous influence. China's only empress regnant, when her husband fell ill, her power as the head of the Zhou dynasty became absolute. Although Chinese tradition didn't allow a woman to reign, Wu Zetian did just that. She crushed her opponents and secured the throne, displaying a ruthlessness that she would later employ to press her foreign policies. China went to war again and again, winning victories as its empire grew. Weakened by ill health, Wu Zetian was deposed just before her death.

Isabella I of Castile
Spanish 1451 – 1504

Reigning as queen of Castile for three decades, Isabella left an indelible mark on her kingdom and that of her husband, Ferdinand II of Aragon. Isabella inherited a realm that was awash with crime and corruption and reformed it, establishing the first known police force and taking a tight hold on Castile's mismanaged finances. She oversaw the conquering of Grenada and in 1492, financed Christopher Columbus' expedition to the New World. She presided over the creation of an empire and worked tirelessly to build relationships with other dynasties.

Queen Wilhelmina
Dutch 1880 – 1962

Though her near six-decade rule ended in abdication, Wilhelmina of the Netherlands reigned longer than any other Dutch monarch. When Germany invaded the Netherlands, the royal family was evacuated to England. From her new home, Wilhelmina controlled the Dutch government in exile, but the relationship was an uneasy one. When she learned that her prime minister was seeking to negotiate with Germany, Wilhelmina had him removed and spoke out as a voice of resistance, earning her the love and respect of her subjects.

Christina of Sweden
Sweden 1626 – 1689

Christina of Sweden succeeded the throne upon the death of her father and reigned for more than 20 years. Passionate about religion and philosophy, Christina decided early in life to devote herself to learning and the arts. Frequently dressed in a masculine fashion, she was a controversial figure for those who wanted a traditional queen. When she decided to convert to Catholicism, Christina abdicated her throne. She travelled Europe and ultimately settled in Rome, where she pursued her love of politics, science and theatre.

Maria Theresa
Austrian 1717 – 1780

Maria Theresa was the only female ruler of the legendary House of Habsburg and the last of its line. She commanded vast swathes of European land as Holy Roman Empress by her marriage to Francis I. When her father, Charles VI died, Maria Theresa inherited his impoverished lands. Though her husband took the title of emperor, in practice the power lay in the hands of Maria Theresa. Her reign was beset by war but she implemented reforms that transformed Austria's administration and finances and improved education, healthcare and civil rights.

CLAPHAM
W.S.P.U.
CROYDON
W.S.P.U.
FULHAM
&
PUTNEY
W.S.P.U.
W.S.P.U.
THE WOMEN'S
AND POLITICAL
PUBLIC
LONDON
Thursday,
(At 8.15 p.m.
ADMISSION FREE.